Travel with Purpose

Travel with Purpose

A Field Guide to Voluntourism

Jeff Blumenfeld

ROWMAN & LITTLEFIELD
Lanham · Boulder · New York · London

Published by Rowman & Littlefield
An imprint of The Rowman & Littlefield Publishing Group, Inc.
4501 Forbes Boulevard, Suite 200, Lanham, Maryland 20706
www.rowman.com

6 Tinworth Street, London SE11 5AL

Distributed by NATIONAL BOOK NETWORK

British Library Cataloguing in Publication Information Available

Library of Congress Cataloging-in-Publication Data

978-1-5381-1532-9 (cloth)
978-1-5381-1533-6 (electronic)

∞™ The paper used in this publication meets the minimum requirements of American National Standard for Information Sciences—Permanence of Paper for Printed Library Materials, ANSI/NISO Z39.48-1992.

Printed in the United States of America

To my young grandson,
Wyatt Fowler Couperthwait.
The future is in your hands.

Contents

Acknowledgments

$\mathscr{I}$t is with gratitude that I acknowledge the assistance provided to me in preparation of this guide to voluntourism. Certainly, I am appreciative and in awe of the numerous voluntourists who took the time to share their most memorable experiences, provide advice to prospective voluntourists, and offer a glimpse at their future plans.

Each interview I conducted, either by telephone or in person, provided insight into what drives these people, what gets them up in the morning, particularly the benefits they gain personally while doing good for others.

I'd also like to thank those selfless folks from the nonprofit community who took me under their wing and allowed me to participate in their own life's work. A shout-out in particular to George "Chief Cook" Basch of Taos, New Mexico, founder of the Himalayan Stove Project, who felt there was a better way to clear the air in Nepal, one fuel-efficient cookstove at a time. George opened my eyes to the unique challenges of fundraising.

Scott Hamilton of Stamford, Connecticut, president of Dooley Intermed International, asked me to serve as director of communications on two separate eye care missions to Nepal. He also taught me how a well-run expedition can achieve its mission safely and responsibly. I also learned from him important life lessons, not the least of which was avoiding salads or tuna fish sandwiches served by sketchy Nepalese street food vendors.

Then there's my literary agent, Terry Whalin of Highland Ranch, Colorado, who, when we first met ten years ago, told me how to write a book proposal, based upon his own book, *Book Proposals That Sell* (2005). He has shepherded me through the process of writing my first book, *Get Sponsored*, followed by this one. I've long valued his sage advice.

Finally, there are two mentors from my Wonder Bread years who have my undying gratitude for instilling in me a love of storytelling. First is Madeline Conway, who edited *Monti Matters*, my weekly high school column in the local Monticello, New York, *Evening News*. I still have the strip of hot type used to headline the column, back when it was set by linotype machine. Conway was first to show me how molten lead was transferred into my words using this now-outdated hot metal typesetting system. What magic it was to watch.

And Mike Greenstein of the *Syracuse New Times*, who let me write about a variety of quirky topics while attending Syracuse University, including a bizarre visit to a local casket factory. Both Conway and Greenstein apparently saw promise in a budding young cub reporter willing to accept a salary of ten cents per column inch. Back then the pay was so low, I might as well have been volunteering. But it was a great start to a career.

Introduction

A World of Voluntourism Opportunities

*I*magine yourself in a schoolroom in Nepal, one of the most remote areas of one of the most hard-to-reach countries on earth. The Lower Mustang region to be exact.

Traveling there requires a fourteen-hour flight from New York to Doha, Qatar. Then four-and-a-half hours by air to Kathmandu, one of the world's worst airports.[1] From Kat it's a 127-mile flight to Pokhara, followed by a jarring, eight-hour Jeep ride over a vertiginous dirt road—one side is a mountain wall, the other side a two-hundred-foot vertical cliff.

Finally you arrive, but it's not just any schoolroom. It has been disinfected with formalin, an aqueous solution of formaldehyde (mean stuff but highly effective), and converted into an operating room so that doctors from New York Eye & Ear Infirmary can provide the gift of sight to twenty-four blind Nepalis. Prior to this, they lived in a world of darkness for no other reason than they had cataracts, the clouding of the eye's lens, easily corrected.

I know. I was there to tell the story of Dooley Intermed's "Gift of Sight" Expedition. That right there was my aha moment. I was in a foreign land as a tourist, but also as a volunteer.

A voluntourist, if you will—a mix of both travel and volunteering. The term is credited to travel writer Alison Gardner who wrote a feature article in 1994 about volunteer vacations for older travelers. She cites some of the earliest players in the fledgling field, including Earthwatch and Habitat for Humanity, both of which remain steadfast short-term voluntourism models to this day.[2]

Today, Gardner is publisher and editor of the *Travel with a Challenge* web magazine,[3] read by 1.742 million senior travelers worldwide. Recently she tells me it was quite an honor in 2012 when she received a call from the publishers of the *Oxford Dictionary* in the UK, saying they were trying to trace the origin of the word, voluntourism, before they accepted it.

"They asked if I could send them a copy of the article in which I had first used the term in 1994. All done, and now it is an official entry in the *Oxford Dictionary* which is about as authoritative as it gets, I suppose."

Indeed. There it is, "a form of tourism in which travellers participate in voluntary work, typically for a charity."[4]

Over the past thirty years, voluntourism has grown with such momentum that both nonprofit organizations and for-profit advisory services and tour operators are scrambling to match many different agendas.

"With a firmly-entrenched Western world mindset of 'rest and relaxation = vacation,' who would have dreamed that working while on vacation would become such a fast-growing segment of the travel industry today?" asks Gardner.

I am a lousy vacationer, bored silly sitting on a beach or touring umpteen churches on cruise ship excursions. Being a regular tourist is not enough for me. I want a meaningful role when I travel and perhaps you do as well.

Average plain vanilla tourists returning from a do-nothing beach vacation like to tell family and friends where they traveled. Nothing wrong with playing Robinson Crusoe, sprawled on a lounge chair, umbrella drink in hand, salty breeze ruffling their hair as they post palm tree images to Instagram.

Voluntourists, on the other hand, not only describe where they've been but explain how the world became a better place as a result of their time and dedication on the road.

While lying on a beach marinated in Johnson's Baby Oil and iodine has its merits, I'm guessing you'll find voluntourism more meaningful, more memorable, and perhaps transformatively life-altering. What's more, many voluntourism opportunities you'll read about in the following pages allow visitors to devote only a portion of their trips to service, leaving time aside for sightseeing, dining out, or yes, even vegging out on a tropical beach with that fancy drink.

Volunteering has been a part of my life, well, for as long as I can remember. As a prepubescent Cub Scout on New York's Long Island, I participated in beach cleanups. For the Boy Scouts I built check dams to reduce trail erosion.

In tenth grade, once I moved to the Catskill Mountain resort community of Monticello, New York, a group of us belonging to Key Club International, the high school service program, provided physical therapy on Sunday mornings to a young child with cerebral palsy. The exercises we performed were meant to repattern his neuromotor function. I've long wondered what happened to that little boy named Izzy.

In later years, I would go on to volunteer for the local ambulance corps, then the local Civil Defense office, manning headquarters at the tender age of seventeen when the full-time staffer elected to go home as that hippie tsunami, the 1969 Woodstock Festival, engulfed nearby Bethel, New York.

If you're like me, you're a participant in life, not merely a spectator. As a volunteer, I thrive on special access—working the high school theater lights from backstage, distributing newspapers at rock festivals, always organizing, planning, activating.

Voluntourism represents the combination of voluntary service and travel and tourism. By adding travel to the mix, no matter whether in the United States or abroad, you benefit from the best of both worlds. You get the opportunity to meet new people and better understand their way of life, experience different cultures, and help improve their lives.

In my case, voluntourism has included supporting a North Pole expedition, chaperoning high school students to Antarctica, and most recently, serving as director of communications for a second eye care mission to another impoverished village in Nepal—this one a grueling eight-hour trek from the nearest road to the epicenter of the devastating spring 2015 earthquake. More on that later.

My previous book, *Get Sponsored* (2014), was designed for hard-core explorers and adventurers, but after over forty book talks, I saw the need for a handy guide that helped everyone not only see the world but also make a lasting impact as they traveled. People asked me during presentations at bookstores, libraries, and travel clubs how they could participate in voluntourism if they didn't have the necessary outdoor skills to hike the Appalachian Trail or trek to Everest Base Camp.

There are millions of people who enjoy the outdoors and try to build adventure into their day-to-day lives yet would never dream of taking off from their jobs, leaving their families, or otherwise put their lives on hold—and possibly at risk—to scale Everest, K2, the Seven Summits, or trek to the North Pole. Those trips can generate lots of media exposure, sure, but they can also get you killed.

Voluntourism is open to anyone who wants to see the world and make a difference during their all-too-short time on Earth. It doesn't require great strength, or wealth, or connections in the travel business. It doesn't have to necessarily be time-consuming either. You can play an important role volunteering for a few hours, a day, a few days or a week, while also enjoying local sights, exotic cuisines, and fascinating culture as an everyday tourist. You don't have to devote an entire trip to it.

In fact, as we'll see further on, voluntourism doesn't even require a passport, or you traipsing off to some region of the world you're likely to see on TV's *Survivor* or *The Amazing Race*. There are still plenty of volunteer destinations in the United States.

Isn't it hard work building wells, schoolhouses, or excavating ancient fossils? Thank you for asking. The quick answer is "very."

Voluntourism requires the drive, the resourcefulness, and, if possible, a particular skill you can share with others, be it music, art, sports coaching, or simply proficiency in speaking and writing English.

As for me, sadly, I'm not particularly gifted with any sort of teachable skill, although I can move English words around coherently (one hopes you'll agree by the time you finish this book). Oh, I'm proficient in Morse code, dating back to my days as an amateur radio ham operator, but dots and dashes don't come up too often in conversation.

Luckily, my expertise as a writer, blogger, corporate fundraiser, and publicist is something I've leveraged successfully to be invited along on volunteer projects.

If you've perfected a skill, even if it's a strong back and willingness to work hard, or maybe not, maybe your best skill is math or science or art, there are causes that would welcome you along, especially if you have the wherewithal to assist with funding or can pay your way.

One voluntourist you'll read about later, Houston real estate developer Joe Watson, sums it up simply, "Voluntourism sure makes traveling more interesting and meaningful and you have better stories when you get home."

Voluntourists are not necessarily celebrities, nor are they otherwise rich and famous. This book contains stories of inspiration from everyday people, everyday voluntourists, perhaps some just like you. These are the stories about the pitfalls, the rewards, and the hardships likely to be encountered. There are stories of ordinary people with extraordinary volunteer projects both in the United States and abroad. They all have definite opinions about the best way to approach that first volunteer vacation.

If you spend time considering your options, you'll find the door open to untold voluntourism opportunities. This book is written for you and hundreds of thousands of others who heed the words of Albert Schweitzer (1875–1965), the French-German physician and humanitarian and winner of the 1952 Nobel Peace Prize:

> *Wherever you turn, you can find someone who needs you. Even if it is a little thing, do something for which there is no pay but the privilege of doing it. Remember, you don't live in a world all of your own.*[5]

Jeff Blumenfeld
Boulder, Colorado
January 1, 2018
editor@expeditionnews.com

· 𝒥 ·

Why We Travel

*Travel is fatal to prejudice, bigotry, and narrow-mindedness, and
many of our people need it sorely on these accounts. Broad, wholesome,
charitable views of men and things cannot be acquired by vegetating
in one little corner of the earth all one's lifetime.*[1]

—Mark Twain

𝒥 couldn't imagine life without travel. After all, the world is a huge and
amazing place. It makes you feel alive when, through travel, you're touching
as much of it as you can, gaining valuable insight on what's important to other
people and why.

"The world's a rough-and-tumble, growing, fascinating, diverse place,
and I think it's an exciting ride, and we can be part of it," travel book writer
Rick Steves tells the *Wall Street Journal*.[2]

Amazon chief and space buff Jeff Bezos has famously said, "We know
about the Solar System now. We've sent robotic probes all over the Solar
System. Let me assure you, this is the best planet."[3]

But the global perspective that travel would eventually offer—the memories, the friendships, the business opportunities, the family memories—was
a mere blip on my radar growing up in a small town ninety miles northwest of
New York. Especially in the days before the Internet. What I knew about the
world came from geography lessons in middle school and my singular mission
to read through all A to Z volumes of the *World Book Encyclopedia*. With a
Swanson's TV dinner balanced on my lap, my worldview expanded exponentially as I watched *Mutual of Omaha's Wild Kingdom* on television featuring
host Marlin Perkins and his sidekick, a young Jim Fowler, who, decades later,
I came to know as a fellow member of the Explorers Club based in New York.

Then came the YMCA Tour-a-Camp program in the mid-1960s, and I hit the road in a bus alongside another forty teenagers on a tour of the United States. We alternated between campsites and hotels, heading as far west as San Francisco, before making our way back through Disneyland, then proceeding to the country's major national parks. The Grand Canyon, Mount Rushmore, Zion and Arches national parks—they were all on the itinerary.

Later, in a typical college boneheaded plan, I would drive to Aspen nonstop from Syracuse, New York. A stupid college marathon of driving, drinking copious amounts of coffee to stay awake, and eating gas station hot dogs cooked on those ubiquitous grease-filled roller grills. Just recalling the taste of those belly bombs creeps me out.

Those trips were rather straightforward. The only beneficiary was me. Traveling in this manner did nothing to help others.

Significant volunteer trips would elude me until I entered the working world, starting at two public relations agencies before establishing my own boutique PR agency. It was then that my horizons broadened. I was no longer a kid from the Catskills. I was experiencing the world and working on a number of worthwhile projects.

I promoted historic expeditions to the North Pole and across Antarctica; spent two weeks in Nome and Anchorage to serve as communications director of an expedition across the Bering Strait; in 2010 I was chosen as a volunteer chaperone on an international high school students trip to the Antarctic peninsula where I lectured on the subject of exploration; and later that year, I volunteered as the media relations director of history's longest sea voyage, a nonstop 1,152-day self-sufficient journey by extreme sailor Reid Stowe.

I was traveling at that time as a participant in someone else's project rather than as a spectator or tourist. Which isn't to say there's anything wrong with tourism.

By all accounts, despite terrorist attacks, political upheavals, and natural disasters, tourism in the last decade has continued to grow, demonstrating its resilience in an unpredictable world, according to the Adventure Travel Trade Association (ATTA) report, *20 Adventure Travel Trends to Watch in 2018.*[4]

The World Travel & Tourism Council (WTTC) found that in 2016, travel and tourism was responsible for just over 10 percent of global GDP and 10 percent of the world's jobs—one of every ten jobs on earth. Visa estimates that by 2025, 280 million households will be traveling internationally, with much of that growth fueled by emerging markets. Tourism is also growing faster than the global economy and other industries such as manufacturing, retail, and financial and business sectors, reports the ATTA.

The ATTA, which serves over one thousand tour operators, tourist boards, and other travel organizations in one hundred countries, reveals that many destinations that experienced declines in 2016, such as Turkey and

France, recovered in 2017, and China continued to produce staggering numbers of outbound travelers (136.8 million in 2016 alone).

International tourist arrivals globally grew to 1.3 billion in 2017, according to the United Nations' World Tourism Organization. The *Wall Street Journal* reports that figure is up from 674 million in 2000 and 278 million in 1980, propelled by the rise of budget air travel, social media, the emerging Chinese middle class alluded to above, and technologies that make distant places easy to navigate.[5]

"Tourism, which many countries once considered a business niche that could yield easy revenue, has become a mega-industry," writes the *Journal*. "And those millions of tourists who descend each year on small towns, once-lovely beaches and historic sites are generating a global backlash."

This becomes evident when you try to make reservations during peak travel periods. Summer in Iceland, for instance. You're not going to get rooms in the best hotels or at the best prices when the weather is the most favorable and you have to compete with thousands of other people hoping to check that scenic island off their bucket list.

The *Journal* points to an overtourism crisis in New Zealand, where rented camper vans leave trails of waste, tens of thousands of helicopter trips land on glaciers once the realm of expert climbers, and double-decker tour buses clog two-lane roads.

One thing about voluntourism will become crystal clear once you read further: many of the destinations that need volunteer help the most are often unvisited, sometimes unknown destinations, frequently in Third World countries. Overtourism is generally not an issue. Your priorities become remaining safe, comfortable, well fed, and well rested.

Travel in general has made me a better person; travel to Third World destinations in particular have been life-altering experiences that have helped me better cope with everyday challenges back home. Decidedly First World issues such as a fender-bender, a missing mortgage payment, and lost concert tickets pale by comparison to how millions of underprivileged people struggle to survive, such as the woman I met in Nepal who was blind for three years because she lacked the resources to pursue outpatient cataract surgery.

The experience of travel can be transformative, it can actually be beneficial to health, and for younger generations, a great resume builder, especially now that trends indicate this is a great time to travel, as you'll learn below.

TRAVEL IS TRANSFORMATIVE

The latest buzzword in travel is *transformational*, slowly replacing *experiential* and *authentic*. The Transformational Travel Council (TTC) is an industry group founded in 2016 that uses research, speaking engagements, consulting, media interviews, and workshops to help tour operators and their traveling clients understand how travel can transform lives.

"In today's world of cultural turmoil, spiritual chaos, and global unrest, we find ourselves over-connected at a shallow level and under-connected at a deeper, more meaningful level. We have allowed digital addictions to pull us away from what's important: ourselves, family, community, and our planet," according to the TTC website.[6]

The TTC believes that now more than ever, we need travel to do what travel has always done: build bridges, foster understanding, enlighten humanity, and bury fear, insecurity, and intolerance. For some people, whether young or simply young at heart, the TTC believes travel is the best and most exciting way to foster real growth, change, and transformation in your life.

The process of transformational travel involves, in part, venturing off to a place that is dramatically different from home, purposefully engaging with the local people to learn about their culture, which is where voluntourism often comes into play.

"Simply put, the end goals of any transformational travel experience are to inspire, empower, and support people in using travel experiences to create positive changes in their lives," cofounder Michael Bennett, EdD, tells travel editor Everett Potter of EverettPotter.com.[7]

TRAVEL IS GOOD FOR YOUR HEALTH

It may be a significant disconnect, one of those hard-to-believe factoids you see embedded in online clickbait, but travel is actually good for us. Hard to comprehend, I know, especially after traveling to Nepal for seventeen hours while trying to survive on airline food, airline terminal snacks, and otherwise subjecting myself to a digestive assault upon my delicate Western stomach.

Travel can actually help boost your well-being and reduce the stress of everyday life. Traveling somewhere new can enable you to immerse yourself in new surroundings, boost your brain power, and fully recharge. It can help you get back in shape, especially if there's a lot of walking or other physical exertion involved, and it can improve your emotional state.

According to a 2014 study conducted by Nielsen on behalf of Diamond Resorts International, those who commit to taking vacations on a regular basis are generally happier, healthier, and have better relationships than those who don't. The study, titled "Vacation Integration towards an All-Inclusive Lifestyle" or VITAL, has become a key part of Diamond Resorts' message on why vacations are important.[8]

The VITAL survey compared the happiness, health, vitality, relationships, and job satisfaction of two groups of survey respondents: those who reported that they vacation at least once per year, and those who reported that they never vacation. More than two thousand respondents aged twenty-five and older participated in the survey, which yielded compelling conclusions—a significant majority (at least 76 percent) of annual vacationers are more satisfied and happy with their lives overall, compared to people who never vacation.

Dr. Dale Atkins, Diamond Resorts International's so-called Vacation Doctor, states, "Vacations should not be considered a luxury—they are a must for our happiness and health in an increasingly stressful world."

The study also shows that vacations can make you feel energized: 72 percent of yearly vacationers report feeling "energized and full of life all the time," compared to just 34 percent of those who never take a vacation, the study shows.

STUDENTS CAN EXPAND THEIR HORIZONS

Traveling abroad offers a unique opportunity for students to become global citizens as they experience and learn about life in different parts of the world. I think back to my semester abroad between my junior and senior years at Syracuse University. Living in London to study international broadcasting, my classmates and I seemingly had the world—or at least Europe—in the palms of our hands. Frequently, we would travel to Dublin, Paris, Copenhagen, or Rome on long weekends, getting a sense of the world at the tender age of twenty.

Traveling expanded our understanding of other cultures, helped us better appreciate life in America, increased our self-confidence, and bolstered our sense of independence. While volunteering wasn't part of the game plan at that time, what I learned from the trip helped me discover my true north.

"For college students, studying abroad offers the chance to travel, earn credit and gain work experience. Students may opt to take language-immersion courses or even earn grants for working on subject-based projects (for example, doing scientific research on the Great Barrier Reef or filming a documentary in Egypt)," says Maya Wesby, writing in *Newsweek.*[9]

"Yet one type of study abroad involves volunteer work in developing nations, and willing participants can travel the world while gaining a sense of community alongside fellow volunteers and the native population."

Happily, the time has never been better to travel, believes "Travel Detective" Peter Greenberg, a multiple Emmy-winning investigative reporter and producer and the travel editor for CBS News.

In early 2018, Greenberg came to the Denver Travel & Adventure Show and impressed an audience of four hundred with his encyclopedic knowledge of almost every corner of the globe. What are the best countries to visit this year that are off the beaten path? Greenberg recommends Faroe Islands, Malta, Portugal, and Rwanda. The white-bearded celebrity talks knowledgeably about the cost of passports (they're going up), requesting hotel rooms no higher than the fifth floor and away from noisy booster pumps, and the importance of travel insurance. He was like a walking Google search engine.

"Every nation wants a piece of the (travel) pie—especially when those numbers are expected to continue to grow," Greenberg posts on his website.[10]

While the numbers of foreign travelers coming to the United States are down substantially due in part to the Trump administration's immigration policies, this actually works to the benefit of volunteers looking to serve overseas.

"What would have been foreigners' return seats are now our outbound seats, and the law of supply and demand rules—lower airfares because there are fewer folks flying. Those lower airfares are expected to continue on foreign routes throughout this year," he reported in early 2018.[11]

This suggests that travel to overseas destinations will be easier on the pocketbook, which, in turn, may encourage more people to consider foreign volunteer destinations where previously their focus was solely on opportunities in the United States. That said, less costly airfare is only one of the factors leading to the growth in voluntourism, as you'll read in the next chapter.

The Growth of Voluntourism

$\mathcal{D}$arryl Salerno and I go way back—to the mid-1970s when we both worked at a large public relations firm in New York City. What I didn't know then was what impresses me most about him now: his decades-long commitment to voluntourism.

He shares with me the parable of the starfish:

One day, an old man was walking along a beach that was littered with thousands of starfish that had been washed ashore by the high tide. As he walked he came upon a young boy who was eagerly throwing the starfish back into the ocean, one by one.

Puzzled, the man looked at the boy and asked what he was doing. Without looking up from his task, the boy simply replied, "I'm saving these starfish, sir."

The old man chuckled aloud, "Son, there are thousands of starfish and only one of you. What difference can you make?"

The boy picked up a starfish, gently tossed it into the water, and turning to the man, said, "I made a difference to that one!"[1]

The parable says much about how Salerno, a strategic consultant in marketing communications based north of New York, views his role in the world today. Since 1999, sometimes alone, sometimes with family, Salerno flies to Tegucigalpa, Honduras, hops on a bus with the rest of his group and their personal luggage packed with aspirin, prenatal vitamins, toothbrushes, and other supplies, and travels for hours to Rancho el Paraíso in the Agalta Valley in Central Honduras. There he stays for one week at a time working with Honduras Outreach (HOI), the Tucker, Georgia, nonprofit that organizes mission trips to Honduras and Nicaragua.[2]

HOI volunteers work side by side with Hondurans on a variety of community projects. Salerno's group, based at Rancho el Paraíso, poured cement floors and helped build two schools, a library, soccer field, and a highway bridge. They have also taught English and music, worked in nearby clinics, and installed new water filtration units and a computer room purchased through their fundraising efforts.

Salerno has accompanied dentists, audiologists, and veterinarians there to neuter dogs. Through this model, he believes short-term mission teams can make a long-term impact.[3]

"There was something in me that said I had to do this," Salerno recalls, explaining that his purpose in Honduras became vividly clear when he visited a ramshackle home in a nearby community.

"It started to rain, both the humidity and the temperature was in the 90s, and we took shelter in a run-down, single-room shack. A mud floor, two hammocks, and three benches. That was it. The family of six cooked outdoors on an open fire. Through a translator, our host asked if the homeowner, a middle-aged man who looked way older than his years, had anything to say.

"He wanted to thank Honduras Outreach for making the life of his family so much better over the past years," Salerno remembers.

"I couldn't help think, if this is what his life is now, what was it like before HOI arrived?

"The fact that the man was living in what most people would consider to be total squalor, and yet felt his life had improved dramatically, I knew I had to keep coming back."

Salerno has visited the Rancho el Paraíso almost twenty times over the years and has worked on efforts to help underprivileged Hondurans become more self-sufficient.

"We had success bringing in a potter to show the locals how to use a potter's wheel. Now, instead of making crude bowls and cups to sell to tourists, they make clay rings for vent pipes to sell to other Hondurans, pipes that vent smoke from their homes.

"Look, I'm a lucky human being to have been born in the United States. I could have been born anywhere else in the world and struggled to exist. Anyone can volunteer while traveling. It doesn't take any sort of specialized experience. The best I can offer are my muscles and brainpower. This costs me just $850 for food and lodging for the week, plus airfare, and whatever supplies I carry in my luggage.

"I'm not trying to save the world. I believe it's better to make a big change in a small place than a small change in a big place. I can witness the progress we're making in this region of the country. I see the same kids year

"There was something in me that said I had to do this," explains New York–area marketing communications consultant Darryl Salerno about his two decades of volunteer work in Honduras. Photo by Meryl Salerno.

after year; they remember me and I've been watching them grow and improve," Salerno says.

"One week a year in Honduras sets my mind straight."

Salerno's experience points to a growing trend: of travelers looking to make a difference, to become better tourists, to leave the destinations they visit a little better, whether it's through mission trips, volunteer vacations, mornings helping the underprivileged in cruise ship ports, or by simply bringing donated supplies in their baggage.

While numbers are hard to determine, and there are many definitions of voluntourism, as you'll learn within these pages, the industry in 2014 was estimated at about $2 billion annually by *Wilson Quarterly*.[4] That's based upon an estimated 1.6 million active voluntourists per year, according to NPR.[5]

Within sub-Saharan Africa alone, the youth travel market, including volunteer tourism, is one of the fastest-growing tourism niches and offers potential for continued development.[6]

Travel writer Alison Gardner created the term *voluntourism* in 1994 in an article she wrote about "volunteer vacations."[7] Another early use was by the Nevada Board of Tourism in 1998 to honor residents of Nevada who volunteered to support travel and tourism in the state. Before the 1990s, the term simply didn't exist, according to the Voluntourism Institute.[8]

Today voluntourism is a growing sector of the travel industry. It has been studied by academics, covered endlessly on social media, and is the subject of a variety of books.

There are a number of factors leading to its growth.

THE RISE OF CITIZEN DIPLOMACY

As we learned from Darryl Salerno, volunteer vacations can change your perspective on the world, teach you new skills, and greatly affect the lives of others.

"A 'citizen diplomat mindset' means being intentional when interacting with individuals from a different country by believing that one of your roles is to positively represent the United States," Jennifer Clinton, former president of citizen diplomacy nonprofit Global Ties, tells *Travel & Leisure* magazine.[9]

"Our reality today is that citizens around the world are having much greater influence on local, national, and international relations."

Being a citizen diplomat means not only representing your country but also engaging in meaningful interactions across cultures to create shared understanding.

Preston Sowell, an experienced expedition leader from Boulder, Colorado, believes: "People should contribute to the world. It's a privilege to go to these remote areas. It can be an enriching experience to engage in an altruistic activity away from the traditional tourist routes, then bring that perspective back home to your own culture.

"Too often, tourists never walk much beyond the main street. If you want to see a place and experience it, roll up your sleeves and get your hands dirty," Sowell says.

Adds Richard Bobo of Cultural Vistas, an international exchange nonprofit, "It's OK to have balance. Spend a few days in a resort. Then spend a day or two out in the country to really experience the culture," he tells *Travel & Leisure*.[10]

VOLUNTEERING HAS POSITIVE HEALTH BENEFITS

Assuming you don't become sick or injured, as I'll warn about in a coming chapter, volunteering is actually one of the many paths to good health. According to a 2013 study called "Doing Good Is Good for You," conducted by UnitedHealth Group, volunteers feel better—physically, mentally, and emotionally.[11]

Volunteers told researchers they are convinced their health is better because of the things they do when they volunteer. People who volunteer manage their stress better and feel a stronger connection to their communities. Some 96 percent of respondents reported that volunteering enriches their sense of purpose in life. In all of the pathways taken to good health, being a volunteer can help to make a meaningful difference, according to the study.

Wait, wait. There's more. Emerging science about the health benefits of volunteering help keep people engaged and stimulated, especially those in their retirement years. One seventy-three-year-old retiree from the bridal gown business, now a fifteen- to twenty-hour-per-week volunteer in New York, tells the *Wall Street Journal*, "You have to interact with people or your brain really dries up."[12]

A 2017 study by UnitedHealthcare and VolunteerMatch found employee volunteerism positively affects the health and well-being of the people who participate and strengthens their connections to their employers.

The report, titled the *"2017* Doing Good Is Good for You Study," reveals 75 percent of US adults feel physically healthier by volunteering. The mental and emotional benefits of volunteering are even greater, with 93 percent reporting an improved mood, 79 percent reporting lower stress levels, and 88 percent reporting increased self-esteem by giving back. Also, volunteers are significantly more likely to feel they have greater control over their health and well-being.[13]

Another study, this one involving more than sixty-four thousand subjects age sixty and older from 1998 to 2010, suggests volunteering slows the cognitive decline of aging. The author of the study, Sumedha Gupta, an assistant economics professor at Indiana University–Purdue University Indianapolis, found that an individual who is volunteering one hundred hours a year scores on average about 6 percent higher in cognitive testing than a nonvolunteer.[14]

Unlike paid work, there is a "different subjective well-being" or "warm glow" that a volunteer experiences from helping people. Volunteering is also unique "because it supplies mental, physical and social stimulation in one package," Gupta tells the *Wall Street Journal.*

"You have to move around, you interact with people, you think about activities."

Whereas completing a Sudoku puzzle offers one type of intellectual stimulation, she says, volunteers get all of these types of stimulation simultaneously.[15]

One logically concludes that combining the health benefits of travel mentioned in the previous chapter with how volunteering positively affects mind and body creates a win-win opportunity, the best of both worlds. Besides, as I hope you gather by now, it's the right thing to do.

TODAY'S MILLENNIALS
ARE MORE INTERESTED IN VOLUNTEERING

Millennials aren't just staring at their smartphones all day. OK, maybe many are. But they're also getting shit done. One study indicates they are more likely than their older counterparts to travel with a purpose. Eighty-four percent of millennials say they would travel abroad to participate in volunteer activities, according to a 2015 survey by Marriott Rewards Credit Card. Furthermore, 32 percent of millennials are interested in taking a charitable trip, while only two in ten Generation X travelers (18 percent) and baby boomers (17 percent) are interested in doing the same. Moreover, female travelers (28 percent), regardless of age, tend be more interested in taking a charitable vacation compared to their male counterparts (17 percent).

"Other generations may not assume millennials would use their most precious assets, their time and money, to give back to international communities they visit, but today's young travelers are reframing that mindset," said Vibhat Nair, general manager, Chase Card Services.

"We've seen in the past that this generation of travelers value rewards and perks from travel services, and now we're seeing how they could be using those rewards for a larger purpose."[16]

When Sam Daddono was a junior at Rumson-Fair Haven High School in New Jersey, his whole Spanish class relocated to Antigua to sharpen their Spanish skills. They also hiked up the side of a volcano every morning to help tend to a coffee plantation—and learn about what life is like in Guatemala, according to an NPR report by Carrie Kahn.[17]

"The way I view things now is a lot different than before," Daddono tells NPR. "I've visited other countries, but I've never done hands-on work or really talked to the people about the problems that they face in their lives."

That worldview for many American teens is a lot different than it was two decades ago, says Ken Jones, who owns Maximo Nivel, a volunteer tourism company based in Antigua. He got his start in the travel business, offering only Spanish-language classes. But young people today, he says, want a richer experience.

"It used to be beach and beer," Jones tells NPR. "And now it's, 'Well, I want to come down and learn something and figure out how to help or be a part of something.' It was more superficial twenty years ago, maybe."

Matt Wastradowski writes in RootsRated.com, "This new generation of travelers is traveling abroad to earthquake-proof buildings, teach in schools, paint classrooms, and install toilets.

"Volunteer travelers are looking for culturally immersive experiences. Volunteer tourists are no different than most travelers in one key regard: They want to see new, different parts of the world, and doing so while doing something good for the local community makes the experience all the more appealing," states Wastradowski.[18]

Dr. Marc Mancini, a travel industry consultant, agrees. He writes in a 2015 post for the Travel Institute an article titled, "The Five Things You Must Know About Millennials," "One of the most admirable Millennial traits is their desire to make things better, to fix the society they're inheriting. That explains why they're attracted to 'voluntourism.' They want to help hurricane-ravaged towns get back on their feet, do something about poverty in developing nations and experience authentic places, not tourist-enhanced ones."[19]

ADVANCES IN TECHNOLOGY
ENCOURAGE CITIZEN SCIENCE

Today's volunteer field researchers are more likely to wear baseball caps than pith helmets, and instead of lugging large wooden cameras and tripods, they're carrying handheld Garmin GPS units and data loggers, some no more complicated than an iPhone.

Later in the book, we'll explain how scientists seek field research from tourists who travel the world. One woman studies plastic pollution in the seas. Other volunteers collect information about wildlife–vehicle collisions, and even study animal feces.

Tourists at the Maasai-owned Il Ngwesi Group Ranch in northern Kenya, a local conservancy, are collecting data on animals they observe and study the state of the soil, while still enjoying traditional sightseeing activities such as participating in game drives, sunbathing near the pool, or visiting the in-house beauty/massage therapist.

In short, technology is opening the doors to extraordinary data collection by ordinary travelers.

Nigel Winser, an environmental consultant based in Oxfordshire, England, one hundred miles west of London, has a front-row perspective on technology's role in encouraging citizen science. For ten years he was executive vice president at Earthwatch, which has helped over one hundred thousand citizen scientists participate in impactful field research that disseminates world-class scientific research. Winser also serves as a trustee of the

Nekton Mission,[20] which is studying the bathyal zone, the largest and least understood ecosystem in the known universe, located 3,300 to 13,100 feet below the ocean surface.

"Volunteer tourists without any formal science training can play a significant role in our understanding of the planet. It's becoming easier and easier to collect meaningful data from the field using handheld smartphones and laptops," Winser says.

"Volunteers can record field observations and capture their exact locations down to one single meter."

Using the right tools, anyone can study water anywhere in the world, for instance, then feed the data to an organization such as Earthwatch Freshwater Watch, a research project investigating the health of global freshwater ecosystems.[21] All it takes is a smartphone with the FreshWater Watch App or paper data sheet and a collection bottle.

"Millennials have become increasingly knowledgeable about the state of the world and are particularly adept at using social media, which can share concepts such as voluntourism exponentially across boundaries," he says, citing the growing popularity of the so-called Three Minute Rule practiced in the Arabian Sultanate of Oman, where Winser often consults. Local environmental groups, including the Environmental Society of Oman, ask for just three minutes per person to clean up plastic from local beaches, hoping, of course, for more time than that.

"Ten people volunteering for three minutes equals a half-hour's work and a carload of beach litter, all carefully documented on Facebook, Twitter, and Instagram, thus promoting the concept to several thousand online visitors."

Winser cites the increased popularity of global databases, especially those focused on the planet's biodiversity, such as the UK's National Biodiversity Network (NBN), a nonprofit composed of UK wildlife conservation organizations, government, country agencies, environmental agencies, local environmental records centers, and many voluntary groups.[22] The NBN Atlas holds over 217 million biological records, the largest biodiversity database for any country in the world, according to the NBN website.

Winser also recommends a similar database called the Encyclopedia of Life (EOL), a free, online collaborative encyclopedia intended to document all of the 1.9 million living species known to science. It works with iNaturalist.org so that anyone can share observations from their schoolyard, backyard, from their walk to work and around town, or as part of a structured citizen science activity.[23]

In September 2016, Winser, a former deputy director of the Royal Geographical Society (with IBG), wrote the Society's *Geographical* magazine review of Harvard conservation biologist E. O. Wilson's book, *Half-Earth: Our Planet's Fight for Life* (2016).[24]

Winser writes, "Respected internationally as the 'father of biodiversity' [Wilson] has witnessed first-hand global habitat loss and the impact this is having on the estimated eight million species of the world.

"Sadly the trends of habitat loss, species extinction, global warming and ocean acidification continue to threaten the functioning of our life-sustaining biosphere. To give nature a chance, Wilson advocates a collective commitment to aim much higher than the level that the global conservation movement is currently achieving."

Winser's book review continues: "And so, with increased moral reasoning, helped by global messaging platforms and our individual hand-held devices, all of us can take a much greater interest in our landscapes and vote for increased protection. In short, now is the best of times to work collaboratively and innovatively to keep biodiversity at the top of the political, scientific, teaching, economic, and conservation agendas, for food, water, and energy security for all."

Recently, Winser shared with me his opinion that "improvements in technology and field-guided apps are allowing average tourists without specialized training help collect pieces of the geographical jigsaw."

GROWING ACCEPTANCE OF FAIR TRADE LEARNING

The voluntourism industry has increasingly adopted the concept of Fair Trade Learning, a framework for ethical engagement by host communities, nonprofit organizations, and (potential) volunteers alike. It arose out of criticism over young voluntourists more interested in sightseeing and partying than a true partnership with local communities.

The subject of a number of studies, Fair Trade Learning is a global educational partnership that prioritizes reciprocity in relationships through cooperative, cross-cultural participation in learning, service, and civil society efforts. It fosters the goals of economic equity, equal partnership, mutual learning, cooperative and positive social change, transparency, and sustainability.[25]

Fair Trade Learning involves participants who give and receive something from others that they would not otherwise have. By volunteering in economically marginalized communities, participants contribute otherwise unavailable (human) resources. This may include English language tutoring, infrastructure development, and a variety of other skilled and unskilled contributions.

Volunteers offer direct labor and share resources. Community members share housing, cooperate in labor projects, tell stories, and orient volunteers to other ways of being.

Fair Trade Learning also involves the sharing of knowledge between the voluntourist and the local participant, and it's the process whereby participants produce something new together that would not otherwise exist.

Significantly, community members have a strong participatory voice in planning and implementation, reducing the risk of unwanted projects and paternalistic assumptions. Volunteer projects must be community driven to be effective.[26]

In effect, it's a code of conduct that encourages utmost respect on both sides to help create a more just, equitable, and sustainable world.[27]

VOLUNTOURISM BUILDS RESUMES

Think back to your college application. I can remember padding it with as many extracurricular activities and jobs as I could conjure up. Counter man at a Catskill Mountains bowling alley. Check. Bar waiter at the famed Concord Hotel in the New York Borscht Belt. Check. I even worked with comedians Don Rickles and Milton Berle, although they were entertaining on stage and I was serving club sodas in the back of the nightclub to senior citizens. No matter. Technically, we worked together, at least together in the same room.

The process hasn't changed much for college and job applicants. If college applicants, admission officers, and potential employers can agree on one thing, it's that international experience can improve a person's chances of college acceptance, and later, finding a job and succeeding in the global workforce.

Graduates with international experience find employment faster than those without it, and they find that their languages, intercultural awareness, and overseas contacts are valued by their employers, according to the 2016 Kaplan study, "Going Global: Are Graduates Prepared for a Global Workforce?"[28]

"Respondents who had gained international experience during their studies were twice as likely to be employed within six months of graduation than those who did not have the same opportunities," says Kaplan, which serves over 1.2 million students globally each year through its array of higher education, test preparation, and professional education services.

Keith Bellows, the late editor-in-chief of *National Geographic Traveler*, believed that "true learning happens between the poles, not just between the ears."[29]

When young students expand their horizons by volunteering, no matter whether domestically or internationally, they come away with far more than they give.

Alice Hawkes fondly recalls her own travels to Fiji at age eighteen, conducting volunteer work for three months during her gap year between high school and college. Today she's director of marketing for Global Vision International (GVI), a British company based in Cape Town, South Africa, that organizes conservation and community development programs worldwide.[30]

"We're keen for young people to become volunteers and develop personally and professionally as they make a difference in the world. In addition to providing employable hard skills like collecting scientific data in the field, learning to dive, and studying the health of coral reefs, volunteering abroad also helps develop soft skills such as confidence, teamwork, problem solving, and cross-cultural fluency, that they'll use their entire career," Hawkes says.

GVI offers 150 different volunteer projects in thirteen countries around the world, attracting approximately 2,500 volunteers a year, ranging in age from the teens to the eighties. Projects last anywhere from one week to six months. All volunteer work abroad projects are run in collaboration with local partners and communities. For the volunteer, costs are generally $1,700 per week (minimum one week), including food and accommodations. Airfare is additional.

"Participation in GVI programs in 2017 have grown from the previous year, with particularly strong numbers signing up for GVI's under eighteen projects that attract high school students interested in building their resumes, understanding different cultures, and learning specific skills while they gain confidence in themselves," Hawkes adds.

"It's also an affordable way to give back. Young people today are keenly aware of issues in the world. They see plastic pollution in the oceans, they see the effects of rising oceans and greenhouses gases, and the polar ice cap melting. They like to know they're contributing and doing their part. Even if they only volunteer for one week, we show them how their work fits into the bigger picture."

VOLUNTEERING DEVELOPS A
MORE DIRECT HUMAN CONNECTION

Voluntourists today seek direct human connections, which Discover Corps, a volunteer travel program based in San Diego, provides annually to nearly one thousand travelers to fifteen countries since its founding in 2013. It's part of

Terra Education, a certified B-Corporation, a new type of corporation that uses the power of business to solve social and environmental problems.

Andrew Motiwalla, founder and director, believes, "Voluntourism organizations offer authentic experiences, something mainstream 'follow-the-flag' and 'lie-on-a-beach' tours fail to deliver. One reason is human connections are hard to predict and hard to scale up to accommodate the large number of people who are traveling today."

Sharing economy services featuring peer-to-peer guided experiences such as Airbnb Social Impact Experiences (which I'll cover shortly), Adventure Local, and BonAppetour promise hands-on travel opportunities but fail to deliver on the potential benefits of volunteer travel, which Motiwalla believes is the intersection of authentic experiences, personal development, and donor-directed philanthropy.

The company allows travelers to get to know a region of the world in a way that would be difficult, if not impossible, for tourists. Travelers connect directly with local people and service organizations to help with problems they might not see closer to home, he says. Discover Corps partners with service organizations who are already doing good, sustainable work in their communities.

"We do not parachute in with our own projects. For instance, in Peru, our volunteers visit a family-owned lodge outside of Cusco where travelers can spend an afternoon with a local women's group, go to their homes to learn how to cook a Peruvian meal, share that meal together, then volunteer four afternoons that week at an after-school program to teach conversational English, play educational games, and provide tutoring.

"The lodge benefits from the revenue, the women's group receives a stipend for the meal, and the children benefit from conversing with visitors fluent in the English language.

"The enthusiasm of the visitors is energizing for the staff at the school—many are located in marginalized communities that don't experience much support from their fellow Peruvians. Meanwhile, it's a catalyzing experience for travelers," says Motiwalla, a former Peace Corps volunteer in Central America.

"Considering the amount of noise in society, what with the onslaught of social media, work and family obligations, this becomes one of the few opportunities to totally unplug, go into a community with an open heart, and make a difference while seeing a new country, learning about new cultures, and, yes, even having fun."

He might also add falling in love.

That was the case with Katherine Cassidy of Lubec, Maine, a widow, and a Maine State Representative who lost her reelection campaign in 2014 and was ready for the next chapter in her life.

When she was introduced to volunteer work in Kenya and Uganda in 2015, the trajectory of her life changed dramatically. She employed her skills in leadership and group dynamics to train farmers receiving assistance from the USAID's Farmer-to-Farmer Program that provides technical assistance to farmers, farm groups, agribusinesses, and other agriculture sector institutions in developing countries.

Shortly thereafter, she found herself consulting with sweet potato, vanilla, coffee, and rice farmers, not knowing very much about agriculture, although she would come to learn more after six trips to Africa.

She wasn't seeking love when she traveled to Sierra Leone, the fourteenth poorest country on Earth according to the International Monetary Fund.[31] Instead, love found her in the form of thirty orphan girls, ages eight to seventeen, and a widower named Emmanuel Kamara. He is the charismatic head of the Home of Hope, run by the Touch the Sky Foundation, in the Sierra Leone town of Kambia on the Guinea border.[32]

She writes about that first trip to Sierra Leone in an op-ed published in the Maine *Ellsworth American*: "I considered Sierra Leone the most challenging place I had ever been, both physically and emotionally. The heat and humidity were a sweltering, unforgiving combination. There is no power to recharge laptop or mobile phone batteries, except by generator at night. There is no refrigeration, and food options are mostly white rice with fish sauce. Cold showers (and bathing from a bucket) are the norm in a guesthouse, and toilets tend not to work. There are harsh limitations and few comforts."

Cassidy continues, "For all its tragedies and sadness, Sierra Leone fascinated me from my first moment. I felt drawn here. During my work with the farmers in the rural village upcountry, I realized I was truly needed and appreciated."[33]

Since 2013, Kamara has provided each girl in the Home of Hope program with school fees, school uniforms and shoes, and school materials.

"They are precious and amazing and lucky to have Emmanuel in their lives," Cassidy tells me by telephone during a visit back home to Maine for fundraising.[34] In Sierra Leone, it's a rare household in which children have something to eat in the morning, or later at school. Mostly children might eat a bowl of rice with some sauce once a day. When there's not enough money in the household to buy rice, the children go to bed hungry, Cassidy explains.

"The best volunteers are optimists, open to all possibilities, and not defeated by experiencing extreme poverty."

In August 2017, Cassidy moved to Kambia under a residency permit and is now engaged to be married to Kamara in 2019. It's something she would never have imagined during her years in the Maine State House arguing about politics and policies. But her position on the legislature's Health and

Human Service Committee helped her prepare for a world where empathy makes for smooth transitions.

IT'S MORE ECONOMICAL

You can easily spend $13,000 per person to go on a Grand African Safari for eighteen days or $6,600 per person to spend ten days in China with Kensington Tours. In comparison, volunteer vacations offer good value to those on a tight budget because they are priced to reflect living conditions and meal delivery at a lower expectation level than traditional vacations, says senior travel editor Alison Gardner of Transitions Abroad.[35]

In other words, since you're not paying to stay at the Ritz-Carlton, don't expect a mint on your pillow each night.

"Dormitory-style or shared accommodation with shared bathrooms, billeting in local homes, different levels of camping, as well as cafeteria- or family-style food preparation and delivery may all be part of a particular project. Some may offer a surprising level of privacy and physical comfort—with air conditioning, private rooms, and gourmet chefs in the kitchen. Some provide educational lectures and entertainment in the evening, or organized group excursions to explore surrounding areas on days off," Gardner writes.

Earlier in this chapter, voluntourist Darryl Salerno said it only cost $850, plus airfare, to spend a week enriching his life by assisting the people of Honduras. Clearly, travel, and voluntourism in particular, is not just for the well-to-do.

AIRBNB IS MORE THAN HEADS IN BEDS

Seemingly out of nowhere in 2008 came Airbnb, which has disrupted the hospitality industry, caused housing shortages for local workers in resort areas, and now has a huge following. The numbers are staggering for this travel juggernaut: over 4 million lodging listings in 65,000 cities and 191 countries, with over 260 million check-ins and counting, according to its website.

My experience with the service has been spotty. I can recall one home my wife and I booked in Breckenridge, Colorado, that was in a messy double-wide trailer, with a shared bathroom and an enormous cat that we had to kick out of bed frequently during a sleepless night.

Other people rave about the service, which today offers more than simply a place to rest your head. It is introducing thousands to the concept of voluntourism.

Airbnb Social Impact Experiences inspire activities that support local causes around the world. It allows hosts to partner with nonprofits to create transformational interactions for local and global causes. As such, the service is sort of voluntourism *lite* for those with limited time, limited funds, or, in some cases, limited interest in traveling far. There are two-hundred-plus social impact experiences in over fifty cities, according to the website.[36]

One definite advantage to using the website is that Airbnb waives its service fees so that 100 percent of the earnings go directly to the nonprofit.

You can hike Runyon Canyon Park in Los Angeles, a 160-acre park at the eastern end of the Santa Monica Mountains, with a rescue dog, and know that 100 percent of the $45 per person fee goes to Free Animal Doctor, a nonprofit animal welfare organization. "Your photos will be used to help bring in donations for the pups' care and generate adoption interest," writes the organizer.[37]

In Amsterdam, you can participate in a two-hour Plastic Fishing Adventure for $32 per person and help make the city's famed canals plastic-free. Proceeds go to Plastic Whale, reportedly the first professional plastic fishing company in the world. They are a social enterprise hoping to make the world's waters plastic-free by creating value from plastic waste. The plastic that volunteers collect is turned into boats and furniture. Fishing nets and gloves are provided.[38]

Traveling to New York? You can kayak the Brooklyn shoreline for two hours for $50 per person, knowing that your experience helps fund the all-volunteer Red Hook Boaters, a nonprofit organization that provides free walk-up kayaking to the general public in the low-income Red Hook, Brooklyn, neighborhood.[39]

VOLUNTEERING IS A FAMILY AFFAIR

In the past, the number of programs that accepted volunteers under eighteen were few and far between. That is starting to change, with organizations such as Children's Global Alliance[40] and GoEco,[41] both focused on trips for teens.

For parents reluctant to allow their children to travel out of the United States alone, many are considering taking their children along on multiweek and multimonth trips that are more education than a typical vacation, and as such offer opportunities to instill important volunteer values.

There's no better place to demonstrate such virtues than on extended family trips, well away from daily distractions, peer pressure, and especially ever-present smartphones that are seemingly duct taped to the hands of every child in America starting in their preteens.

Travel industry professional Susan Farewell, founder and owner of Farewell Travels LLC in Westport, Connecticut, is a travel designer.[42] No, not a travel agent. Not a tour operator. She customizes independent trips by appointment only, from the moment her clients arrive in a foreign land to their safe return home, and she does so with an eye toward responsible tourism and a determination to help people learn more about the world through travel.

Airport transfers, personalized tours, waterski rentals, surfing lessons, and restaurant reservations are some of the services she provides in return for a commission from the various local businesses and a planning fee paid by the client that depends upon the complexity of the trip.

Farewell reports her company plans an increasing number of itineraries for families taking their young elementary and middle school students out of class for extended trips lasting many weeks or months.

A former travel editor at Condé Nast in New York, Farewell continues to write about travel for both magazines and newspapers such as the *New York Times* and the *New York Post*. She's also author of several travel books and has been interviewed about travel frequently on radio and TV.

"Parents see their friends on social media taking their children on multicountry educational trips and want to do the same, often with a volunteer component baked into the schedule," Farewell says.

"My first question is whether parents want it to be a vacation or an educational experience. Usually, it's the latter. Rather than lie on the beach and play tennis or golf, they're looking for ways to engage with the local community and teach their children something about the world and the importance of giving back. That often means volunteering for at least part of their visit."

One of her client families returned this year from a three-and-a-half-month trip through Central and South America. Their three preteens were roadschooled—they worked on homework assignments almost every day and participated in Skype lessons from their hotel rooms. They also filed periodic trip reports back to their classrooms to remain engaged with their school during their long absence.

Most of her clients traveling with children want to volunteer at local schools, a request Farewell is happy to facilitate so long as the families refrain from acting like voyeurs.

"Schools are not tourist attractions, and they're not there to make North Americans feel especially privileged due to their wealth. Sometimes these visits can feel manufactured and disruptive.

"We work with local nonprofits, including one in Peru and another in Ecuador, to make sure a school visit is appropriate, meaningful, and respectful. We try to make visitors feel less like tourists and more a part of the community. For some clients, they report that interacting with local schoolchildren was the best part of their trip," she recalls.

"When creating a family budget, take your vacation dollars and instead allocate them to your education budget. Treat this important family travel time as an eye-opening education about the world."

Rainer Jenss, a married father of two young boys, echoes Farewell's sentiments about the redeeming value of family travel. After a thirteen-year career as a vice president with the National Geographic Society, including a stint at *National Geographic Kids* magazine, Jenss realized not enough parents were taking full advantage of all the opportunities that voluntourism has to offer.

To help create a broader awareness of all the possibilities, he launched the Family Travel Association, a coalition of the travel industry's leading suppliers, resources, and experts on the subject of traveling with children. Its mission is to inspire families to travel by (1) promoting all the child-friendly experiences that families can share together, (2) educating the public on all the positive and lasting benefits travel affords young people, and (3) simplifying the process of planning a trip.[43]

"The places you can travel to and the things you can do shouldn't shrink when you have kids," he believes. "We've found that the demographic most predisposed to wanting to volunteer while traveling are families. When you travel with a child, you're not traveling for yourself, you're traveling for others. You're more selfless when you're a parent; it's a more compassionate mindset. For parents, the experience of volunteering is something they want to pass onto their kids."

Jenss did just that when his family traveled to the Beqa Lagoon Resort in Fiji. In addition to typical tourist activities, he and his sons—all three are certified divers—helped rehabilitate coral reefs through the Beqa Lagoon Initiative, a project that Beqa Lagoon Resort collaborates with the Pacific Blue Foundation, focusing on ecosystem-based management of marine and coastal environments.[44]

Resort guests harvest healthy "fragments of opportunity"—dispersed coral fragments, broken from the mother coral colonies that otherwise would have a very low chance of survival. These fragments, approximately five centimeters in diameter (about two inches), are then mounted on a base and placed on an underwater coral nursery to recover and grow. Routine maintenance at the nursery cleans and removes sediment, algae, and other fast-growing invertebrates, which would otherwise jeopardize the survival of the corals,

On a volunteer vacation in Fiji, resort guests harvest healthy "fragments of opportunity"—dispersed coral fragments, broken from the mother coral colonies that otherwise would have a very low chance of survival, according to Sefano M. Katz, project manager for the Beqa Lagoon Initiative. He's pictured above delivering a tray with coral nubbins to the coral nursery. Photo by Frankie Rivera.

according to an email from Sefano M. Katz, project manager for the Beqa Lagoon Initiative.[45]

"Guests are able to adopt the corals they deploy to the nursery, giving them a much more personal experience, and the donated funds support the project," Katz says.

"Months later, after the corals grow large enough—over ten centimeters in diameter (approximately 3.9 inches) in the nursery—they are transplanted onto a location with low live coral cover."

Jenss recalls, "It was like planting a tree—eventually healthy corals would surround it and grow, helping to rejuvenate that portion of the reef. It only took about four hours, and was definitely 'soft' volunteering, but we decided that instead of leaning back and lying on a beach, we would lean forward and help the boys connect in a small way to protect the environment."

HELP RESTORE CORAL REEFS IN MALAYSIA AND BALI

Other resorts that offer voluntourists the opportunity to help restore coral reefs include the Andaman, a Luxury Collection Resort, on Malaysia's Langkawi Island, and the Alila Manggis, a secluded seaside resort in Manggis, East Bali, Indonesia.

A fringing reef located in the bay fronting the Andaman is estimated to be between six thousand and eight thousand years old. While not ideal for snorkeling, it provides a trail for guided reef walks where one can learn more about marine biology, according to the Andaman website.[46]

The 2004 Indian Ocean earthquake and tsunami resulted in the destruction of thousands of coral colonies on the Andaman Reef. The dead corals that were detached from the reef by the impact of the tsunami now move around through wave action, causing further destruction to living corals and inhibiting regrowth.

Once or twice monthly, at times of low tide, guests and resort ambassadors gather to clear away the dead corals from the reef, giving the living corals a better chance of survival. The resort calls this activity "gentle laboring." The dead coral material is then recycled through the construction of mini artificial reefs at the coral nursery. Coral fragments are attached to these structures, and after four to twelve months of nurturing, they are returned to the sea where it's hoped they will blossom as part of a healthy new coral garden.

In 2014, the Andaman partnered with Lafarge Cement and the National University of Malaysia (UKM) to introduce ARMS (Artificial Reef Module System) as an addition to the many coral-related activities at the resort. It involved Lafarge manufacturing concrete structures that will act both as a coral substrate and as a living space for juvenile fish. Eventually, the project hopes to develop a sustainable fishing resource for the people of Langkawi.

"What started out as a voluntary activity for the Andaman associates (employees) during low tides is now a highlighted activity for guests. It all started with a few guests watching as the team carefully removes dead coral from the sea that were rolling over and damaging live corals. When we explained what we were doing, we were pleasantly surprised at how many adults and children wanted to help and do their little bit to save the environment—one polyp at a time," says Carlos Tarrero, general manager of the Andaman.

Environmental consultant Gerald B. Goeden established and now supervises marine conservation activities at the resort. He told me recently, "Surveys indicate that the programs increase tourist bookings by 10 to 15 percent and have a strong, positive influence on returning guests, especially families. From a resort perspective, this is very good business from a small investment."

At Alila Manggis, divers and snorkelers can also help restore the local reef. Based on the rapid assessments of Bali's reefs conducted by Conservation International, the reefs around the Candidasa area, namely Gili Tepekong, and West and East Gili Mimpang, are reefs of high conservation value. Alila Manggis, in conjunction with Zen Dive Bali, organize a periodic beach and underwater cleanup of the "Underwater Garden" artificial reef. Volunteers, either certified divers or snorkelers, can help when the resort visits the site weekly to maintain the garden, plant new coral, and monitor coral growth.

Guests who support the project are credited on name tags placed underwater by Zen Dive Bali and are emailed updates on coral growth.

The resort also organizes a Plastic-Free Oceans cleanup involving local residents, the Alila team, and resort guests. The session begins with an interactive presentation explaining how the resort contributes to the worldwide debris database with its cleanup, explaining the reasons and needs behind such an initiative.[47]

Stories about voluntourism appear in the media frequently. Books, such as this one, continue to be published. The benefits of family voluntourism is spreading but still has a long way to travel before it goes mainstream.

In its 2017 US Family Travel Survey, the Family Travel Association asked respondents if they ever took a volunteer vacation. Just 7 percent responded affirmatively versus 73 percent reporting they visited a theme park in the last year. However, according to the study, 30 percent reported wanting to take a vacation that included at least some element of giving back to the communities visited.[48]

Why don't more families go on volunteer vacations? Jenss believes it comes down to awareness. "There's confusion about which programs are better than others. Besides which, they range in price, from free to many thousands of dollars a week," he says.

Despite the obstacles, Jenss points to the benefits of family voluntourism.

"It helps kids develop skills such as compassion, empathy, and self-confidence. Travel opens the doors for youths to discover the world and discover themselves. It instills values and can build a strong foundation for children. The younger you travel with kids, especially if it includes a community service component—the more profound, more memorable, and more impactful the experience becomes," Jenss says.

"When you learn to travel, you'll travel to learn. Volunteer vacations should be just as transformational as they are recreational. After all, you don't have to give up sightseeing to volunteer on vacation. You can do both."

Jenss adds, "Parents want to set their children up for success, and volunteer travel is one way to do it. And it doesn't have to be a heavy lift. Often voluntourism involves real life, human interaction. It's a personal connection versus a digital one. For that one brief, shining moment, they're fully engaged and not buried in their smartphones."

Jenss points to the challenge of picking the right volunteer project that will resonate with you and your travel companions. One volunteer found his calling in Nepal, while another—uh, me, in fact—found a Nepal volunteer trip particularly grueling. Luckily, volunteer opportunities range across the board, as we'll learn in the next chapter.

· III ·

Selecting the Right Project

No book is going to tell you what notable cause to support. It has to come from your heart. Consider what's most important to you—fighting cancer, curing blindness, helping animals, ensuring people have access to books, schoolchildren have desks, or would you rather volunteer to help local African communities gain access to clean drinking water? Voluntourists can learn much from others who have found their life's mission through travel with purpose.

Realize that this is an investment of your time, effort, and money. You will likely pay your own expenses, plus be required to make a financial contribution to the host nonprofit. If the experience is positive, be prepared: you'll probably become even more committed and start raising funds once returning back home.

On the other hand, this may be the one and only time that you ever take such a trip. If that's the case, give yourself every opportunity to have the best experience possible.

Ask whether the project will take you where you want to go. Does it meet a personal yearning to see more of the world before you slough off this mortal coil?

What social issues do you care most about? Wherever you're going, there are people who are exploring innovative solutions to similar issues. Importantly, consider your age and health. Are you up to the task?

"You're going to be working hard and likely staying in bare-bones accommodations, so you need passion to stick with your commitment," says Courtney Regan, the founder of the San Francisco travel company Courtney Regan Travel.[1]

Voluntourism attracts more than bark-eating, Birkenstock-wearing, bivouac-on-the-side-of-a-cliff outdoor elites. It appeals to a broad range of the traveling public: senior citizens volunteering to build libraries in Uganda, former airline flight attendants, high school English teachers, millennials, and retired baby boomers alike.

There are numerous opportunities to volunteer as a tourist. The right project for you, the one that has the potential to be transformational and life alerting and launch you on a career of service to your fellow human beings, depends upon your willingness to commit time, energy, financial resources, and sometimes even sheer brute strength on behalf of others.

For inspiration, consider the stories of the following dedicated volunteers. Their experiences provide direction on the various forms of voluntourism available. Some opportunities are as close as Las Vegas or Denver. Others require a passport and inoculations. But all attract everyday people who strive to make the world a better place.

FOCUS ON A SPECIFIC NEED

Joe Watson is an affable Texas real estate developer I met for the first time alighting from a helicopter in a remote, roadless village in Nepal. He's wearing one of those safari jackets you often see on TV adventure programs, the ones emblazoned with patches. A serial adventurer, the seventy-three-year-old Houstonian is a member of the Explorers Club, the international exploration society whose members have included Sir Edmund Hillary, Thor Heyerdahl, and Neil Armstrong.

Watson is a proud glider and aerobatic pilot who boasts, "I poke holes in the sky for fun." He's also traveling with a veritable camera store worth of gear—expensive Canon cameras and lenses, two drones, and lots of camera bags and accessories.

In 2014, Watson was introduced to Dooley Intermed International,[2] a multinational nonprofit established in 1961 to continue the humanitarian work of Dr. Thomas A. Dooley III, the so-called jungle doctor, a charismatic medical missionary from a comfortable St. Louis suburb who in the 1950s captivated the American public with his aid to the people of Asia. During the Eisenhower years, Dooley's remote medicine missions—seventeen in all—were established in impoverished areas of fourteen Asian countries using millions of dollars donated by those he had inspired, according to the Dooley Intermed website.

In short order, Watson became a significant supporter of Dooley's Eco Home for Orphaned Children outside Kathmandu, a home for twenty-eight children who live at the facility while they attend an on-site school.

"I love people, I love children, so support of an orphanage made the most sense to me," he says as a mule train, the long-haul truckers of the Himalayas, pass us with bags of rice lashed to their sides, bells around their necks softly pealing.

Watson learned of the need for a reliable supply of fresh milk from the Eco Home manager, who explained how the children often became ill due to a lack of fresh protein. After much research, Watson realized that water buffaloes are preferable to dairy cows and set about to donate two.

There are 130 million domesticated water buffalo, according to the Dooley Intermed website. More humans rely on water buffalo than any other domesticated animal. Water buffalo are suitable for tilling rice fields, and their milk is richer in fat and protein than that of dairy cattle. Through his contacts in Texas, Watson raised a modest $10,000, which was enough for two animals and a shed they nicknamed the "Cow Palace."

In his endearing Texas twang, he tells me, "I put the big britches on some wealthy friends, and after buying the water buffaloes, had money left over for the shed, then raised even more money from my 'Buffalo Buddies' to pay for a full-time caretaker who grinds up their feed. It was more complicated than I thought."

This is Watson's third mission to Nepal, and he's on a personal mission to check the status of the two donated water buffaloes named Sterling and Sydney, in honor of the children of one of his donors. Later that day, Watson provides a tour of the corral, admonishing me to remove my red parka, explaining that water buffalo are agitated by that color.

He continues, "We also provided room and board for the caretaker's wife and enrolled his son in the Eco Home's school alongside the other young residents."

The Eco Home's water buffalo milk is boiled, then used for drinking, cooking, cheese, and yogurt.

"The kids take to it like a milk shake at McDonald's," laughs Watson, who the kids have come to call "Buffalo Joe."

"Our next goal, which seems entirely possible after I ran the numbers, is the opportunity to create a profit center and selling the milk. There is a ready market for both excess milk and extra calves."

The future holds the possibility of a second Eco Home for Orphaned Children, this one containing fifty beds, more water buffaloes, and chickens that would provide an organic food supply for the kids. He jokes, "I just sure hope they don't change my name to 'Chicken Joe.'"

Watson takes the long view: "People need to stop worrying about where their wine comes from and wearing chic clothing. They need to start worrying about sustaining this planet. If we're not careful, it's going to become really temporary."

This water buffalo is named "Sydney" after the daughter of one of its donors. The massive beasts are suitable for tilling rice fields, and their milk is richer in fat and protein than that of dairy cattle. Photo by Joe Watson.

Volunteer efforts to raise funds for two water buffaloes for a childrens' home near Kathmandu earned Texas real estate developer Joe Watson (left center) the nickname "Buffalo Joe." Photo by Jeff Blumenfeld.

It doesn't take a successful career as a Texas real estate developer with wealthy friends to raise $10,000. That's a number within reach of many industrious voluntourists.

Watson is making a major difference in the health of twenty-eight Nepali children, focusing on a specific need in one corner of the Third World, where a little effort goes a long way. His success shows that one small, relatively low-cost idea can have a magnifying, expanding, ultimately even a generational impact over time.

George Basch, a well-known philanthropist in the outdoors industry (think hiking boots, backpacks, and tents), had his own eureka moment. The year was 2001 when Basch was part of the team that supported athlete Erik Weihenmayer's first blind ascent of Mount Everest. During the eight-day trek to the 17,500-foot-high base camp, he was astounded by the primitive Stone Age cooking conditions in many impoverished homes.

Upon his return back to Taos, New Mexico, where he lives in an adobe-style home with an expansive view of the Sangre de Cristo mountains, the property tax and financial consultant learned that Nepalis cooking over unvented stoves or over indoor fire pits were subjecting themselves to excessive amounts of fuel while polluting their indoor air to dangerously unhealthy levels.

On a global scale, deadly Household Air Pollution (HAP) is responsible for 4.3 million premature deaths annually (7.7 percent of global mortality in 2012).

Three billion people (42 percent of the world's population) cook primitively, causing widespread destructive environmental impacts—deforestation and emissions of black carbon into the atmosphere, thus accelerating glacial snowmelt and global warming.

Says Dr. Maria Neira, head of public health and the environment for the World Health Organization (WHO), "We have 3.7 million people dying a year from outdoor air pollution, and 4.3 million from household pollution. Almost half the world is still cooking like in the Stone Age."[3]

In 2010, Basch founded the nonprofit Himalayan Stove Project (HSP),[4] a humanitarian and philanthropic program dedicated to preserving the Himalayan environment and improving the health of the people living in the trans-Himalayan region.

Determined to improve living and health conditions among the people of Nepal, he sourced clean, fuel-efficient Envirofit cookstoves that reduce household air pollution by 90 percent and consume up to 75 percent less fuel while cooking 50 percent faster.

The Envirofit stoves support the environment through dramatically reduced fuel consumption and reduction of black carbon in the air. It also

Fuel-efficient Envirofit cookstoves distributed by the Himalayan Stove Project reduce household air pollution by 90 percent and consume up to 75 percent less fuel while cooking 50 percent faster. Founder George Basch is helping to clear the air in Nepal one stove at a time. Photo by George Basch.

increases home safety, as there are numerous, tragic instances where children have fallen into open cooking fires.

Over the eight years since founding the HSP, through a sustained major fundraising effort, the HSP shipped over five thousand individual and institutional cookstoves to Nepal, thus positively impacting the lives of an estimated forty thousand Nepalis. In fact, immediately following the 2015 earthquake that resulted in the loss of nine thousand lives, he raised an estimated $100,000 in emergency supplies, which were delivered directly to those in need, circumventing ponderous (and often corrupt and inefficient) government relief efforts.

His organization deployed tents, tarps, building materials, water purification systems, solar lights, and twenty Envirofit institutional stoves for mass-feeding efforts, principally in Gorkha, the epicenter of the quake.

I follow him around the massive Outdoor Retail Winter Market trade show in Denver, and there's nobody this spry eighty-one-year-old doesn't know. A shameless advocate for the people of Nepal, he wears an embroidered chef's toque and calls himself the "Chief Cook" of the stove project. HSP sponsors welcome him with open arms—they provide room for a stove display in their booths, schedule meetings to discuss further support, and two even sponsored cakes to celebrate his eightieth birthday in 2017.

Basch's work has not gone unnoticed. He has been recognized by *Costco Connection*, the twelve-million-circulation magazine for the membership buying club. Basch received a Citation of Merit from the Explorers Club and has been covered on the *Forbes* website and various Rotary International publications, according to his HimalayanStoveProject.org website.

He tells me the need in Nepal alone is for an estimated one million stoves and admits he has a long way to go. But considering the tens of thousands of Nepalis he's helped breathe easier, he is gratified to be clearing the air in Nepal one stove at a time.

WHAT HAPPENS IN VEGAS: VOLUNTEERING AT TOURIST DESTINATIONS

Using a free service such as VolunteerMatch,[5] the budding voluntourist can pick almost any destination in the United States as a site for worthwhile projects. Take Las Vegas, for instance, a city of 630,000 residents, which balloons in size as an estimated fifty million people[6] visit each year, as they have since the first casino opened in 1931, to gamble, eat to excess, drink, watch name entertainment, and otherwise forget their worries for a few days in the desert sun.

Most of the money is concentrated on the Strip, that four-mile stretch of conspicuous consumption. But travel just a few miles away, and Las Vegas reveals itself as a city facing rising suburban poverty due in part to low-wage service jobs at the casinos.

"The growth of suburban poverty in Las Vegas was faster than what was going on nationwide. Between 2000 and 2014, the nationwide poverty rate in suburbs grew by 65 percent; in Southern Nevada it grew 123 percent," Elizabeth Kneebone, a fellow at the Metropolitan Policy Program at the Brookings Institution, tells KNPR.[7]

The harsh reality of life in the Entertainment Capital of the World is echoed by Kim Amato, founder and executive director of Baby's Bounty,[8] a nonprofit providing low-income southern Nevada residents with supplies for their newborns.

"This is a town where you come to misbehave. People think there's lots of money, they see the Strip, but that's just one road dripping in money. Go farther down the road and you have families living on the street," Amato tells me during a visit to her nondescript strip mall office and warehouse in central Las Vegas.

Kim Amato, founder and executive director of Baby's Bounty in Las Vegas, is in constant need of volunteer help. Photo by Jeff Blumenfeld.

"Pregnant teen mothers who find themselves homeless are especially at risk. They don't know how to navigate the system for help since many of them are not even from here. Our clients are at the edge, they are in serious survival mode," she says.

Baby's Bounty started from her home in 2008, when she and her husband, Guy, would scour Craigslist for donated baby items. Many families were leaving the hospital without any newborn supplies whatsoever. The babies had no safe place to sleep and no clothing or diapers. She laments that too many infants were leaving the hospital wrapped in a father's shirt and put to sleep in bed with young siblings or in a drawer on the floor.

Since then, the organization has become what is essentially a citywide baby shower as Amato and a part-time assistant solicit clean, gently used baby clothes and portable cribs and infant bathtubs in working condition; car seats must be brand new. Recipients include babies born into families recovering from domestic abuse, teen pregnancy, mental health issues, and unemployment or underemployment.

Volunteers help collect, sort, and store the items and prepare them for distribution to new mothers, at the rate of approximately sixty per month.

Now, each baby receives a Baby Bundle with new and gently used infant clothing, receiving blankets, bottles, toiletries, portable crib, bathtub, brand-new car seat, and a front chest carrier—all valued at approximately $375. In 2014 alone, they helped 733 babies, including nineteen sets of twins, according to Amato.

Baby's Bounty is in constant need of volunteer help, which they often receive from casino employee groups, from local business such as Zappos, and tourists who have spare time during their visit. The process is straightforward: call or email in advance, explain when you're available, and Amato and her team will put you to work for as long as you have time. Sometimes you'll be asked to help "wrangle" (organize) the warehouse. You'll be asked to sort baby items, assemble Baby Bundles, or help with administrative duties such as filing or making follow-up phone calls to new parents.

"Every baby deserves to be wrapped in love," she says.

My tour of southern Nevada nonprofits continues with a stop at Lighthouse Charities,[9] which helps refugee and at-risk families become self-reliant through English classes, job training, and donations of clothing, household supplies, and furniture. Lighthouse partners with both of the Las Vegas Valley's resettlement agencies, Catholic Charities of Southern Nevada and the Ethiopian Community Development Council.

I meet Cindy Trussel, an immigrant from Australia, who came to the United States in 1980 at the age of eleven. Since then she's lost all traces of her original accent. A member of the Mormon faith with eleven children—five biological, three adopted, and three stepchildren—she became aware of the local food rescue program that diverted discarded food from supermarkets, restaurants, and casinos to the needy. During the first year, Trussel kept accurate records of how much food she personally rescued in the family minivan: an impressive 1.4 million pounds, including other household products that could not be sold for one reason or another.

Her home overflowing with food and apparel, it looked like a hoarder's residence. To alleviate the clutter in her living space, a $50,000 donation allowed her to rent a vacant home to serve as storage. She incorporated Lighthouse Charities in 2015 to help families in need, particularly refugees from various nations. She recalls her own early experiences in this country as her father searched for six months for work.

"We struggled in the early 1980s—I slept on the floor for months because we had no furniture. We had no money for school supplies. It was hard on us, and we spoke English," she tells me. "Imagine how hard it is for refugees who are illiterate and speak no English? The current dreams of refugees coming to southern Nevada are the same dreams I had when I was new to this country."

To make ends meet, Trussel learned how to lay flooring and eventually worked her way up to membership in the Bricklayers and Allied Craftworkers Local #13 as a professional floor installer. Today she hopes her blend of job training and English lessons will provide a lifeline to women refugees. She's taught them how to handcraft jewelry, crochet, work with wood, and use their basket-weaving skills to create products sold in the charity's retail boutique called Nafasi Designs, which means "opportunity/favorable circumstance" in Swahili.

In 2016, Lighthouse Charities served an estimated 170,000 underprivileged residents of the Las Vegas area through food pantries, jobs, and English as a Second Language (ESL) classes. Schoolchildren are provided with backpacks, notebooks, and supplies.

There's a small screening room where she shows YouTube instructional videos that help teach various skills. Refugees make cookies for local charities, are taught how to write resumes, are provided with professional clothing to wear to interviews, and are instructed how to act when seeking employment.

Cindy Trussel's Lighthouse Charities serves an estimated 170,000 underprivileged residents of the Las Vegas area, through food pantries, jobs, and English as a Second Language (ESL) classes. Photo by Jeff Blumenfeld.

According to the charity's website, "We have learned that many of our refugees lack basic knowledge of very simple things such as how to use a spray bottle, how to use a mop, how to clock in for work, etc. These are all things that have often been deprived of them their entire lives while living in a third world country, and because many of them spend at least half, if not all, their lives in a refugee camp where living conditions are so poor, many die every day from starvation and disease."[10]

Work skills are also taught to refugee women in a job-training space across the alley behind the store. Lighthouse "clients," as they are called, create rags from donated casino towels, which are then sold at a profit. Both men and women refugees are making $150 to $600 per month cutting rags to supplement their income, Trussel reports. Huge bundles of clean rags sit ready to be shipped to local restaurants and hotels.

"They may be just rags, but we're using them to teach self-sufficiency," she says.

Volunteer support is needed to sort through gently used donated clothes and shoes and to inspect donated toys, school supplies, and hygiene products in the organization's eight-thousand-square-foot warehouse behind the store.

Trussel asks of just one thing in return from her clients: that they come back and donate one hour of service to the organization; she reports they gladly comply.

Complete an online volunteer form and you'll know in short order how Lighthouse Charities can best use your volunteer time.

You can only spend so much time at the casino gaming tables, or eating at lavish buffets, or watching Penn & Teller perform. My tour of Las Vegas volunteer opportunities continues with a visit to Three Square Food Bank, Southern Nevada's only food bank that provides assistance to four counties.[11]

Three Square's mission is to provide wholesome food to hungry people while passionately pursuing a hunger-free community. They do this by combining food banking (warehousing canned and boxed goods), food rescue (obtaining surplus or unused meats, bread, dairy, and produce from hospitality and grocery outlets), and preparing ready-to-eat meals to fight food insecurity, which occurs when people are unable to secure enough food for a healthy diet and active lifestyle.

Three Square was founded in 2007 by the late Hilton Hotel heir Eric Hilton. A decade later, it was distributing more than thirty-six million meals annually, the equivalent of more than forty-four million pounds of food and grocery product, calling upon help from the gaming industry, local businesses, nonprofit agencies, food distributors, higher education institutions, school districts, government entities, the media, and thousands of volunteers and donors. And that's only in four counties in southern Nevada. There are food

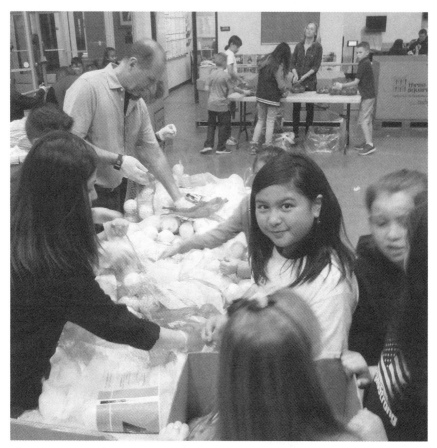

Three Squares needs an astounding one hundred to two hundred volunteers each day, including these local youngsters, who took time to pack onions. Photo by Jeff Blumenfeld.

banks nationwide that need volunteer help. Pick a city you're already planning to visit, and VolunteerMatch can provide numerous suggestions.

It came time to roll up my sleeves. I jumped in at Three Square, joining about sixty students ages ten to twelve packing apples and white onions into orange nylon mesh bags earmarked for food insecure families. Nearby, another crew was packing tangerines.

The work was hard, somewhat tedious, bending over a cardboard bulk bin containing twelve bushels—about 1,500 apples—from Washington State. We had to inspect each one, placing the rejects into a plastic bucket for delivery to a local pig farm.

Loud music played, turning the warehouse space into a party as the youngsters beside me chatted about their friends and funny viral videos. During a break, I take a look at literally hundreds of digital images lining the walls showing previous volunteer groups who came to donate their time—8 × 10 photos plastered as thick as wallpaper. There were years of volunteer photos of casino employees, conventioneers, youth ministries, University of Nevada Las Vegas sororities, birthday parties, singles meet-ups, school groups, and even thirty Miss Universe contestants in the city for a competition.

Later I would take a tour of the Three Square kitchen, home to Kids Cafe, a program of Feeding America, designed to ensure children without access to regular nutrition receive a healthy meal after school. An impressive ten thousand to twelve thousand after-school meals are prepared here every day along five assembly lines, each food item placed into a see-through bright orange plastic clamshell box before shipment to 220 local community and school groups. Depending upon the day, the kitchen might be preparing from scratch grilled chicken salad, turkey veggie wraps, chef salads, or chicken tacos.

Elsewhere, volunteers were working to prepare "Backpacks for Kids" containing nutritious, single-serve, ready-to-eat foods to sustain youngsters over the weekend. Sadly, when the school bell rings on Friday, many of these children would otherwise go hungry until school resumes on Monday morning.

Three Squares prepares and distributes "Backpacks for Kids" containing these nutritious, single-serve, ready-to-eat foods to sustain food-insecure youngsters over the weekend. Photo by Jeff Blumenfeld.

In all, the program is highly efficient—for every dollar donated, Three Square is able to distribute three meals.

Three Squares needs an astounding one hundred to two hundred volunteers each day. This keeps Mikell Goheen, the volunteer engagement manager, and her eight-person staff occupied full-time sourcing volunteers, processing volunteer applications, and greeting them upon arrival so they can have a rewarding experience. She obviously loves her job, but the task is daunting.

"We need approximately eighty volunteers every morning, and thirty in the afternoon, around one hundred each evening, Mondays through Fridays, and sometimes we struggle. In 2016, we had over thirty-two thousand volunteers donate their time," says Goheen, who has been known to pitch in herself when there were meals to pack and not enough extra hands available.

To volunteer, one starts with the Three Square website and fills out an application and schedule to come in to help at a convenient time. Volunteers may be standing, bending, lifting, and walking on concrete in non-climate-controlled areas. The website advises to dress warm in the winter months and cool in the summer months.

"Come for a couple of hours or come for the entire day. We'll take all the help we can get and won't waste your time," Goheen says.

As I leave, I read an inscription by US quotation anthologist Terri Guillemets on the wall of the lobby. It reads simply: "The world is hugged by the faithful arms of volunteers."

Watching Las Vegas recede in the rearview mirror, I head two-and-a-half hours south through the desert to reach Lake Havasu City, whose motto is "Home of the London Bridge." Indeed, it was here in 1971 that real estate developer Robert P. McCulloch reconstructed a bridge purchased in London and moved it stone by stone to the shores of his proposed planned community along the lower Colorado River.

Since then, Lake Havasu City has grown to fifty-four thousand residents and attracts spring breakers, powerboaters, fishing anglers, and retired snowbirds who reside there in the winter by the thousands.[12]

DeeDee DeLorenzo came to the area in 1978 from western Pennsylvania. Lured to the desert for an elementary schoolteacher job, she taught for over thirty years before retiring to pursue her passion as an avid birder. In fact, she's recorded 635 birds on her life list, a tally of all the different types of birds she's seen in the wild, including the endangered Ridgway's rail and a rare California condor. Each bird is carefully recorded in her well-worn copy of the *Birder's Life List & Diary* published by the Cornell Laboratory of Ornithology.

Today, DeLorenzo conducts bird studies for Arizona Game and Fish, the US Geological Survey, and is president of the nonprofit Friends of Bill

Williams River and Havasu National Wildlife Refuges, which extend one hundred miles along the Colorado River, the border between Nevada and California to the north, Arizona and California to the south.

A National Wildlife Refuge System does what the name implies: it is the system of public lands and waters set aside to conserve America's fish, wildlife, and plants. Havasu National Wildlife Refuge is comprised of 37,515 acres adjacent to the Colorado River, Topock Marsh, Topock Gorge, and the Havasu Wilderness. The Bill Williams National Wildlife Refuge is home to over six thousand acres of habitat, 355 species of birds, 34 documented reptiles, 40 species of butterflies, 57 species of mammals, 7 amphibians, and a plethora of indigenous wildlife, according to the Lake Havasu City tourist bureau website.[13]

The Friends group is ready to put you to work. There are volunteer projects that last a few hours, a day, or a week or more, including trash cleanups and staffing fundraisers, such as the group's spaghetti dinner.

Periodically, the seven-year-old nonprofit solicits volunteers for their Bird Counts. "There's no special training. You don't have to be a biologist. All you need to do is spot birds and help keep a list for us," DeLorenzo says. "If volunteers can kayak, all the better. We'll even provide the kayaks."

DeLorenzo also needs help pole cutting and planting. The process is simple: volunteers cut willow and cottonwood branches, soak them in water, then plant them in eight-inch holes. In time, the poles will grow into trees.

"That doesn't take much skill," she advises. "If you can use a pair of loppers and walk, you're good to go."

Her only request to prospective volunteers is to call in advance so the Friends group knows you're coming and can plan to put you to work. A volunteer calendar on their website indicates when volunteers are most needed.[14]

As you might suspect from the organization's name, volunteering here is also a good way to meet the locals and make "friends" for life.

Baby's Bounty, Lighthouse Charities, Three Square, and Friends of Bill Williams River and Havasu National Wildlife Refuges—four organizations, located in just one area of the United States. These are just a few examples of how the opportunities to volunteer at America's leading tourist destinations provide plenty of options for vacationing travelers.

BECOME AN ADVENTURE SCIENTIST

There are times when a particular need for volunteer assistance falls right into the voluntourist's lap, as was the case with Joe Watson and George Basch. But it's not limited to travel to Nepal. Wherever you travel, there are scientists desperate for data from around the world. You can provide an invaluable service—becoming the eyes and ears of researchers worldwide—by simply collecting data and shipping it back to a nonprofit organization based in Bozeman, Montana, called Adventure Scientists.

Since its founding in 2011, Adventure Scientists has sent thousands of volunteers on missions to collect data from remote, difficult-to-access locations for its conservation partners. These partnerships have led to the discovery of more than three dozen new species, provided key information to guide climate change decision making, and helped protect threatened wildlife habitat around the world.[15]

Consider Expedition 196, an attempt to visit all the countries of the world. Without a purpose besides setting a Guinness World Record, it would have been merely an expensive stunt. But Cassandra De Pecol, twenty-seven, wanted to achieve more. She added legitimacy to her travel adventure by filling thirty-three separate liter-sized water sample bottles along her route and shipping them all back to Adventure Scientists for its study of the insidious proliferation of microplastics in the world's oceans.

The sources of these often microscopic particles can be from washing nylon apparel, cosmetics, toothpaste, and debris such as plastic bottles and bags. Circulating currents have created immense rotating patches of waste, mostly plastic, in subtropical regions. Wave action and sunlight break floating plastics down into smaller pieces, called microplastics; some of them are slow to degrade chemically and are toxic. As such, they pose a significant environmental risk.[16]

De Pecol's Expedition 196 project visited 193 UN member states in one year and 193 days between July 24, 2015, and February 2, 2017, making her the female record holder for the fastest time to visit all sovereign countries, according to Guinness World Records.[17]

Sadly, Adventure Scientists find evidence of microplastics in an average 74 percent of samples received worldwide—89 percent for saltwater samples, 51 percent for freshwater. The data is part of one of the largest microplastics studies on Earth.

"The numbers are absolutely shocking," Adventure Scientists founder and executive director Gregg Treinish tells the 2017 National Geographic Explorers Festival on June 16, 2017, in Washington, D.C. Treinish, thirty-six, a wildlife biologist and backcountry guide who has hiked the 2,200-mile Appalachian Trail and spent nearly two years hiking 7,800 miles along the Andes, wanted his journeys to make a difference, considering the enormous problems the world faces from coral bleaching, illegal timber harvests, deforestation, and shark finning, to name a few issues.[18]

"It's important that this data is used to influence change," Treinish says.

Take roadkill for instance, a sad fact of life for millions of animals each year. According to Treinish, researchers need annual data about wildlife–vehicle collisions (WVC) across the United States. In 2011 to 2012, there were 1.23 million deer–vehicle collisions in the United States, costing more than $4 billion in vehicle damage, according to State Farm,[19] a fact that makes me think back to the two deer I struck on two separate occasions in my car—an awful experience that could have been worse had I swerved. With the necessary data, Treinish says they can identify which species are at most risk, whether any "hot spots" exist that are extraordinarily perilous to animals, and where to place wildlife underpasses and overpasses that in some locations have reduced roadkill deaths by 80 percent.

Treinish, named a *National Geographic* Emerging Explorer in 2013, said he founded Adventure Scientists in 2011 to link adventurers in hard-to-reach places to scientists who needed data from those locations.

"I started biological and ecological expeditioning, using my outdoor skill sets to make a difference in the world. I was sure that given the proper tools and a similar skill set, there were others like me.

"I have been proven right thousands of times ever since. Explorers come to us to have an adventure with a purpose. We send them on missions worldwide," Treinish says.

In addition to the study of roadkill and microplastics, the organization has collected data about animal feces (scat) to study the antibiotic resistance of *Enterococcus* bacteria, which exists within every animal on the planet, including humans; studied pikas in high alpine environments; researched how butterflies can be biodiversity indicators for ecosystem health; and is creating a genetic reference library of endangered trees along the US West Coast.

Participating in an Adventure Scientists project requires no particular technical experience. "The majority of our projects are for hikers, bikers, and skiers," Trenish tells me.

"Whether voluntourists are sailing, kayaking, hiking, rowing, or simply vacationing on a mega cruiseship to a remote location, we'll tell them how to collect and ship proper samples, take GPS coordinates, and document the effort with photos and video."

Becoming an Adventure Scientists volunteer could possibly help you raise funds for your effort, and certainly provide much-needed data for researchers. It all starts by visiting their website and telling them where and when you plan to travel. There is no cost to participate. Adventure Scientists will even pay shipping costs for the return of field samples.

A similar organization voluntourists can consider is Science in the Wild, an adventure citizen science company that leads immersive and educational expeditions around the world.[20] Where they differ from Adventure Scientists is that these are guided research missions, led by an engaging Ukrainian American named Ulyana N. Horodyskyj, PhD. I first met Uly when she came to one of my book talks at the American Mountaineering Museum in Golden, Colorado. Since then we've become close friends and fellow Explorers Club members. She is one extraordinary young woman.

Uly, as she's called, is a Colorado resident barely in her thirties who has amassed an impressive resume. At age thirteen, she started working on a science fair project examining travel in space without fuel (using solar sails instead), which earned her enough scholarships to attend college. She meshed her interests in the outdoors and science as a geology major at Rice University in Houston. By the time she turned twenty-three, she had traveled to and worked on all seven continents. Through her twenties, she was employed by National Geographic Student Expeditions as a geology/climate change instructor in Iceland, and as a glaciology/volcanology instructor on Mt. Baker, Washington, and on the Gulkana glacier in the eastern Alaska range through the "Girls on Ice" program.

She has tested commercial spacesuits in a Falcon 20 "vomit comet" and ridden a human centrifuge at the National Aerospace Training and Research (NASTAR) Center in Southampton, Pennsylvania.

In fall 2016, she climbed inside a windowless 636-square-foot pod housed in a warehouse at NASA's Johnson Space Center, switched off her phone, high-fived the three strangers accompanying her the next thirty days, and watched the doors shut tight. She was there to serve as mission commander of the Mission XII crew of NASA's Human Exploration Research Analog (HERA) project, a multiyear endeavor to study what happens to people's bodies, brains, and psyches when they're isolated with other adults inside a confined space on a simulated long-duration mission to an asteroid.

In other words, this is a woman to be reckoned with.

Travel on a Science in the Wild mission and you'll learn how to collect, analyze, and interpret data in the field alongside professional scientists.

"We show you how to think like a scientist, and provide you with scientific tools and training. Education is at the heart of what we do—providing you a chance to enrich your experience by exploring wild landscapes like a scientist," Horodyskyj writes.

Her teams have used unmanned surface vehicles (USV) to study glacial lakes in Nepal; traveled by Cessna 210, snowmobile, sled, and skis to study snowmelt in the Canadian Arctic; and determined the extent of melting snowpack surrounding the Andes mountainside site of the plane crash in 1972 depicted in Piers Paul Read's 1974 book, *Alive: The Story of the Andes Survivors*. She guides the expeditions and is a certified Wilderness First Responder if anything goes wrong.

Her field projects attract citizen scientists ranging in age from sixteen to sixty. The trips can be physically grueling, so it helps to be in physical shape with some experience in the outdoors, either as a runner or hiker. You'll be asked to attest to your fitness level and complete a standard medical form. A training regimen is sent months in advance so you can get ready to hike with scientific instruments to remote locations.

Depending on the location, you'll pay anywhere from $2,000 to $4,500 plus air transportation for these citizen-scientist missions, which includes money to publish the trip's findings in science publications that will credit all team members, including its hardy band of voluntourists.

"This passion of mine for exploration has been there from a young age to operate at the intersection of adventure travel, citizen science, and low-cost expeditions," she tells me. "To study the environment as closely as we do, we need as many extra pairs of arms and legs as we can find."

TRADE A SKILL AND JOIN THE TEAM

Often you can serve on a humanitarian mission by trading a particular skill.

In most cases, you'll still have to pay for your own airfare and may be asked to pay for expenses on the ground, but chances are it will be less than if you were to travel with a commercial tour operator that offers a day or two of voluntourism.

What kind of skill? You'd be surprised. If you're coming out of the business world, volunteer organizations need your help.

John Ward, a retiree from Dallas, spent his career working in the military and defense industry. His last job was in aerospace business development for Lockheed Martin, the global military contractor. Ward was consumed with marketing military hardware, missile defense systems in particular, to the world's armed forces.

Once retired, he found a way to apply his business skills to a different purpose: fundraising for an American doctor, Rick Hodes, MD, MACP, who has lived and worked in Ethiopia for nearly thirty years, serving as medical director for the American Jewish Joint Distribution Committee (JDC), a century-old NGO.[21]

Hodes, who has been featured on CNN, HBO, and was honored as ABC-TV "Person of the Week" in 2010, delivers comprehensive medical services in Ethiopia, Rwanda, Zaire, and Tanzania, with a specialty on people suffering from spinal deformities. His programs, which also treat congenital and rheumatic heart disease, some forms of cancer, and rare diseases, has reached tens of thousands of patients.

Ward tells me, "In the business world, I was solely focused on reaching customers. Now I've found that the techniques for attracting donors are quite similar.

"You need to target donors, strategize how best to reach them, create events that introduce financial supporters to the cause, and build lasting relationships with Dr. Hodes's life-changing work."

Ward has been to Ethiopia six times in the past four years. While not a medical professional himself, he has played an important role in the doctor's mission, serving as an extra pair of arms and legs while more trained staff members tend to patients. He's also secured visas and arranged transportation for physically handicapped Ethiopian patients to travel to Ghana where the spinal corrective surgery is performed. The logistics are immense because airlines and airports in the country are not handicap accessible as they are in the United States.

Ward stays at a basic guesthouse in Ethiopia's capital city of Addis Ababa during his volunteer stints. "The accommodations are pretty Spartan. In fact, they remind me of my days as a poor college student," he laughs.

Ward points proudly to a yearlong effort to digitize thousands of medical records, again using his skills as a former Lockheed Martin executive. Instead of a room full of paper files and X-ray film, the doctor can access patient histories online from anywhere with an Internet connection.

Ward continues, "The need is great and this has brought a new phase of volunteering to my life. I definitely get more out of it than I put in. Working in the defense industry, then to be eventually volunteering at an African spinal clinic, was the furthest thing from my mind. But now I realize, the more money we raise, the more spinal surgeries can be performed. I use my business training often to help keep ringing the gong for Doctor Rick.

"Besides which, I have great conversations with the Ethiopian community in Dallas who are surprised how much I know about their country."

As a result of his volunteer work, Ward has accumulated more in-depth knowledge of Ethiopia—its geography, culture, and politics—than one could gain as a simple tourist.

"Being able to observe, firsthand, the work that Doctor Rick is performing makes me better equipped not just to give myself, but to really encourage other donors as well."

Another volunteer with much-desired skills is Mike Pizzio, a former Special Agent for the FBI who served three rotations in Iraq and seems to have no problem getting invited on volunteer projects.

He's a certified Dive Instructor Trainer, one-hundred-ton Master US Coast Guard captain, and has blown bubbles within a few feet of the most iconic shipwrecks in history, including the Civil War–era *Monitor,* the *Andrea*

Doria, and *Britannic*. A single father of two grown children, he has led dives to find a missing World War II aircraft, a P-51D Mustang lost in 1944 off what is now Los Angeles International Airport.

Pizzio is also a licensed private investigator, working with plaintiff attorneys on cases that include diving liability, and he has been a member of numerous diving expeditions for the *History Channel, National Geographic*, and *Learning Channel*.

Yet besides those dive and law enforcement skills, admittedly pretty impressive by themselves, the Port St. Lucie, Florida, volunteer admits he's really not an expert in anything else. But he knows a little bit about a lot of things.

He's not licensed to fly an airplane but has been in the right copilot seat enough times to take a stab at landing safely in an emergency.

His advice for getting invited on a volunteer project: "Learn as much as you can about everything to make yourself as valuable as you can."

Pizzio is the kind of team member you want by your side—a MacGyver who can rely upon his twenty-six years of FBI training to get almost any job done. Eat lunch with him and he insists on sitting facing the door—that's after he's scanned the room for exits.

"I don't want to be anywhere I'm absolutely worthless," he says.

For that reason, he travels with three forms of communications: EPIRB, Iridium Extreme sat phone, and a SPOT Messenger to access three communications satellites. He learned from military friends who used to tell him, when it comes to redundancy, "Two is one, one is none."

At one point, while sidelined for four months by an abdominal condition, what did he do? He took a 160-hour EMT course and passed at the top of his class.

"I want to be the guy people turn to. Am I an expert in emergency medicine? No. But I know a lot more than the average guy who can only use a Band-Aid."

How does he pay for his volunteer travel?

"I'm not a rich guy. I live on a retired government employee salary. Sometimes my expenses are paid, as in the case of the cable network projects. Other times, I pay. The importance is to know up front what the trip will cost. No surprises."

He suggests the best way to receive an invitation to join a volunteer project is to expand your skill base. "You want to have as many skills and abilities as you can," he says.

"Look, at my age I'll never be an accomplished rock climber. I don't have the physical capability or years of experience. But I've learned basic climbing skills so that I can be of value if I need to ever belay someone."

He adds, "Whenever I can, I try to add a new skill to my toolkit. I want to be the Swiss Army knife of team members. Become a jack of all trades even if it means you'll be the master of none."

Doctors, in particular, will find the doors wide open to join volunteer projects.

"One of the most sought-after skills on an expedition is that of medical professional," says Kenneth Kamler, an orthopedic microsurgeon and extreme medicine specialist. He is also the author of *Surviving the Extremes: What Happens to the Body and Mind at the Limits of Human Endurance* (2004, 2006).

It was Kamler who attended to victims of the 1996 Everest disaster during which time eight people died on their descent, an account immortalized in Jon Krakauer's book *Into Thin Air* (1999).

Team members have relied on Kamler to treat bear bites in the Arctic, frostbite in the Antarctic, set fractures in the Andes, and perform surgery in the mud of the Amazon rainforest.

"Having a doctor along is especially critical on volunteer projects in the Amazon, the most competitive arena on earth, where everything is trying to kill everything else," he tells me.

I've known In-Hei Hahn, MD, for two years now, having been impressed by her calm professionalism and dedication to providing volunteer medical support to a number of projects. An emergency medicine physician affiliated with hospitals in Utah, New York City, and California, her subspecialty is medical toxicology. Get bitten by a snake out in the field, and you'll want Hahn by your side.

Being an inveterate traveler has allowed her to explore the world and deliver health care to people ranging from the Indians in the Brazilian Amazon jungle, ultramarathoners racing all over the world, and even race car drivers at the Lime Rock Park NASCAR track in Connecticut.

Her favorite assignments are the annual paleontological expeditions to the Gobi Desert in Mongolia and Transylvania, Romania.

As a volunteer expedition physician, she has been called upon to treat heat stroke, seizures, dehydration, head trauma, infections, severe bleeding, diarrhea, and what sounds simply ghastly: foreign body extraction. She's there to help volunteers and locals alike, whomever needs medical attention.

Constantly trying to improve her skill base, she is currently working to acquire her fellowship in Wilderness Medicine.

"My goal is to be able to take care of anyone everywhere. As an emergency physician, it appears as if I can volunteer almost anywhere project leaders need to ensure the health and safety of their participants. I enjoy being part of a team and love taking care of people in their specialty environment, especially serving as expedition physician to a group of 'rock star' paleontologists from the departments of paleontology at both the American Museum of Natural History and the Smithsonian Institution," Hahn tells me.

"The challenge to develop a system of having the maximum amount of medical capability with the minimum amount of gear is unique and allows me to think outside the box whenever an emergency arises. I am passionate about learning about new fields, meeting amazing people, and travel.

"Variety is important. It's what keeps me going and avoid burnout. I'm reminded about a favorite quote from mythologist and writer Joseph Campbell: 'If you follow your bliss, you put yourself on a kind of track that has been there all the while, waiting for you, and the life that you ought to be living is the one you are living.'"

Hahn adds, "My volunteer medical work is incredibly gratifying. I'm so glad I have a skill that project leaders value. What's more, I get to hunt for dinosaur fossils, which is pretty fun and cool."

Don't be intimidated by the stories of highly skilled medical professionals. Sometimes all it takes is basic first aid.

When an international relief organization needed help overseas in the 1960s, it made perfect sense to turn to airline flight attendants, called stewardesses back in the day. They were traveling the world anyway, were good with the public, and knew first aid. Over twenty-six airlines were involved from 1961 to 1988, sending approximately three hundred pilots and flight attendants to provide humanitarian assistance to remote health clinics on behalf of Dooley Intermed International, based in New York.

The airline volunteer program was conceived in 1961 by Dooley Intermed's then president and founder, the late Dr. Verne Chaney, to provide volunteer assistance to its medical and educational programs. He unabashedly approached Juan Trippe, founder of Pan American World Airways, and secured his agreement that any employee sufficiently interested in supporting humanitarian projects would receive an airline ticket and three months leave of absence without pay, at no loss to their seniority within the company. Trippe's staff was aghast. "They told him they were running an airline, not a charity," Chaney remembers during an interview I conducted with him a few years before he died.

International Stewardess News began calling them "Dooley's Dollies," while Pan Am provided transportation to and from the volunteer sites.

The airline employees worked alongside Dooley Intermed's doctors and nurses in its clinics, hospitals, orphanages, and schools or wherever there was a need for extra help. The women were assigned to Dooley Intermed project sites in India, Nepal, Vietnam, Laos, and Thailand.

"Besides being of immense value to patients, the program provided enormous positive awareness for the airlines involved," says current Dooley

Intermed president Scott Hamilton. "Pan Am ran ads headlined, 'When your Pan Am stewardess isn't serving you, she may be serving mankind.'"

Within the past few years, the program was revived in partnership with Washington, D.C.–based Airline Ambassadors International (AAI), and its network of airline personnel, students, medical professionals, families, and retirees.

"Airline personnel are well trained and highly motivated for volunteer assistance that meets a clearly defined need in a country severely impacted by poverty and natural disasters," Hamilton tells me.

Barbara Price, retired director of corporate travel for UBS Investment Bank in New York, fondly remembers her time in the field with Dooley Intermed. As a Pan Am employee, she spent three months in remote areas of Nepal assisting a registered nurse. In the late 1970s many villages could only be reached on foot.

Price was sleeping in tents and trekking with a group of Sherpas for five to six hours per day to reach off-the-grid villages and provide badly needed health care.

"Frequently, we were the first Westerners the inhabitants of these villages had ever seen and, consequently, winning the confidence of the Nepalese people was a large part of the job," she recalls.

Price performed vaccinations, measured blood pressure, gathered blood samples for further study, and conducted health education classes with a battery-powered filmstrip projector.

"Oh, my goodness. It was the experience of a lifetime," she tells me. "Pan Am's volunteer program in Nepal, combined with Dooley Intermed's know-how, allowed me to positively influence hundreds of lives."

Former Dooley volunteer Kate Jewell, a retired naturopathic doctor from Orcas Island, Washington, and former American Airlines employee for thirty-seven years, is the current director of the Air-Intermed Volunteer Program.[22] She organizes two-week volunteer vacations to the Dooley-supported Eco Home for Orphaned Children near Kathmandu, Nepal. Voluntourists, mostly women in their fifties and sixties, stay on the grounds in the newly built Happy Shepherd Guest Cottage and meet with the children each day.

The trip includes local sightseeing, hotel accommodations in Kathmandu, restaurant meals, and local transportation for about $1,100 plus airfare (which in this case is highly discounted for current and former airline employees). Non-airline-affiliated volunteers are required to have Global Entry, the US Customs and Border Protection (CBP) program that allows expedited clearance for preapproved, low-risk travelers.[23]

"The volunteers immerse themselves in the Nepali culture, teach the children music, art, jewelry making, or whatever their skills may be," Jewell says. They also share games, health education, geography lessons, and more. Through their interaction, the children sharpen their English language skills, and volunteers even learn a few words of Nepali. Mainly, we are trying to teach the children things that will help them gain employment when they are older . . . and have fun!

"The experience is all about sharing who you are and learning more about their lives. It's a totally secular experience, without any religion involved. You're not there to convert, you're there to interact and enjoy, and teach and learn and be," Jewell adds.

"Instead of visiting Nepal as a tourist, for that two-week period at least, you're part of the childrens' daily lives."

I can't cook. OK, maybe scrambled eggs. I have only basic first aid skills, and my technical background is limited to a few years as a ham operator before I discovered girls in my teen years. But I do know my way around a camera, and some might say I have a way with words. That allowed me to sign on as director of communications for two humanitarian missions to Nepal with a group of superstar ophthalmologists traveling with the Dooley Intermed International team to the epicenter of the 2015 earthquakes.

Around 253 million people live with vision impairment worldwide, of which 36 million are blind. The vast majority live in low-income settings, yet more than 80 percent of all visual impairment can be prevented or cured, according to the World Health Organization (WHO).[24]

"Lack of access to eye care prevents billions of people around the world from achieving their potential and is a major barrier to economic and human progress," Madeleine K. Albright, the former secretary of state, told the *New York Times* in May 2018.

The WHO has estimated the problem costs the global economy more than $200 billion annually in lost productivity.[25]

Blindness is a severe public health problem, especially in Nepal's relatively inaccessible areas, my destination in 2017 with the Dooley Intermed medical team.

My job was to post daily trip reports that were read by donors and volunteers following along from home. It was my second trip to Nepal with Dooley Intermed and the most grueling, especially when hiking sheer-drop, sphincter-clenching rocky trails where the wheel simply has no function. I was asked to convey what we were all facing as we traveled halfway around the world to perform cataract surgeries on impoverished Nepalis.

Dooley Intermed's Gift of Sight eye care mission toured Kathmandu before their journey to the remote Upper Gorkha region of Nepal, site of the devastating 2015 earthquake. It was the author's (second from right) second volunteer trip to Nepal with Dooley Intermed and the most grueling. Photo by Jeff Blumenfeld.

My intention was not to sugarcoat but rather share the sense of hardship, the physical exertion, the long hours in Third World conditions. As you read my trip reports, consider whether helping impoverished people in this manner is right for you.

THURSDAY, DECEMBER 7, 2017:
KATHMANDU AT LAST—THE DOOLEY INTERMED OPERATION RESTORE SIGHT TEAM ARRIVES

What do you do for twelve hours in the air? Frankly, whatever you can to pass the time: watch two movies, begin reading *Annapurna* by Maurice Herzog, eat three meals, read the airline in-flight magazine, clean out your wallet, make space by deleting iPhone photos, sleep in an upright position (good luck with that), play iPhone blackjack, and rip articles out of magazines to read again, maybe never.

We have a four-hour layover. While Dan Byers, our videographer, and Yale ophthalmologist Christopher Teng walked off their jet lag at the ultra-modern Hamad International Airport in Doha, Qatar, I was on a singular mission to determine whether this rich country on the northeast coast of the Arabian Peninsula is called "cutter" or "cuh-tar."

A stately gentleman in a long, flowing white tunic called a *thawb*, sandals, and keffiyeh headpiece settled it for me: it's "cuh-tar," which vaguely rhythms with "gui-tar."

The Qatar Airport, with its high-end Rolex, Coach, Harrods, and Swarovski shops, was a sharp contrast to what we experienced in Kathmandu this evening.

Kat is the loud, raucous, polluted capital of Nepal. A city of 1.2 million that assaults every sense from the moment you arrive at Tribhuvan International Airport.

Our driver presents us with marigold garlands we wear like Hawaiian leis. Nice touch.

We pass hundreds of tiny store fronts, mopeds seemingly coming at us from all directions, dogs everywhere in the streets, and pedestrians wearing dark clothes on dark, poorly lit washboard streets. Not the best idea.

It's election day, and private vehicles are banned from the city. Our local guides proudly show us ink-stained thumbs that indicate they voted today in the national election. They have secured special permits, and we breeze into the Marriott free of traffic. The hotel will be our home base for two days, as we decompress from our nonstop journey to the other side of the world.

FRIDAY, DECEMBER 8, 2017: *STRANGERS ARRIVE*

Imagine you live in a remote Nepali village one day's trek from the nearest road. Now imagine a group of strangers arrive with sharp instruments and want to operate on your eyes. It requires an abundance of faith.

For their part, the communities know we're due to arrive. Thus, it was important for the Dooley Intermed–ORS team to understand a bit more about the rich, if somewhat enigmatic, culture of Nepal and its people.

Such was our goal today.

First stop was Pashupatinath Temple, a UNESCO Cultural Heritage Site and sacred Hindu temple on the banks of the Bagmati River. From across the hill we watched as a half-dozen families cremated their deceased loved ones. Red-bottomed monkeys, stray dogs running through the river, and vendors selling all matters of trinkets added a festive air.

We pay to pose with a sadhu, a colorfully decorated Hindu holy person said to renounce all worldly possessions. However, our guide tells us this particular fellow's insistence on being paid for photos makes his piety somewhat suspect.

We see evidence of the spring 2015 earthquake that killed nine thousand Nepalis—numerous construction sites and still cracked walls—as we head to Boudhanath Stupa, the holiest Tibetan Buddhist temple outside Tibet. Dating to the fourteenth century, from above it looks like a giant mandala—a diagram of the Buddhist cosmos.

Nearby we tour the Rinchenling Thanka Gallery and Art School, an artist co-op. It specializes in *thangkas*, Tibetan Buddhist paintings, some with twenty-four-karat gold and natural stone colors, used as an aid to meditation and prayer.

We next tour the Healing Bowl and Therapy House where, bizarrely, heavy, hand-hammered bowls made of seven different metals are placed on our heads and over our bodies, then are struck repeatedly, thus summoning the healing qualities of both sound and vibration. The procedure dates back to the Bronze Age, about 3000 BCE.

"It's not magic, it's physics," we're told by the singing bowl therapist staffing the store.

Perhaps. As I request treatment for my weak back, I'm reminded what my mother used to say about the medicinal value of chicken soup: "It couldn't hurt."

With some free time, I snake my way through the popular Thamel neighborhood, the labyrinthian center of Kat's tourist industry for four decades. Shops offer $200 sightseeing flights to view Mt. Everest, restaurants prey on timid Western stomachs, and outdoor stores offer $35 down jackets, most counterfeit, most filled with anything but natural feathers.

There are cobwebs of wires everywhere, rubber-coated spaghetti on every pole. One for telephone, one for power, one for Internet, one for TV, one for who knows what, leading to every apartment.

Like much of everything else in this country of twenty-nine million, no one knows how, but it all seems to work.

Tomorrow we travel by Jeep eight hours into the hills, then trek from there on foot for ten hours with mules. It's in these remote areas at the end of the road—and beyond—that Dooley does its best work. Me, not so much.

DECEMBER 9–10, 2017:
MAYTAGGED ALONG WASHBOARD ROADS

Bone-jarring. There, I've said it. How else to describe an eight-hour 4WD kidney-rattling drive from Kat to Soti Khola about eighty miles away?

Dust kicked up by the bus ahead inhibits our vision. Leaves are coated a mocha brown. The roads are more like trails. You can't read; you can't sleep. As you're Maytagged on rutted dirt roads, you hold on and try to absorb the shocks as if riding a bucking bronco.

What appears to be hay bales with legs are women along the side of the road carrying enormous bundles supported by straps to their foreheads. Frequently we see elderly Nepalis pounding rocks by hand to create piles of gravel to sell.

We arrive at our teahouse along the Budhi Gandaki River, our rooms enveloped in the incessant white noise sound of rapidly flowing water.

Sunday morning the plan blessedly allows us to leave the claustrophobic 4WDs behind and trek on foot two hours and one thousand feet higher to Lapu Besi, our stop for the night. The porters and cooks follow behind, aided by pack mules to carry our personal and medical gear.

I marvel at the speed of one porter who passes me at a good clip. I'm kitted out in Sherpa brand fleece, LEKI collapsible trekking poles, and Hi-Tec boots with soles that mimic car tires. Yet I'm smoked by an elderly gentleman loaded down with a camera case and medical equipment while wearing open-toed rubber sandals, both of his heels listing to either side.

These are strong, resilient people for sure.

The Dooley Intermed–Operation Restore Sight eye screenings begin this afternoon at the Shree Prabhat Kiran Secondary School in Lapu Besi with eye tests using a tumbling E eye chart and a retinoscopy test to determine the need for correction.

The school had been completely rebuilt after the spring 2015 earthquake, in part through the help of Prince Harry.

After just two days in this underserved region of Nepal, it's easy to see the need for quality eye care here where medical care must travel in on the backs of humans and mules.

DECEMBER 11, 2017: *SHARING THE PATH WITH MULES*

For decades, Dooley Intermed has been providing health services to those in need in the remotest regions of the world. That never became more apparent to me than here in one of the world's poorest countries.

The only way to reach our final destination, the hillside village of Machhakhola, was another four-hour trek along this undulating, rocky terrain, making this impoverished settlement a total eight-hour hike from the nearest road.

Four hours today doesn't sound like much, and the elevation is only about 2,800 feet, but the trail at times narrows to a footpath on precipitous cliffs above the rushing Budhi Gandaki River. We see the carcasses of two pack mules that failed to successfully navigate particularly hazardous sections.

Piles of mule crap line the trail, making passage particularly tricky.

Speaking of mules, we share the trail with numerous mule trains, some carrying large containers of explosive propane cooking gas. Best tip when faced with an oncoming mule: stand on the uphill side; I was already whacked once by a bag of rice hanging on the side of one particularly large beast—the painful sideswipe got my attention.

Gingerly crossing a tremendous landslide caused by the earthquake, we're welcomed to Machhakhola by resounding applause from a crowd of one hundred Nepalis eagerly awaiting our arrival. Marigold garlands are ceremoniously placed over our heads.

Dozens of villagers crowd the central square—old men hunched over with walking sticks, women in brightly covered clothing, young mothers carrying babies on their backs, some nursing. There's a young man leading an obviously blind parent by the hand.

We're told some walked a day to get here, an impressive feat considering most locals wear a pair of open-toed sandals, certainly not the modern hiking boots or trekking poles that we couldn't imagine going without.

Dozens of Nepalis crowd our makeshift examination room. We hit the ground running.

DECEMBER 12, 2017: *ISOLATED FROM THE WORLD*

These people have so little, their lives made harder still by the spring 2015 earthquake whose epicenter occurred here, directly below this rural hillside village.

We awaken this morning at 5 a.m. to the beating drums of a funeral ceremony in the distance. Our unheated teahouse rooms are luxurious by Nepal standards. There is electric power for three hours at night, padlocked doors to secure our possessions, two single beds with one-layer foam mattresses, and a single squat hole toilet down the hall, which admittedly, requires a certain skill to successfully employ.

During a morning walk I cross a swaying steel footbridge and look back at a scene of particular desperation. Smoke from poorly ventilated tin roof shacks billow out; mules, chickens, a pig, and goats roam freely; and a one-room store sells a few dusty household necessities.

A single water tap in the central square provides water for drinking, washing, cooking. Those of us with hair-trigger Western stomachs give it a wide berth as we frequently apply Purell sanitizer to our hands.

We are, some might say, blissfully isolated from the world. Our Kat-bought SIM cards are temperamental, there's no Internet and no newspapers. One consolation is an inReach emergency satellite device that allows us to send 160-character texts and summon emergency aid if necessary. Otherwise, this blog has to wait until I return Friday to the city.

Into all of this arrives the Dooley Intermed–Operation Restore Sight team. In short order, the volunteer ophthalmologists find patients with facial skin cancer, blocked tear ducts, droopy lids, and chronic eye infections. Over seventy-six operations are scheduled, mostly to remove mature bilateral (both eyes) cataracts that are rendering these patients sightless. So far it's been a grueling but intensely satisfying trip.

DECEMBER 13, 2017: *BANDAGES REMOVED, SIGHT RESTORED*

Often during our stay in Machhakhola, schoolchildren we meet will clasp their hands together, say "Namaste," and in the next breath ask for chocolates, money, or pens. Our Nepali hosts say this engenders a beggar mentality, and that donations should be made through schools. Besides which, we're told, the kids don't need chocolates due to concerns about their dental health.

Numerous patients speak a local dialect called Tamang instead of Nepali. This necessitates one Tamang-to-Nepali translator working with a Nepali-English translator so our doctors can communicate with them. This complicates matters for videographer Daniel Byers, who is documenting the project.

This morning was the reveal for forty-six surgery patients; bandages were removed, doctors performed a final check, and sunglasses were distributed.

These are not particularly emotive people. Their reactions to regaining sight were quite subdued, just a few smiles here and there, especially among family members who now no longer have to lead their loved ones by hand.

Tomorrow: another reveal, patient follow-up, and the docs will handle any walk-ins from the surrounding communities.

DECEMBER 14, 2017: *PASSING THE FINGER TEST*

Chinja Ghale, sixty-five, is a proud Nepali who became blind three years ago. For five hours yesterday, her son-in-law guided her along serpentine footpaths to the Dooley Intermed–Operation Restore Sight eye camp here in Machhakhola. Cataracts in both eyes turned her world into darkness. She walks barefoot to better feel the ground.

Yesterday, the mature cataracts were removed from both eyes, replaced by intraocular lenses.

As expedition leader Scott Hamilton, a certified ophthalmic technician, removed both bandages, a smile came over her deeply lined face.

Chinja Ghale (far right), sixty-five, is a proud Nepali who became blind in 2014. Overnight, Dooley Intermed and ophthalmologists at the Operation Restore Sight eye camp restored her to perfect vision, one of the most gratifying procedures in medicine, both for the patient and the doctor. Photo by Jeff Blumenfeld.

She passed the finger test; she was asked the color of the jacket on a volunteer.

"Hariyo (green)," she says in Nepali, now able to see colors again.

Then suddenly she jumps up and begins walking in the dirt and hay-covered courtyard of our makeshift eye hospital, walking for the first time in three years totally unassisted.

Through a translator, she tells videographer Daniel Byers she is looking forward to returning to the fields. Her son-in-law, for his part, no longer has to serve as caretaker.

She was carried in piggyback style and walked out like a spring chicken.

Ophthalmologist Christopher Teng was astounded. "I started residency in 2005 and this is the first time I've seen someone with bilateral mature cataracts make such a complete recovery. In the States you typically don't see cataracts this advanced."

Another twenty-four patients, some who had single cataracts removed, others with infections and other eye ailments, were also sent home this morning.

Down the hillside below the eye camp, a woman squats next to her home pounding rocks into gravel that she'll later sell to support her family. We see numerous other women throughout our eight-hour trek, also pounding rocks, making gravel, trying to eke out a living in this unforgiving remote landscape.

We can't help everyone in this impoverished village, but over these past four days, for over eight hundred eye patients (seventy-one surgeries), the quality of their lives forever changed for the better.

Friday is our planned extraction by helicopter. The sooner our doctors return to their US practices, the better.

Months later, team member Daniel Byers of Skyship Films created an eleven-minute documentary about the trip. It's used during presentations to existing sponsors and their employees, and in pitches to potential sponsors. It can still be seen online.[26]

VOLUNTEER WITH A SERVICE ORGANIZATION

Drive into any medium-sized town in America and there along the roadside, at the gateway to the city, is a welcome sign packed with logos. I've seen them hundreds of times during road trips across America. They contain the names of local service organizations—American Legion, Kiwanis, Lions, Rotary—and sometimes brag about local citizens who left town and made a name for themselves elsewhere.

For one fifty-year-old volunteer in Florida, Rotary International would help set a personal course for years to come.

John Freeman, the married father of two young children, left a thirteen-year career as a financial advisor to seek a PhD in a career he felt more passionate about than stocks and bonds. He wanted more meaning in his life. He wanted to work at something greater than himself.

It was at age forty that he followed his father and mother's lead and joined the local Rotary Club in his hometown of Lakewood Ranch, Florida. Situated on the state's West Coast, it's about a two-hour drive southwest of Orlando.

Rotary International is a global network of 1.2 million neighbors, friends, leaders, and problem solvers who see a world where people unite and take action to create lasting change. For more than 110 years, its members, affiliated with thirty-five-thousand-plus clubs worldwide, have tackled some of the world's biggest issues, from literacy and peace to water and health.

It was as a Rotarian that Freeman first learned about ShelterBox USA, a nonprofit that provides emergency shelter and tools for families displaced

Volunteering for ShelterBox USA profoundly and positively impacted the life of Florida Rotarian John Freeman. Freeman was on a ShelterBox Monitoring & Evaluation field assignment in Agadez, Niger, seen here interviewing a head of household in front her ShelterBox emergency relief tent. Photo by John Freeman.

by natural disasters. Volunteering for the group profoundly and positively impacted John Freeman's life.

Since 2000, ShelterBox[27] has helped 1.2 million people by providing emergency shelter following more than three hundred disasters in ninety-five countries. ShelterBox responds urgently to earthquake, volcano, flood, hurricane, cyclone, tsunami, or conflict by delivering emergency shelter and other aid, including blankets, water filters and carriers, solar lights, and other essential tools for survival.

The aid comes in the form of ShelterBoxes and ShelterKits. Sturdy green ShelterBoxes contain family-sized tents specially designed to withstand the elements and provide disaster victims with temporary shelter until they are able to start the process of rebuilding a home.

ShelterKits contain all of the essential tools people need to immediately start repairing and rebuilding homes and contain items that help transform a shelter into a home, such as cooking equipment, solar lights, and activity sets for children.

Freeman became an on-call, trained member of the ShelterBox Response Team whose main requirement is that volunteers be available to assist over a five-year period by deploying during disasters anywhere in the world. What's more, they are required to serve at least twice each year for three weeks at a time, often under trying conditions.

"My ShelterBox Response Team experience in Rwanda, Democratic Republic of the Congo, Niger, and Peru changed my worldview and my life. Seriously, it made such an impact and shaped what I would like to do the second half of life," Freeman says.

"I think the experience of hearing disaster survivor stories made the difference. These families were the poor and marginalized. This was especially the case in Peru following severe flooding of the Amazon, and landslides in the Andes."

Now with the ShelterBox experience under his belt, and as a member and former president of the eighty-member Rotary Club of Lakewood Ranch, Freeman is one of thousands of Rotarians involved in the international service organization's humanitarian relief projects. As a current professor of Environmental Science and Policy at the University of South Florida Sarasota-Manatee, access to clean water is a particular passion of his.

"One out of eight people on the planet lack access to safe water, and 90 percent of water-related diseases occur in children," he says.

These dire statistics are what drove the Lakewood Ranch Rotarians to organize an April 2018 Walk for Water event that raised $15,000. While only one-mile long, the fundraiser symbolized the daily trek many women and children endure to obtain water for their homes—water that is dirty and filled with common waterborne disease, bacteria, and viruses.

Freeman emphasizes, "It's full of nasty stuff. We walked to raise money to provide clean water and sanitation, to save lives, to improve school attendance and economic conditions."

In the planning stage is a late 2018 fact-finding mission to Iquitos in the Peruvian Amazon. It's one of the largest cities in the world accessible only by plane or boat.

Freeman and his Clean Water and Sanitation Projects Committee are seeking donors to accompany them, help conduct community assessments to determine future needs, and visit some of the country's famed tourist attractions, not the least of which is Machu Picchu. Dating to the fifteenth century, this mountaintop citadel is the most familiar icon of Inca civilization.

Working with other nongovernmental organizations (NGOs) such as Water Mission[28] in North Charleston, South Carolina, his planned $80,000 construction of a Living Water Treatment System in Monte Castillo, Piura Province, in northern Peru, will impact all two thousand families—approximately twelve thousand people—who were previously sourcing their household's drinking water from agricultural irrigation ditches, subjecting themselves to untold numerous waterborne diseases.

Freeman, who considers himself an adventurer and humanitarian, advises, "Everyone has heard of the Rotary or Kiwanis, but not every potential volunteer realizes that becoming involved with these and other service organizations can open the world up to them.

"My worldview totally changed once I became involved in international service projects. I am much more self-aware of the world around me and how I can make a difference, both individually and as part of a global service organization such as Rotary International."

CONSIDER CORPORATE VOLUNTEER PROGRAMS

Check with your employer. Companies large and small offer programs that allow employees to take time off for the greater good, encouraging employee involvement in volunteer trips and promoting responsible travel. For instance, backpack and luggage manufacturer Eagle Creek, based in Carlsbad, California, has a campaign called Live.Work.Travel.

As a participant in Eagle Creek's Creeker Volunteer Trip Program,[29] company employees have an opportunity to take five additional days off with pay to travel and volunteer with a nonprofit organization of their choice outside of the state they reside in.

If you work at a company that is particularly woke to the role it can play in improving lives near and far, look into volunteer opportunities with co-workers or others in your profession. Or start a trip yourself. One easy way to do this is to pull together a group for a volunteer cruise where tour operators handle all the logistics.

TRAVELING TO A TRADE CONVENTION? PITCH IN

From the massive Consumer Electronics Show, the World of Concrete Show, and the Shooting, Hunting, Outdoor Trade Show (SHOT Show) and Conference, down to the smaller The Running Event for running shoe retailers, or the American Optometric Association's Annual AOA Congress, there are millions of businesspeople attending thousands of US trade shows and conferences each year.

In fact, consider your own professional organization—associations account for more than 315,000 meetings held in the United States each year, with 59.5 million participants in attendance.[30]

Increasingly, these conferences plan activities to encourage attendees to spend a few hours on volunteer projects in the host city. For instance, the American Society of Association Executives (ASAE), consisting of thirty-nine thousand individual members from 7,400 organizations, run Community Connections events that coincide with its annual meetings. In 2017, volunteers at the ASAE convention in Toronto helped plant trees honoring Canada's fallen veterans and visited the Toronto Humane Society.

During ASAE's 2018 convention in Chicago, attendees assisted the Greater Chicago Food Depository with food collections and Little Brothers: Friends of the Elderly by decorating bags for birthday deliveries and packing toiletry kits for homebound elders.[31]

If you're part of a trade group and plan to attend one of these business events, consider spending a few hours away from the show floor to help local residents. If a volunteer program is not part of the conference agenda, organize one.

TAKE A CRUISE

Imagine pulling into Antigua on a mega cruise ship, the 3,690-passenger *Carnival Breeze* for instance. You know the kind: there's a midnight buffet, limbo contest, umbrella drinks, daily bingo, and shopping.

Within minutes, you disembark, then have your photo taken next to a large ring buoy at the bottom of the gangway. But instead of being steered through T-shirt shops and overpriced jewelry stores, you hop a local taxi and ride a few miles inland where, unfortunately, despite the influx of tourism-related wealth, 22 percent of the occupants of Antigua and nearby Barbuda live below the poverty line, according to the World Travel & Tourism Council.

The need for volunteer assistance is as great here as it is anywhere else in the Caribbean. With tourism comprising 60.4 percent of Antigua and Barbuda's GDP, wealthy visitors could help alleviate the challenges faced by the locals, if only tourists knew how best to help.[32]

"Voluntourism, a longtime travel industry niche, is rising in popularity as a way for travelers to give back and make a difference in the communities they visit," writes John Roberts, a Cruise Critic contributor.[33]

"The effort has spread to cruises, where itineraries offer charitable initiatives on board and excursions with an eye toward volunteering in port. Cruise lines have long been proud of their good deeds on the corporate level, but the cruise industry is increasingly involving passengers, on and off the ship, and offering sailings dedicated to supporting individual charities."

This trend toward giving-while-on-a-cruise is the impetus behind HopeFloats, a nonprofit started by two medical professionals in Lodi, California. It's the Match.com of cruise-based voluntourism.

Once your cruise is booked using any cruise line sailing to the Caribbean, simply log on to the organization's website[34] and scroll through the numerous lists of existing charity organizations at the different island ports you'll visit. Choose the organization you'd like to help, and HopeFloats will connect you with a local nonprofit that is desperate for an extra pair of hands.

In Tortola, for instance, your services are needed to help prep and serve lunch to thirty-five elderly shut-ins. During another island stop you may be asked to assemble and pack disaster first aid kits, sort materials at a recycling center alongside locals, or walk dogs at an animal shelter, all either a short walk from the ship or within a fifteen-to-twenty-minute drive.

HopeFloats was started in 2008 by Cathleen Huckaby, mother of four sons and a registered nurse, along with her husband, Bill, a cardiovascular perfusionist. They were introduced to cruising as guest speakers, trading an enjoyable week at sea in exchange for talks about medicine, healthy eating, and memoir writing.

During my recent interview she almost jumped through the phone; her energetic, fast-paced speaking style signals a woman out to make a difference in the world.

Huckaby's aha moment occurred in 2007 during a port stop in St. Thomas.

"There were all these expensive jewelry stores, yet three blocks away residents were living in abject poverty, digging through garbage. The disparity between cruise passengers and locals was pervasive—poverty, sanitation, and environmental issues confronted us blocks from every pier during our cruises.

"We both felt that if more cruisers knew about volunteer opportunities just fifteen minutes from their cruise ship and were assured it would be a safe and guided experience, it would entice them off the ship for a satisfying shore excursion," Huckaby recalls.

Exit surveys and testimonials conducted by HopeFloats of singles, families, and community groups praised this as a "win-win"—helping locals in very tangible ways while the cruisers achieve immense satisfaction in giving back.

Fast forward eleven years. Today HopeFloats offers sixteen different volunteer opportunities on ten Caribbean islands, with organizations specifically selected for their name value—among them the Salvation Army, Humane Society, Rotary International, Meals on Wheels, and Red Cross.

"HopeFloats prefers 'name brand' nonprofits. We realize that cruise passengers are more likely to volunteer if they know the organization," says Huckaby, who runs the service with her husband and son Josh, a thirty-year-old pastor, who provides technical computer advice.

HopeFloats will email you written instructions of how to reach the nonprofit, what to wear, what to bring, and a general description of the tasks you'll be asked to perform. Volunteers will then receive the name and telephone number of the contact person at the charity who will greet them upon arrival and be with them during their service time.

"If they'd like, all volunteers can pack needed items to donate to each nonprofit. For instance, at the Humane Society of St. Thomas, US Virgin Islands, simple supplies like leashes, pet toys, and cleaning materials are warmly appreciated," Huckaby tells me.

"'Wish lists' of suggested items to bring are available from all the nonprofits we serve. Charities welcome the support," she says. "During the morning that the cruisers are in port, the nonprofits' staff receive well-rested and eager volunteer help, as families, employees, and college students dive in to help with projects large and small. Without exception, passengers tell us it's one of the most memorable activities of their entire cruise. Voluntourists know that no matter how tough their stint may be, in a few hours they can be back on board eating lobster sandwiches and knocking back cold beers.

"What's more," Huckaby adds, "passengers get to interact with the locals and benefit from their knowledge of the best beaches, best restaurants, and places where residents shop."

Volunteer activities, for individuals, couples, or groups, are scheduled Monday through Friday from 9 a.m. to 1 p.m.—plenty of time to return to the ship before it departs, usually that same evening. The registration cost is a modest $30 per person, with discounts for groups. All participants are required to sign a liability waiver. No money changes hands between volunteers and charities; this is considered service time, so you won't be pitched for donations, although once passengers return home and decide they would like to donate financially, their support is gratefully accepted, according to Huckaby.

It's also possible to book volunteer experiences directly through cruise lines, but the opportunities are somewhat limited since there isn't as much money to be made offering volunteer shore excursions versus, say, a rainforest tour or sunset snorkel and cocktail cruise.

The savvy voluntourist can find so-called impact sailings on Princess Cruises and Fathom Travel, two of ten leading brands from Carnival Corporation, the world's largest leisure travel company. The Travel Deep program to the Caribbean connects cruisers with locals for in-depth immersion into island life and a connection with local communities. Optional activities involve rebuilding homes, beach cleanups, reforestation, and therapy through arts.[35]

"These purpose-driven groups allow travelers to get closer to the places we visit with a chance to come alongside local communities and have more authentic, immersive experiences with locals," says Tara Russell, Fathom president and Carnival Corporation global impact lead, in an announcement issued in early 2018.

For instance, in St. Thomas, the Fathom Travel group on *Crown Princess* handed out nearly $14,000 worth of baby items, purchased by travelers, to more than two hundred young families from the island. In the afternoon, the group helped the local Boys & Girls Club, where they built game tables and repainted facilities.

On St. Maarten, cruisers participated in a cleanup at Guana Bay, a beach important to three species of sea turtles that nest on the island. More than 1.5 tons of trash were collected and removed. In addition, travelers visited the National Institute of Art, where they interacted with locals and supported the Art Heals program with a donation of $1,500.

At Amber Cove, Dominican Republic, one group of fifty travelers took part in the construction of two homes by pouring concrete floors for families who lost their homes during hurricanes. Another group of fifty travelers visited a local school and spent time visiting with students. Later, the group planted four hundred mahogany tree seeds.

Holland America rolled out its first shoreside volunteer activities in Alaska in 2009 with a program called "Cruise with Purpose." Passengers boarded research vessels to document humpback and orca whale populations. They also measured ocean temperatures, gathered plankton, and collected water samples—readings that serve as a barometer for the annual salmon-run season in the state.

For those not willing to work up much of a sweat, there are excursions focused on simply introducing cruisers to local communities to see how they live, encouraging the purchase of local handicrafts.

For instance, Holland America's Cruise with Purpose program offers brief visits called Viva the Kids to the Betania Foundation, a ten-acre property that is host to four hundred children in Corinto, Nicaragua.[36]

Excursions to Panama take a journey into the lives of the Emberá Native tribe—a proud people who maintain their traditions and lifestyle as it was before the Spaniards colonized Panama.[37]

Holland America guests can head into the residential communities adjacent to the Huatulco, Mexico, resort area, learning about authentic cultural and social characteristics and getting acquainted with local habits and customs.[38]

Cruise with Purpose passengers stopping in Dubrovnik, Croatia, can learn about the ancient craft of silk production, from cocoon boiling to thread reeling, dyeing, plying, reeling, weaving, and embroidering.[39]

In Amber Cove, Dominican Republic, cruisers can visit RePapel, a recycling microbusiness founded by women, and help produce paper products and jewelry. At DIY workstations, they work alongside the staff to make new products for sale.[40]

"This all raises the important questions about the complicated nature of development work and whether these voluntourists actually cause more harm than good," writes Lucas Peterson in the September 29, 2016, *New York Times*.[41]

"Why, some argue, encourage untrained tourists to spend thousands of dollars to go on one of these trips when far more good could be accomplished using that money to, say, hire trained local workers?"

Gil Lang, impact guide manager for Fathom, tells *The Times*, "This is development 'lite'—we're not claiming to be anything else."

Lang, who spent nine years doing development work in South Africa, said he became disillusioned and frustrated with traditional development work. He believes that getting large corporations, like Carnival, involved ultimately helps more than it hurts. "Whether the intentions are altruistic or not, it doesn't matter," he said. "If even a tiny sliver of corporate profits can be funneled toward a good cause, it has a net positive effect."

MAKE ROOM FOR SUPPLIES

If you learn anything from this book it's that in many cases, becoming a voluntourist isn't a heavy lift after all. Whether traveling by cruise ship, or trains, planes, or automobiles, if there's room in your luggage, you can profoundly influence the life of someone less fortunate.

Ingenious is the best way to describe Rebecca Rothney's nine-year-old website, Pack for a Purpose,[42] based at her Raleigh, North Carolina, home. The site enables tourists to earmark suitcase space for donated products that fall within five general areas: education, health, child welfare, animal welfare, and socioeconomic development. These can include everyday items, such as over-the-counter medicines, clothing, books, sports gear, and school supplies.

Rothney, a retired schoolteacher and former custom cufflink manufacturer, established Pack for a Purpose in 2009 after she and her husband realized during an earlier African trip they had airline weight allowances they weren't using. The idea has become so successful that in 2014 she was recognized as one of only ten people honored that year as a National Geographic Traveler of the Year.[43]

The process is simple: you log on to the organization's website, select your destination country from a list of approximately sixty, then drill down further to identify one of 440 local tour operators or accommodations on

Pack for a Purpose makes it easy for voluntourists to dedicate suitcase space for donated products such as over-the-counter medicines, clothing, sports gear, school supplies, and in the case of this young volunteer, children's books. Photo by PackforaPurpose.org.

the website. You then select a nonprofit and are told what specific items are needed.

In Costa Rica, for example, the Safari Surf School needs colored pencils, crayons, erasers, and glue sticks. Visiting New York City? The Chatwal luxury hotel is looking for acrylic paint brushes and paints, beads for beadwork, and buttons for the project they support, the Children of Promise. If you've always wanted to visit Botswana, pack some colored pencils, rulers, crayons, and world maps and carry them to Little Vumbura Camp, where they will be delivered to the Children in the Wilderness Program.

While children love candy, it's not something they need, certainly not when a simple pencil will be more practical and help them learn. Over-the-counter (OTC) medicines need to be current for at least eight months after your arrival date.

The supplies are delivered to the school, the medical clinic, orphanage, or other nonprofit at no charge. Travelers can enjoy their stay in the country knowing they helped in a small way, although for the local organization the donated supplies often make a big difference.

"We ask people to carry at least five pounds of supplies, hoping they will wind up carrying more. After all, a stethoscope weighs less than a pound but can touch ten thousand hearts. A tube of antibiotic ointment can help heal the skin of a classroom of children," says Rothney, who works fifty hours a week with a tiny staff of volunteers that she'll often reward with homemade chocolate mint chip cookies.

Participating nonprofits, including a number located in the United States, are required to report every four months about the supplies they receive. Since it was founded, this has amounted to over 115 tons of supplies, all transported as part of regular checked baggage or carry-ons.

Rothney adds, "Pack for a Purpose is a simple, easy, and meaningful way for travelers of all ages to express their gratitude to the communities they visit. It requires only a small amount of space, takes little effort, and makes a big impact."

GET YOUR HANDS DIRTY

If you like the outdoors like I do, there is no shortage of volunteer projects to consider right in your own backyard. You can help restore trails on the Continental Divide Trail, Pacific Crest Trail, and in dozens of city, county, and state parks nationwide.

For example, the Appalachian Mountain Club, headquartered in Boston, offers volunteer vacations from the White Mountains to the Delaware

Water Gap to the Virgin Islands. You arrive, are assigned a trail crew, and receive training in safety procedures, the use of hand tools, and trail construction and maintenance during four days of trail work. It might feel strange, but you have to pay the club to volunteer for them. The cost for a one-week adult Base Camp Volunteer Vacation in the White Mountains, for instance, where volunteers will be called upon to build cairns and scree walls, install drainage, rock steps, bog bridges, and a variety of other projects, is $340 to $370, including bunkhouse accommodations and all meals.

"The program fee doesn't fully cover all expenses for the week and helps us defray costs. Without these funds we would be unable to operate volunteer crews, or to maintain our trails," according to the organization's website.[44]

Another outdoor group to consider supporting is Leave No Trace.[45] For over two decades, Dana Watts has been encouraging America to pick up after itself. As executive director of the Leave No Trace Center for Outdoor Ethics, a national nonprofit organization that promotes stewardship of the outdoors and responsible recreation practices, Watts and her staff of twenty-one have taken their message to Capitol Hill and regularly visit with land managers at the National Park Service, Bureau of Land Management (BLM), US Fish & Wildlife Service, and the US Forest Service.

Maintaining programming in every state and many countries, Leave No Trace annually reaches an estimated fifteen million visitors to public lands with cutting-edge education and a resource-rich website that includes an On-line Awareness Course. "We simply want to protect the outdoors by teaching and inspiring people to enjoy it responsibly," Watts tells me.

Volunteers are needed to be the eyes and ears of the organization, conducting research as citizen-scientists, carefully recording observations about the places they visit. The collected information is shared with land managers and other stakeholders, providing useful insights on the ways that human activities impact particular places and the ways that Leave No Trace can lessen those impacts.

Out in Colorado, nothing irks Boulder native Ann Baker Easley more than people who walk around muddy trails, cut switchbacks, or abandon dog poop bags. For eleven years, Easley has been head of a veritable army of volunteers passionate about maintaining Colorado's outdoor environment.

As executive director of Volunteers for Outdoor Colorado (VOC),[46] a statewide nonprofit volunteer organization founded in 1984, she and her staff supervise ninety-five projects each year. In 2016 alone, this involved 5,400 volunteers and nearly $955,000 in donated labor. These projects take place across Colorado—from city parks and open spaces to grasslands and foothills, to alpine meadows and peaks.

Volunteers seed hillsides after fire, reconstruct trails damaged by flood, remove invasive species, and create new trails that can withstand heavier foot and bike traffic.

Easley, a resident of Denver, remembers when her father would pack a Coleman stove and take the family up Boulder Canyon for an outdoor breakfast.

Food is a large part of VOC's lure. "Come volunteer and our crew chefs will feed you well. There's breakfast burritos, coffee, hors d'oeuvres, a full dinner, even beer at the end of the day," Easley says.

"It's like a camping trip that someone has planned for you, although you will have to work for it."

A handy online calendar allows volunteers to plug in their preferred volunteer dates between April and October and the type of work they're prepared to perform, from flood restoration, gardening and planting, to trail construction and managing evasive species. You can even select an activity according to physical difficulty, from easy to difficult.

"The various land managers, such as the Forest Service or local municipalities, can't do it alone. The public has to own their public lands in terms of caring for them, not just using them. That's the ethic we're trying to grow and sustain," Easley tells me.

"Most of us have desk jobs where the results aren't immediately apparent. When our volunteers return to hike a trail they helped build or maintain, there's a sense of incredible accomplishment, a sense of satisfaction people can't get in their normal working lives.

"Besides your own instant gratification, you get to show off envy-worthy selfies. After all, everyone looks gnarly holding a pickaxe or wearing a hard hat."

JOIN A WORK EXCHANGE

Another approach to voluntourism is to join a work exchange, an opportunity to exchange hard work, sweat, and personal vacation time to live and volunteer in an exotic destination.

For example, through World Wide Opportunities on Organic Farms (WWOOF), board and lodging are offered in exchange for a day's work on a farm.[47]

There are kibbutz experiences in Israel where you get to live in a Socialist community, working in various branches of the kibbutz economy such as agriculture, kitchen, gardening, and factory.[48]

You can find literally thousands of work exchange hosts through online services such as HelpX,[49] an online listing of host organic farms, nonorganic farms, farmstays, homestays, ranches, lodges, B&Bs, hostels, and even sailboats that invite volunteer helpers to stay and work short term in exchange for food and accommodations.

Another service is Workaway,[50] which promotes fair exchange between budget travelers, language learners, or culture seekers who can stay with thousands of families, individuals, or organizations that are looking for help in over 165 countries.

A. Christine Maxfield, a former magazine travel journalist and TV producer for the National Geographic Channel and WILD, now living in Gaithersburg, Maryland, was at a stage in her life a few years ago when the time was right to hit the road. After working for two years at *Arthur Frommer's Budget Travel* magazine, she decided to use her knowledge of travel to spend a year of her life—solo—experiencing work exchanges, one each month, in countries as varied as Australia, India, Peru, and Nepal, just to name a few. She lived with tribes in Africa and the Middle East, indigenous Australians in the Outback, shamans in the Amazon, and nomadic sheepherders in the Alps. Twenty countries in all.

Christine and I have known each other for years, in fact about a decade, when she reached out to me after reading a copy of *Expedition News*. I was immediately impressed that this was a young woman on a mission, not just geographically but professionally as well.

Today, Christine is the media relations manager at the African Wildlife Foundation, Africa's oldest conservation foundation. She's also a recent newlywed and stepmother to two teenagers, and she recalls fondly her year volunteering on six continents.

Working in exchange for food and lodging, often sleeping on bunk beds in simple wooden shacks, she taught piano at a Cambodian orphanage; taught English to Tibetan Buddhist nuns in Nepal; worked on a cattle ranch in the Australian Outback with an Aboriginal family; in Sierra Leone, she helped handicapped victims of war; visited Romania where she taught music to Roma (gypsy) children at the local village school; met President Barack Obama's grandmother in Kenya; and helped staff a black pearl farm in French Polynesia where she received pearls as thanks for her hard work.

At each stop she photographed her experiences and created daily blogs. She has since told her story in newspaper and magazine articles, on a web series,[51] and in personal appearances at travel shows.

It all amounted to 365 days of extraordinary experiences around the world.

Particularly memorable was her thirty-day stint at the ARCAS sea turtle hatchery in Hawaii, Guatemala.[52]

There she joined volunteers from throughout Europe as they combed the beaches at night for evidence of sea turtle nests, wearing headlamps with red filters. The nests were marked, the eggs later unearthed to prevent them from falling into the hands of poachers, and then taken to the hatchery. Two months later the newborn olive ridleys, the smallest of all sea turtles found in the world, were released back into the sea.

"The release of a little olive ridley sea turtle baby is always a miracle to behold on the beaches of Hawaii, Guatemala," she blogs.

"I enjoyed seeing the process of conservation with my own eyes, from the eggs that were laid by the olive ridleys in the sand, to the babies that were hatched and released back into the Pacific Ocean. It was a beautiful example of the circle of life that I can't experience just anywhere."

Her enthusiasm for that year of volunteer travel was contagious, and she recommends the experience to those with the time and passion.

Was it worth it, I wondered? Spending a year with pit toilets and bucket showers?

Maxfield sums up those twelve months as feeding her intensely wanderlust spirit. "Ever since I was a little girl, I had a list of the places I wanted to visit someday. I knew I had to do this and travel solo, which made it so liberating. Now I can go anywhere in the world and find my way around. I really changed and am not as fearful of a person. It was incredibly empowering.

"You are working your butt off, especially since your hosts are providing food and lodging. However, even though you're not making money on a work exchange, you're not spending any money either."

WHEN AN ILL WIND BLOWS

There is seemingly no shortage of volunteer opportunities available when natural disasters strike somewhere in the world.

While a disaster is hardly a time to practice the "tourism" aspect of voluntourism, aiding a US community affected by tornado or flooding, or a foreign country hammered by earthquake or tsunami, provides valuable insight into the lives, the culture, the hopes and dreams, of fellow humans.

In the 1990s I was involved with Americares, the health-focused relief and development organization that responds to people affected by poverty or disaster with life-changing medicine, medical supplies, and health programs.

I ran a kayak fundraiser for the nonprofit around Manhattan Island on September 6, 1997. I remember the date well because it coincided with the funeral of Princess Diana. It was one of the most watched events in TV history.[53] The effect it had on New York City was chilling. Manhattan was eerily quiet—no traffic, hardly anyone on the sidewalks while the funeral was underway. As a result, the volunteer kayak fundraiser lacked spectators, a reminder that any special event, volunteer or not, can be adversely affected by hard news events.

A few years later I would participate in an Americares Airlift to San Pedro Sula, Honduras. The airlift was staged with Hollywood theatricality. Immediately following a black-tie gala in a hangar at the Westchester County Airport in New York, the massive sliding doors slowly pulled apart to reveal outside on the tarmac a chartered jet ready to whisk invited guests, now changed into jeans and sneakers, to visit orphanages and hospitals in Honduras the very next morning. Returning later that afternoon, the exhausted volunteers became evangelists for the work that Americares has performed since its founding in 1979.

Those flights continue to this day. In fact, the Americares Airlift Benefit recently celebrated its thirtieth anniversary.[54]

According to Americares, roughly 80 percent of the Honduran people do not have access to quality health care as they face a high incidence of common infectious diseases and a significant increase in diabetes and hypertension.

Through its longstanding partnership with the Honduran Order of Malta, the organization continues to provide access to medicine for more than eighty health and social service institutions throughout the country with a focus on diabetes treatment.

Volunteers are crucial to the success of the organization. Each year hundreds work in various capacities at its Stamford, Connecticut, headquarters or as part of its Free Clinics community program.

The United States alone has spent $350 billion in the last decade on extreme weather and wildfire events, and climate change will only make the problems worse, according to a CNBC report.[55] "The outpouring of help from emergency responders, volunteers and fellow citizens for victims of the recent hurricanes and wildfires is testament to our nation's immense capacity for compassion and sacrifice in the face of disaster," writes Trent Lott, a former Senate Majority Leader and Senior Fellow at the Bipartisan Policy Center, and Jason Grumet, president of the Bipartisan Policy Center.

Consider for a moment the hurricanes that struck in 2017.

The historic 2017 Atlantic hurricane season produced seventeen named storms, most notably Harvey, Irma, and Maria that left hundreds dead, destroyed communities across the southern United States and Caribbean, and caused an estimated $265 billion in damage—the most expensive hurricane season on record. Hurricane Harvey set a new mark for the most rainfall from a US tropical storm. Hurricane Irma became one of the strongest Atlantic Ocean hurricanes ever recorded. Hurricane Maria was the most powerful hurricane to make landfall on the main island of Puerto Rico in eighty-five years, according to the Americares website.

Americares simultaneously responded to all three storms, deploying seventy-five relief workers who spent more than 2,500 days in the field.[56]

In a little-remembered story by F. Scott Fitzgerald called "Family in the Wind," a second tornado in two days rips through a small Alabama town, causing the story's hero, a local doctor, to remark: "This is worse than a calamity; it's getting to be a nuisance."[57]

Extreme weather and fire-related disasters are becoming more commonplace, more deadly, and more costly. Some models predict that extraordinarily destructive hurricanes and massive wildfires will become the new normal, pointing to the need for increasing numbers of volunteers, often on a moment's notice.

This is especially true in the hurricane-stricken Caribbean. Nonprofits and resorts offer special programs for those who want to assist. Projects might include cleaning up trails in a national park, river and beach cleanups, painting at a local school, and assisting at an animal shelter, according to the *New York Times*.[58]

"Just by visiting, the injection of foreign exchange in the economy is going to help," said Hugh Riley, the secretary general of the Caribbean Tourism Organization. "But some want to come to do something in addition to relaxing on the beach, and we are seeing many opportunities for voluntourism."

Caribbean organizations seeking volunteer help include the Friends of Virgin Islands National Park,[59] the environmental Puerto Rican organization Para La Naturaleza,[60] and Anguilla island cleanups through the Anguilla Stronger Emergency Relief Fund founded by Starwood Capital Group, which owns the Four Seasons Resort and Residences Anguilla.[61]

El Yunque, the rainforest and national park in northwest Puerto Rico, was once a wall of green, the path shaded by a lush canopy of mahogany and ironwood trees. Now hikers squint into the sunlight, and scraggly patches dot the mountainside where Hurricane Maria ripped through, according to *Travel & Leisure*.[62]

In some areas, as much as 40 percent of the forest is gone, says Carlos Rodríguez Gómez, a guide with environmental conservation group Para La Naturaleza.

The nonprofit is connecting visitors with experiences that let them see the country while helping with recovery efforts. There are opportunities to assist with tree planting, coastal cleanups, document the population of the endangered crested toad, restore historic sites, and even excavate the nests of invasive iguanas, making room for native fauna to reclaim their place in the ecosystem, according to the travel magazine.[63]

In the Florida Keys, mercilessly pummeled by Hurricane Irma, no special skills are needed to be a volunteer at the National Key Deer Refuge, home to twenty-three endangered and threatened plant and animal species including Key deer, the smallest subspecies of the North American white-tailed deer. Here volunteers may work full time, a few hours per week or month, or even during a particular season.[64]

In nearby Key West, Casa Marina Resort's director of human resources and voluntourism works with groups staying at the hotel to link them with volunteer projects in the islands, such as rebuilding trailer homes.

Volunteer organizations, says Christine Steinhauser, "are still here, still working, still assisting with projects. They branch off in so many different areas you could take your pick of working in warehouses of food goods, delivering clothing and food and water or helping with reconstruction," she tells the *New York Times*.

Another group that provides assistance in natural disasters is the nonprofit All Hands and Hearts–Smart Response, located in Mattapoisett, Massachusetts.[65] It was formed through the merger of David Campbell's All Hands Volunteers and the Happy Hearts Fund created in 2005 by supermodel Petra Němcová, who was swept away by the 2004 Indian Ocean tsunami and survived by clinging to a tree for eight hours. All Hands addresses the immediate and long-term needs of communities impacted by natural disaster. Its mission is to rebuild safe, resilient schools in impacted areas. This helps families recover faster after natural disasters using a "smart response" strategy—by rebuilding in a disaster resilient manner, they are prepared for future events and, through the process, strengthening both volunteers and communities.

Němcová has been the key motivation and driving force behind rebuilding schools for children forgotten after natural disasters due to lack of sustained response. The organization accepts spontaneous volunteers from any background or faith, providing on-the-job training free of charge.

"We can't control nature, but we can control the actions we take," says Němcová.[66]

To paraphrase the famous saying, next time an "ill wind" comes along, voluntourists can rise to the occasion and do good, helping hundreds, perhaps thousands during their time of need. This is especially true if they spend freely and help the local hotels, restaurants, and shops while on the scene.

The more voluntourists I meet, the more I'm impressed with how these everyday people are wired differently than most. What gets these volunteers, typically glass-half-full optimists, up each morning is the realization that by assisting others, they are enjoying more fulfilling lives. Assuming, of course, that the conditions under which they serve don't make them long for a nice boring beach vacation instead.

· IV ·

Become a Better Voluntourist

*A*nother consideration when selecting the right project is to honestly gauge your tolerance level. Unless you volunteer here in the States, you're in a foreign country. You're hot. You're hungry. You're annoyed by the insects, the incessant sun, the dirt, the pollution. This is where tolerance is a virtue. Ask yourself, "Can I mentally and emotionally process being with children who have no arms or legs, or cleft palates, are blind, or have stomachs bloated by malnutrition?"

Understand the conditions: meals and transportation included? How many hours required? Any free time? What are the sleeping conditions—private room or dorm style? What's your tolerance for primitive sleeping accommodations?

When I traveled to Nepal to participate in Dooley Intermed's Gift of Sight cataract mission, our teahouse accommodation lacked towels. I was drying off with dirty T-shirts. There was no heat, and the bathroom—actually just a hole in the floor of a closet—was down the hall. I was way outside my comfort zone. While this is rather low on the list of human hardships, suffice it to say it's important to understand the availability of creature comforts before you depart.

Ask yourself: What is my personal minimum requirement for accommodations? Do I need running water? My own bed? My own room? Volunteers need to be intolerant of nasty situations. They'll review charming and sweet photos of underprivileged children in the brochures and websites—but they arrive and it's uncomfortable when they see the actual conditions, including smelly, squat hole toilets, lice in the childrens' hair, ripped clothing, and dirty floors and walls.

STAY COMFORTABLE WORKING OUTDOORS

Consider how rigorous you want your volunteer experience to be: Does it involve hiking? climbing? high altitude? steamy rainforest? Arctic cold?

Prolonged exposure to heat and direct sun can be debilitating and exhausting. Even in New Jersey. Especially in New Jersey.

My fellow Explorers Club member, Kenneth J. Lacovara, PhD, is one of the country's foremost paleontologists. In 2014, he published his scientific description of the immense, long-necked dinosaur he discovered in southern Patagonia and subsequently named *Dreadnoughtus schrani*, which is considered one of the largest ever found, a supermassive find he describes in his book *Why Dinosaurs Matter* (2017). Today he serves as founding dean, School of Earth & Environment, and professor of paleontology and geology at Rowan University in Glassboro, New Jersey.

As founder and director of the university's Jean & Ric Edelman Fossil Park, Lacovara is supervising the construction of a $57 million fossil museum not far from Philadelphia, which he expects will open in spring 2021. This suburban quarry is the only major fossil site within a major metropolitan area and is a world-class destination for scientific discovery and citizen science.

The fossil park is within walking distance of a Lowe's home improvement store—"a dream location for any paleontologist needing last-minute supplies," Lacovara laughs. Yet the suburban location, within a day's drive of one-third of the US population, can be a deceptively difficult assignment for volunteers, where temperatures can range from well below freezing to over 100 degrees F.

Volunteers, up to one hundred, are required for annual community Dig Day; the sign-up usually reaches capacity within twenty minutes after becoming available online. Some fifteen volunteers are also needed on days that schools visit the site. Schoolchildren in particular are eager to dig for fossils, which they can keep—there is no shortage of fossilized clams and oysters buried within sixty-six-million-year-old sediment at the sixty-five-acre site. The ancient specimens then wind up on desks, bookshelves, and windowsills of young students for years, silent ambassadors to the thrill of exploration and the joy of learning.

"We couldn't run the fossil park without our volunteers. They help park cars, answer questions, and ensure visitors have a memorable experience," Lacovara says. "They need to be cheerful, helpful, and selfless since one bad experience for a visitor could reflect on the entire facility. Our volunteers must believe in the cause over and above their own creature comforts."

The volunteers also need to demonstrate a certain hardiness and familiarity with working outdoors, even if this is the Garden State.

"Volunteers must be comfortable standing outside in all sorts of conditions, donating time in weather that may be well outside their comfort zones. This means dressing appropriately, wearing a hat, sunscreen, eye protection, proper footwear, and hydrating themselves before they become thirsty.

"Field conditions are never ideal. Contributing to the mission of field science and stimulating youth to pursue STEM careers is more important than the quality of the lunch served that day, or whether their feet hurt. The best reward they receive is the meaning of the work," Lacovara tells me.

"Besides, no good volunteer story ever starts with, 'things were fine and stayed that way.'"

One way to prepare for a volunteer experience is to take yourself to a local outdoor store, explain your project to the sales associate, then ask for recommendations on how to dress. If you as a volunteer are not happy, not comfortable in the field, it will reflect on the experiences of your fellow teammates as well. When volunteers aren't happy, nobody is happy.

CONSIDER TEAM DYNAMICS

Another way to become a better voluntourist is to ask yourself, "Do I play well with others?"

Preston Sowell is an environmental scientist, naturalist, photographer, and explorer residing in Boulder, Colorado. He has led, supported, and photographed expeditions to twenty-one countries around the world, including fifteen scientific expeditions to remote areas of South America. So I turned to him for advice on the importance of team dynamics.

"Remember you are there for something larger than yourself and you have a responsibility to conduct yourself accordingly. Show up prepared and don't misrepresent your skills/abilities," he advises.

"Taking care of yourself is taking care of your team and the larger goal/mission. Understand the chain of command and communication. If you're not sure, ask.

"Know when to communicate issues that could affect the entire team, such as when more water or supplies are needed, who is impaired, sick, hurt, or exhausted, or whether there are team member conflicts the group leader needs to be aware about," says Sowell, a member of the New York–based Explorers Club.

"Maintain a healthy mindset to avoid being a weak link, or even deleterious to the effort."

Sowell adds, "Always be conducting a risk analysis when you're working in extreme environments. For example, how remote are you? What are primary threats in that environment, and what are the implications of an accident? You have to develop a greater awareness, beyond the tourist mindset."

Above all, don't be difficult. Sowell vets his team members carefully, checking their backgrounds, references, field experience, physical fitness, and special skills. "Some people can suck the energy out of an expedition, especially if they don't suffer well or are overly critical of the situation or leadership. Things may not go perfectly on expeditions when there are many factors at play. If you're not happy, communicate that respectfully and be prepared to facilitate solutions."

GET TO KNOW THE NONPROFIT
BEFORE YOU DEPART, THEN STAY INVOLVED

One way to approach a volunteer project in a foreign country is to go in cold. Trust that a tour operator will handle your personal needs for food, shelter, security, and transportation while you tend to the needs of others less fortunate. This is not an ideal way to begin volunteer project work. The preferred approach, one favored by a friend in Boulder, Colorado, is to develop a relationship with an overseas nonprofit, and a destination, before you depart.

Jacquie McKenna, the wife of a fellow Explorers Club member, is a development finance consultant who has been volunteering throughout her life. Today a busy mother of two teenage girls, she recalls fondly some of her early voluntourism adventures. One memorable experience happened just after graduation from the Wharton School of the University of Pennsylvania in 1988, in which she volunteered for Plenty International[1] to help build an automobile repair facility for the Carib Indians in Dominica, a small island republic in the Caribbean Windward Islands. She and a small group of fellow graduates raised money to pay for the building materials and spent two weeks living, eating, and working with the Carib Indians, the indigenous Caribbean people of the Lesser Antilles, while remaining solely focused on helping build the repair facility.

"They could have built it faster without us, I'm sure," she laughs, "but they put up with us. It was a phenomenal way to get to know the island and the indigenous population, besides from just the usual tourist prospective."

Supporting economic self-sufficiency, cultural integrity, and environmental responsibility remains Plenty's mission today. In fact, since 1974, hundreds of Plenty volunteers have worked in nineteen countries on projects such as organic agriculture, food production and nutrition, cooperative businesses, solar energy, communications, health care, disaster relief, fair trade crafts marketing, and ecotourism.

Years later, after Jacquie married her husband, Andrew, an explorer involved in the search for the famed aviatrix Amelia Earhart, the two encouraged their then ten-year-old daughter to choose an organization to which guests to her birthday party could donate in lieu of gifts. She chose the David Sheldrick Wildlife Trust (DSWT), raised over $400, and was able to select two elephants to adopt, one for her and one for her parents. Normally adoptions are available for a minimum donation of $50.

The Trust, based in Nairobi, Kenya, is one of the most successful orphan-elephant and rhino rescue and rehabilitation programs in the world and one of the pioneering conservation organizations for wildlife and habitat protection in East Africa. The DSWT Orphans' Project offers hope for the future of Kenya's threatened elephant and rhino populations as they struggle against the threat of poaching for their ivory and horn and the loss of habitat due to human population pressures and conflict, deforestation and drought, according to the organization's website.[2]

The family continued to support "their" elephants and DSWT. A couple of years after the party, when the McKennas traveled to Kenya, they were invited by the Trust to visit the Sheldrick facility as part of its foster parent visiting program. It was a stopover that made their Kenya tour all the more

Jacquie McKenna from Boulder, Colorado, became a foster parent to an elephant named "Rapa" at the David Sheldrick Wildlife Trust in Kenya. Photo by Jacquie McKenna.

memorable. As they watched baby elephants being fed and had a chance to bond with them, they learned more about the Sheldrick program that eventually releases hand-raised elephants back into the wild herds of Tsavo East National Park.

"Teaching our daughter to give something meaningful by supporting a nonprofit organization instead of being inundated with unneeded birthday gifts was special, and adopting baby elephants was a bonus. Visiting them was magical," she tells me. "It made us feel a part of the fabric of Africa, if only for a couple hours during our stay."

Jacquie's most recent voluntourism experience occurred in October 2017, when the McKenna family combined their interest in sightseeing through Nicaragua with volunteering with Empowerment International (EI), an education-based program founded in the McKenna's hometown of Boulder, Colorado, and one in which the McKennas had been involved for many years.

EI addresses the plight of street children in the impoverished barrios of Central America, home to vulnerable communities and families who have traditionally devalued the role education can play in improving their lives. Instead of being educated, children are sent out to work on the streets selling fruits and vegetables or are required to stay home to help with younger children and chores so the parents can work, according to EI's website.[3] EI has focused its efforts in the city of Granada, located an hour's drive from the capital city of Managua.

The organization works to reverse this trend by getting involved with the students in their program—providing after-school activities to support the schoolwork as well as offer students somewhere meaningful to go after school to stay out of trouble. Home visits are periodically conducted to ensure students stay in school and continue their learning.

"EI has an over 90 percent success rate in graduating its program participants compared to less than 50 percent in Nicaragua overall," McKenna tells me.

To fund its program, EI offer donors, such as the McKenna family, an opportunity to not only support a child but also personally travel to the facility to volunteer their time and energy in person.

"We had been sponsoring a young girl named Lesly for years, corresponding through the mail, paying her school fees and supporting her participation in the EI program. During a planned vacation to Nicaragua, we thought the time was right to meet Lesly, spend time with her, and volunteer with EI. We contacted the nonprofit's staff and they helped us set up an individualized family visit," McKenna recalls.

"We were in Granada for three days, interacting with Lesly, her fellow students, and EI program managers, while still setting aside some time on our own. We assisted the younger children with an art class, purchased school supplies based upon the teachers' wish list, went on a photo tour of Granada with Lesly and the school's photo club, and toured an active volcano, as the students acted as our tour guides. This gave us a kind of 'backstage tour' and an insider's perspective of the city and countryside, one that regular tourists usually never hear or see."

McKenna continues, "The kids were wonderful about answering our questions. The cultural exchange was very special. We were touring with friends rather than some unknown tour guide.

"In addition to the time we spent with EI, we also had time on our own. Our family visited a lake in a nearby volcanic caldera where we spent the day swimming, boating, and relaxing. Aside from taking the students out for lunch one day, we had the chance to eat on our own at various restaurants in Granada and explore the city on our own."

Since the McKenna's visit, the EI program has partnered with a Denver travel agency, Walking Tree Travel,[4] to arrange organized programs that combine sightseeing with meaningful volunteer work. The travel agency provides consistency and insurance for the visits by individual families as well as school groups.

McKenna notes, "It's a more memorable experience when you hit the ground to volunteer and already have a strong relationship with the locals."

Doug Christoph, a beverage industry business development and marketing consultant based in Atlanta, tells me of a similar experience. After traveling to Cambodia in 2011, following his retirement from the Coca-Cola Company, he was exposed to the horrific history of the Pol Pot regime whose Communist Khmer Rouge government led Cambodia from 1975 to 1979. Its disastrous influence remains to this day. Destitute villagers, mostly children living in Phnom Penh, were forced to eke out a meager existence combing through the former Steung Meanchey garbage dump, one of the most toxic environments imaginable.

Their dire situation affected Christoph right down to his core, both emotionally and mentally, which ultimately drove him to want to help in any way he could. Through a friend at Coca-Cola, he met with Scott Neeson, founder of the Cambodian Children's Fund (CCF),[5] a nonprofit organization based in Phnom Penh whose program of education, food, community, and clothing offers a pathway out of poverty. CCF works with families to build plans for escaping debt, educating the children, and developing job skills for parents and older children. The organization believes that a generation of educated children has the power to change a whole society.

Abysmal conditions in Phnom Penh's former Steung Meanchey garbage dump, one of the most toxic environments imaginable, encouraged beverage industry consultant Doug Christoph to donate his time, talent, and resources. Photo by Doug Christoph.

The garbage dump was closed in 2009. However, the need for CCF's services continues as Steung Meanchey remains an entry point into Phnom Penh for destitute families with no option but to scavenge or beg on the city streets, according to CCF's website.

Christoph, and close friend and business partner Tom McNichols, decided to sponsor children and at the same time, conduct development and planning work for CCF to help the organization grow and evolve. When they returned a year-and-a-half later, they were gratified to see CCF had made significant progress in achieving its various missions.

Christoph tells his Facebook followers, "New buildings, over 2,000 children in the program, more donors, and an incredible staff. . . . CCF now provides for them (including) housing, food, education, and the only free medical facility in the country for the kids and their families."

The organization seeks trained volunteers, pulling from the ranks of teachers, doctors, imaging technicians, social media experts, sports coaches, geriatric specialists, or in Christoph's case, fundraisers and marketers. Christoph and McNichols return for visits to CCF and Cambodia as frequently as their schedules allow.

"Today, it is absolutely incredible what Scott and his team have done for the children, their families, and CCF," Christoph says.

PREPARE TO LEARN NEW SKILLS

I was born missing the handyman gene. To this day, my wife talks about the time early in our relationship when I attempted to fix a leaky toilet with a drill. Actually, the drill had a screwdriver bit, so I thought it would help adjust the screws on that floating bobber thingy in the tank. Still, she thought I was going to inflict great harm on the plumbing, and quite possibly myself.

Thus, it was with some trepidation that I volunteered at a Denver-area Habitat for Humanity ReStore, one of 850 nonprofit home improvement stores and donation centers nationwide that sell new and gently used furniture, appliances, home accessories, and building materials to the public at a fraction of the retail price. These independently owned reuse stores, operated by local Habitat for Humanity organizations, help families build a decent and affordable place to call home.[6]

Some ReStores are located near popular tourist destinations, making it easy to donate vacation time. In fact, there are five ReStores clustered around I-70, the main east-west corridor to the world-famous mountain resorts of Aspen, Vail, and Breckenridge. Denver has been setting tourism records over the past few years. Its rise as a top tourism destination continued in 2016 as the city welcomed 31.5 million total visitors for the first time, including 17.3 million overnight visitors. In fact, overnight visitation surpassed 2015 totals by nearly one million visitors, a 6 percent year-over-year increase, according to Visit Denver, the private, nonprofit trade association that markets Denver as a convention and leisure destination.

In addition to skiing and snowboarding up in the mountains, visitors come to see the Denver Mint, Red Rocks Park & Amphitheatre, Denver Art Museum, Denver Botanic Gardens, even the Buffalo Bill Museum and Grave. Thus, it's not much of a disconnect to think these very same visitors could also spend a tiny fraction of their vacation time volunteering at one of the hundreds of Colorado nonprofits listed on VolunteerMatch.org. In fact, last time I looked, there were 359 volunteer opportunities in the Denver area alone.[7]

If you're a visitor to the Colorado Front Range, volunteering at a ReStore couldn't be easier, even if you happen to be born like me with all thumbs.

First, you sign up on their website, pick a location, select a five-hour shift, and print out your assignment. No questions asked. Just register with a user ID and password. I lay out my best yardwork clothes for the one-hour drive tomorrow—nothing special, just jeans and an old T-shirt I don't mind soiling.

At the appointed time, one bright and sunny Sunday morning, I report for duty at a ReStore that shares space with a Goodwill store. The crew chief has my name on an iPad and is expecting me. In front is a retail store, but it's behind the scenes where all the fun happens.

Back surgery years ago means I won't be the guy who lugs around donated sofas. However, I was immediately put at ease—volunteering doesn't necessarily require a strong back. I would be assigned other tasks. As I begin my shift, I am shown the fire extinguishers, emergency exits, and bathroom. Handed a blue ReStore apron and a pair of work gloves, I am asked to watch a rather humorous eight-and-a-half-minute safety video on a computer screen practically buried on a desk cluttered with price lists, hand tools, shrink wrap, plastic tape, and Clorox wipes.[8]

The video warns me about trips, flips, and falls; how to lift heavy objects correctly (with the legs, or slide the object along the floor); and the importance of wearing Personal Protective Equipment (PPE), including gloves and safety glasses. I'm told never to stand on the top rungs of the ladder—get a taller ladder. I'm realizing these are important life skills everyone needs, both within and beyond the volunteer experience.

The video concludes with a pat on the back: "You don't just talk about poverty and homelessness, you do something about it. You are a big deal to us."

ReStore volunteers are often sent out on trucks to pick up donated goods such as new and gently used appliances, cabinets, furniture, flooring, building materials, and household goods. However, this morning, the donations come to us. For five hours, in a constant procession of private SUVs and trucks, ReStore volunteers and staffers greet the drivers, open their hatchbacks or trunks, and load donations onto rolling platforms or hand trucks. Some people were moving, others were performing spring cleaning or home renovations. Still others, unfortunately, treat ReStore as a free dump, and we received some bizarre items.

Still, in this throwaway society of ours, it was good to think that not everything is destined for a landfill. ReStore claims it diverts hundreds of tons from landfills each year accepting the hard-to-dispose-of flotsam and jetsam of everyday life.

All the donors this morning are motivated by the ReStore receipt that allows them to claim a charitable deduction at the fair market value of the goods they were now dropping in our laps. The organization offers an online

Donation Value Guide. It turns out those treasured possessions are not worth as much as one would think. The value of a porcelain bathtub is only $25 to $50; a couch is valued at $25 to $150, based upon condition.[9]

Still, this doesn't seem to deter anyone. It was like Christmas in May.

"Ding, ding," went the driveway bell, which reminded me of the sound of local automobile service stations, back when they still made repairs.

"Ding, ding," a box of CDs.

"Ding, ding," here comes a glass TV stand. An unopened home entertainment system. A set of Harry Potter books.

A Celestron reflecting telescope. A lawn seeder.

The smaller items are processed to be sold in the adjacent Goodwill store; larger items that fall within home improvement—three porch lights, doors, windows, and tile, are rolled back to the workshop where I am stationed.

"Ding, ding," they call me out to pick up two pedestal bathroom sinks that would prove to be my nemesis. But more on that later.

I spend the five-hour shift moving donated goods around, using tape to remove dog hair from a donated sofa (a slightly icky assignment), screwing in table legs, and dismantling those three porch lights—magnetic parts in one bin, nonmagnetic in another, cut the wiring and recycle those, and toss the glass panels. Appliances are plugged in, checked, and cleaned. I'm asked to clean two plastic Adirondack chairs with Clorox wipes. They will later sell for $8 each—a steal.

"Ding, ding." More cars arrive as it gets closer to noon.

It was actually a fun experience. Marcus, the crew chief, is walking around with a pirate's hat on his head; country music is playing on a donated boom box. Ever since moving to Colorado three years ago, C&W songs of drinkin' hard and lovin' hard are starting to grow on me.

My fellow volunteer, a high schooler, is there performing community service. Seems when you go 35 mph over the speed limit and it's your third speeding ticket, paying a fine isn't enough. You're headed to community service. Yes, indeed, right next to a volunteer/book author who has trouble telling the difference between an Allen wrench and a monkey wrench. But I would soon learn.

When the time came to remove the faucets from those two pedestal sinks, I met my Waterloo. I tried an Allen wrench, socket wrench, a vise grip, adjustable wrench, and even a hammer, but couldn't budge the fitting. No dice. I remember the admonition from my high school shop teacher, "Use the right tool for the job."

At least I was getting valuable hands-on experience using the right tool, but this was going to be the wrong job for me.

Luckily, crew chief Marcus said I could leave my disastrous sink project for the next volunteer beginning his shift in a few minutes. I was happy to move on, with the knowledge that the next DIY project I tick off the "honey do" list at home might go a tiny bit smoother.

There are close to a thousand ReStore locations around the United States looking for volunteers. They need help unloading trucks, repairing and refurbishing furniture, pricing inventory, customer service, stocking store shelves, and, as with my experience, dismantling porch lights and sinks.

Besides helping the poor and homeless for a few hours when visiting Colorado, you might also learn a thing or two about maintaining marital bliss during your next home plumbing repair.

YOU'RE NOT ALWAYS GOING
TO BE ASSIGNED THE FUN JOBS

Thoughts of pelicans eating out of my hand and parrots perched on my shoulder as if I were a pirate were soon dashed when I visit the Florida Keys Wild Bird Rehabilitation Center in Tavernier, Florida. I was visiting relatives in nearby Key Largo and knew that volunteers are the lifeblood of this non-profit dedicated to the rescue, rehabilitation, and release of native and migratory wild birds that have been harmed or displaced. The center also provides a humane shelter for birds that cannot be released. Its permanent inhabitants include various owls, hawks, falcons, and turkey vultures that look all the world as if they walked out of a Warner Bros. Looney Tunes cartoon. Some were injured in auto accidents; others were shot by pellet guns and attacked by domestic house cats.

The facility was founded in 1991 by Laura Quinn, who started by providing modest rehabilitation facilities behind her small oceanfront home. What began as a homegrown effort to heal broken wings and remove fish-hooks and monofilament line grew into a 5.5-acre property on which only about an acre is developed to provide habitats for approximately one hundred birds along serpentine walkways. Pelicans, which appear to be the evolutionary offspring of dinosaurs, peer down from rooftops. The rest of the property is lush native vegetation, mangroves, hammocks, and wetlands. The facility was still feeling the aftereffects of Hurricane Irma, which roared through three months before in September 2017.

During my visit, I met with assistant director Jordan Budnik, a twenty-six-year-old educator from Atlanta, standing on the crushed coral driveway of the facility. There's a forty-year-old military macaw named Nikki perched on her right shoulder. She occasionally nuzzles the bird, which likes to dance

Volunteer at the Florida Keys Wild Bird Rehabilitation Center, and you'll help the staff clean bird transfer boxes, scrub boardwalks, assist with academic programs and office/ administrative work, and provide enclosure maintenance. Just don't expect to walk around like a pirate. Photo by Jeff Blumenfeld.

to Latin music Budnik plays on her smartphone (the macaw's top favorite is "Despacito" by Luis Fonsi, featuring Daddy Yankee).

The two are so intimately bonded that Nikki can recognize the sound of Budnik's car wheels when it crunches down the driveway and the bleep-bleep of her remote car lock.

She tells me that volunteers are not allowed to have contact with the birds, more for the birds' sake than the humans, due to the possibility of the animals contracting a human-borne disease. Instead, volunteers help the staff with cleaning bird transfer boxes, scrubbing boardwalks, assisting with academic programs, office/administrative work, and enclosure maintenance.

There are no monetary fees or donation requirements associated with volunteering, but volunteer positions (minimum age eighteen) require the submission of an application, passing a background check, interview, facilities tour, and training by the staff. The process is fairly straightforward, and volunteers are welcome even for half a day, Budnik tells me.

"We'll take whatever volunteer time we can get, no long-term commitment is required, but remember these are wild animals so you won't be interacting with them directly."

Speaking of wild animals, it doesn't help anyone if a volunteer is bitten, takes ill, or succumbs to things that go bump in the night, as you'll read in the next chapter.

· $\mathcal{V}$ ·

Stay Safe Out There

$\mathcal{N}$o matter what project you select, you're not going to be much good if you can't perform at your best. You need to stay healthy and safe. Much has been written about staying safe on the road. A quick Google search will yield advice from a variety of sources, including *Bloomberg*, CNBC, *HuffPost*, *USA Today*, and numerous other mainstream media.

By its very definition, voluntourism often takes you to places far off the grid, far from reliable medical services, and far from the safe sanitation and food handling practices you've come to expect in the United States.

Don't I know it. During my last trip to Nepal I was a good boy: drank only bottled water, used Purell hand sanitizer by the gallon, and ate only food that was hot, hot, hot—cooked completely through and through. But I let my guard down.

During literally the last hour in Nepal, at the Kathmandu Tribhuvan International Airport, I convinced myself that the fruit plate in the VIP Executive Lounge could be trusted. Big mistake. In about twenty hours, during the final flight from New York to Denver, digestive distress kicked in, alleviated only once I arrived home and downed some DiaResQ, a natural diarrhea relief aid made with bovine (cow) colostrum. Sounds awful, but it worked. Eating that last snack in Nepal was a rookie move on my part, as I realized during my eighth trip to the tiny airplane lavatory. Too much information? OK, let's move on.

I've been to every state in the union except Mississippi, and have traveled to thirty-six countries, so while I'm not the world's authority on safe travel, there are certain measures I employ that have worked well for me and might also be appropriate for you.

Check the US Department of State—Bureau of Consular Affairs Travel Advisories and Alerts to make informed decisions about your personal safety. The US State Department recently changed how it issues warnings to US citizens about international travel. Previously the agency released advisories, warnings, or bulletins about specific nations, which caused some confusion. "What's the difference between a travel warning and a travel alert?" people wondered. The system has changed so that each country now has an advisory—not a rule, but instead a "recommendation"—rated on a four-point threat scale. The lower the number, the lower the risk: (1) Exercise Normal Precautions (blue), (2) Exercise Increased Caution (yellow), (3) Reconsider Travel (orange), and (4) Do Not Travel (red). An interactive digital map helps make sense of the information.[1]

Not surprisingly, countries such as Afghanistan, Iran, Iraq, and Syria fall within the highest category because of the likelihood of life-threatening risks and the US government's limited ability to provide help.

CBS Travel correspondent Peter Greenberg criticizes the new program because it's not well defined. "Once you get beyond the first category, I still don't know what that means. Does it mean 'don't trip'? And 'Exercise Increased Caution,' does that mean 'don't trip and fall'?

"Most people, once it gets beyond the second category, decide 'I'm not going,'" he told *CBS This Morning* on January 16, 2018. "My own personal metric is that I will not go anywhere where I don't know who's in control but putting Mazatlán in the same department as Syria and Yemen is not really helping people."

The warnings are split even further by country according to crime, terrorism, civil unrest, health, natural disaster, and time-limited event, which Greenberg thinks is a good idea.[2]

Enter your destination country and the threat level will be displayed along with alerts and visa requirements. Larger countries that have sensitive areas, such as Mexico, where some states report violent crime from gangs, could have multiple rankings depending on the region.

Through its Smart Traveler Enrollment Program (STEP),[3] you provide details of your trip and are then placed on an email list to receive travel advisories and alerts as soon as they are issued.

Staff columnist Stephanie Rosenbloom writes in the *New York Times*, "The smartest way to use the rankings to help decide if a trip is right for you is to read the explicit risks on the country page, which on the overhauled website are more clearly explained."[4]

While you're at it, carry a copy of your passport, leave a copy with a trusted loved one at home, and research the contact information for the nearest US embassy to your destination.

Depending on the destination, 22 to 64 percent of travelers report some illness—generally they're mild and self-limited, such as diarrhea, respiratory infections, and skin disorders. But some travelers return to their own countries with preventable life-threatening infections, according to the *New England Journal of Medicine.*[5] Consult with a medical professional prior to departure and ensure that your inoculations are current.

Before my first trip to Nepal I became a human pincushion after I decided to get trued up after years of lapsed vaccinations. Your needs may be different, for sure. For me, it took doses of Tdap, typhoid, hepatitis A and B, meningococcal meningitis, poliovirus, and a good old flu shot before I was ready to face the world.

Travel health precautions are available from the Centers for Disease Control (CDC)[6] and World Health Organization (WHO).[7] Additional information on vaccines in the form of Vaccine Information Statements (VIS) is available for download.[8]

My go-to resource whenever I travel to a country where health and sanitation is questionable is Passport Health, the referral source for physicians, Fortune 500 companies, tour operators, the US State Department, and local health organizations. According to its website,[9] Passport Health is the largest provider of travel medicine and immunization services in North America and sets the immunization industry standard. There are over 270-plus clinic locations with rigorously trained medical staff. After my visit in fall 2017, I received a thirty-two-page spiral-bound Travel Health Itinerary tailored specifically to Nepal, my destination country.

Also look into the International Association for Medical Assistance to Travellers (IAMAT), a nonprofit organization established in 1960 that will help you plan your trip and connect you with reputable English-speaking doctors in case of accident or illness. There is no fee to join.[10]

Travel insurance will compensate you for the dozens of problems that might arise during international travel (just don't think about it too hard or you may never go). Risks covered by insurance could range from the minute—a delayed flight that leads to the expense of an extra night in a hotel—to a problem far more serious. Travel insurance provides great peace of mind, especially in the case of accident and sickness medical expenses, accidental death and dismemberment, flight accident insurance, lost baggage, baggage delays, cancellations, roadside assistance, and particularly emergency evacuation.

I've had success with AIG Travel Guard, filing a claim only once when an Antarctic passage was delayed one year because the research vessel I was booked aboard ran aground and required repairs. They reimbursed me when I had to cancel my airfare. Students on Ice, the polar education expedition company that accepted me on as a volunteer chaperone, applied my payment to the following year.[11]

Travel Guard plans work anywhere in the world and also covers translation services, prescription replacement assistance, roadside assistance, and cancellation, interruption, or delay coverage.

Says Scott Hamilton, president of the nonprofit Dooley Intermed International, "Trying to arrange medical evacuation, cross-border flights, visas and permits, and making hospital arrangements without professional assistance is close to impossible. Otherwise, your options for local medical care will be severely limited, as in the possibility of fly swatters in the operating room. A medical evacuation to another country with quality medical care can easily cost $100,000 or more.

"The life you save by purchasing travel insurance in advance may well be your own. This is a very prudent expense and should be considered a requirement," Hamilton believes.

It was Hamilton, by the way, who first told me about the so-called Jesus nut, also known as the Jesus pin. There we were, about to board a helicopter in Nepal, and he leans over and explains this slang term for the retaining nut that holds the main rotor to the helicopter's mast; the phrase is also used to refer to any component that represents a single point of failure with catastrophic consequences.

If the Jesus nut were to fail in flight, the helicopter would detach from the rotors and the only thing left for the crew to do would be to "pray to Jesus."

Thanks, Scott, for planting this gruesome thought in my impressionable head.

Volunteer missions to Third World countries require comprehensive support, particularly in roadless areas, and even more care needs to be placed upon food preparation. After all, a distressed ophthalmologist who has to run to a squat hole toilet every hour instead of performing cataract surgery with assembly-line precision isn't performing at maximum efficiency.

For thirty years Nepal's Himalayan Holidays, based in Kathmandu, has provided on-the-ground support to numerous medical missions, expeditions, voluntourists, and everyday trekkers. During their trips, leafy greens are soaked in potassium permanganate disinfectant to destroy the wiggly organisms that can find their way into the food supply, and water is either purified with iodine tablets, thoroughly boiled, or derived from bottled sources.[12]

"These are important safety precautions," Himalayan Holidays founder Bibhu Thakur told me during my 2017 trip.

"Visitors who come here are not used to the local bacteria. Restaurants especially know that if visitors get sick eating there, someone will blow the whistle on TripAdvisor and the place will go down the drain."

Whether traveling with a tour operator or alone, eat foods that are fully cooked and served hot. Stay away from the salads and tuna fish sandwiches and that teahouse cheese plate dotted with house flies that were previously dancing the Alley Cat on some yak dung.

Drink beverages that have been bottled and sealed, and forget the ice. While you're at it, squeeze the bottle first to make sure it hasn't been resealed. (Remember the scene from the 2009 Academy Awards Best Picture *Slumdog Millionaire*, where a water bottle is refilled and the cap was superglued for resale?) Carbonated beverages are much safer than noncarbonated—flat water drinks can be diluted with local tap water.

Fruits and vegetables are always questionable, unless you wash and peel them personally.

Don't let your guard down in the bathroom. That means rinse toothbrushes only in bottled water, and no singing in the shower lest tap water gets into your mouth. Practice for a week before you leave home. It is incredibly easy to slip up and find yourself using tap water out of force of habit.

Do not even THINK of petting the dogs and cats, and certainly never approach the monkeys. They all have sharp teeth—it's not a fair fight. Sadly, in October 2017, a ten-year-old French boy died from rabies after he was bitten by a stray puppy while on holiday in Sri Lanka. The unnamed boy, from Rhône in eastern France, became infected with the virus the previous August after the dog bit him on a beach in Dikwella in the south of the country.[13]

Keep your hands in your pockets. The majority of bites are induced in some way by the visitor. These are not the friendly Labrador retrievers you grew up with. If bitten, wash the wound vigorously and seek professional care and the postexposure rabies vaccine. By the time you discover you have rabies it is generally too late for a cure.

Hand sanitizer is your best friend. Use it frequently and avoid putting your hands anywhere near your eyes or mouth. Let that hangnail wait for a proper pair of nail clippers.

Take a kit of medications with you in your carry-on. My bag contains a small first aid kit, OTC pain relievers, sunscreen, tweezers, ear plugs, an eye mask, and lip balm. Check with your physician for a suggested antibiotic to carry along . . . just in case.

Pack some energy bars for sustenance if you arrive late, the restaurants are closed, and Oreos are your only choice in the hotel vending machine. I especially like Bobo's Oat Bars,[14] which, according to its website, is an artisan, hand-baked alternative to the overcluttered snack bar aisle riddled with overengineered bars made with unrecognizable ingredients. It's best to take a hard pass on those snacks.

Once at my hotel, I check the locks on hotel room doors and windows before unpacking. If I can't lock everything properly, I ask for another room. In

Boston of all places, my hotel room overlooked a rooftop setback and the window didn't lock. I was out of there fast. I use a small motion detector for the doorknob called the Lewis N. Clark Travel Door Alarm. It costs just $12 from Target and provides great peace of mind. If someone is trying to get in, I want to know about it. By the same token, I leave the TV on when I go out to dinner (assuming there is a TV). Make the room appear occupied.

Now for something fairly cringy: check for bedbugs. You can thank me later. The Environmental Protection Agency (EPA) advises that bedbugs can be found around the bed; they can be found near the piping, seams, and tags of the mattress and box spring; and in cracks on the bed frame and headboard. They can also be hiding in the seams of chairs and couches, between cushions, and in the folds of curtains. These are nasty buggers.

Look for rusty or reddish stains on bed sheets or mattresses caused by bed bugs being crushed; dark spots about the size of a period pencil point; eggs and eggshells, which are tiny (about one millimeter or about the size of a period on this page); pale yellow skins that nymphs shed as they grow larger; and live bed bugs themselves.[15]

Speaking of things you can barely see, when Philadelphian Bob Dever retired as a public affairs executive for Land O'Lakes, Inc., he performed humanitarian service for the United States Agency for International Development (USAID) in northern Zambia. From 2001 through 2014, he traveled to Africa eleven times volunteering in the microfinancing industry, founded a women's agricultural cooperative, and taught accounting, among other projects. During one trip he remembers staying in a two-star hotel. Perfectly fine, it was home to a number of people who worked for the United Nations in the country.

After about a week, he sent his clothes to the hotel laundry and was later amused to find all his clothing was pressed and ironed, including his briefs.

"My shorts do not usually get ironed and I thought having them pressed was a bit humorous," he would later recall.

"That night at dinner I was telling some of the guys from the UN my ironed shorts story. They all immediately started to laugh. They said, 'Bob, do you know why your shorts are ironed?'

"Obviously I did not. What they told me was that there is a parasite in the local water and that the only thing that kills it is heat."

Word to the wise voluntourist: keep your guard up.

Make a mental note of what to grab in case of earthquake or fire. It happened to me in southern California. Fire alarm goes off. I grab my laptop, pants, shoes, and wallet; other guests in the lobby are shivering barefoot in their tighty-whities. False alarm, but still.

Before you leave, set up an international calling plan for your smartphone, or buy a local SIM card so that if you have to use your phone in an emergency, the call doesn't cost dozens of dollars.

Carry an inventory of the contents of your checked luggage. That way, it will be easier to file a claim afterward.

Lock your bags with an approved TSA-recognized lock, able to be opened by security officers using universal master keys. In this way, your luggage locks may not have to be cut. These locks are available at most airports and many travel stores nationwide. Look for packaging that indicates whether they can be opened by TSA. This keeps honest people honest and slows down the bad guys.

Avoid looking too prosperous; leave the real Rolex home and buy a $20 Timex instead. Keep money in three different places on your body and create a throw-down wallet—something with a few dollars that looks like you're handing over your real wallet in case of trouble. If you're traveling to a really sketchy destination where robberies and bribes are the local way of life, it can be worthwhile to bring along a fake Rolex or some expensive-looking bauble to help baksheesh (bribe) your way out of a predicament.

Be situationally aware. Stay alert and forego the use of personal headphones when you're walking about. Avoid wearing flashy jewelry and designer clothes. Kathmandu, the capital of Nepal, is a city with a myriad of hazards. There are wild dogs, five lanes of traffic on two-lane streets, a rat's nest of wires hanging from utility poles, open conduits in the sidewalk, and strange locals approaching you to strike up chatty conversations or seeking money for "baby milk" or similar. It pays to know what's going on around you.

That's something the voluntourists in the next chapter know all too well.

· *VI* ·

Stories of Purposeful Travel

$\mathscr{F}$or years I've been hearing stories of volunteer trips from friends, relatives, and business acquaintances. In fact, a recent query to my Facebook friends revealed a dozen more—all people who love to travel and have found meaning in helping others, whether through church missions, as we'll see below, or starting one's own nonprofit. While the projects are diverse and won't by themselves cure world hunger or end poverty, there's a consistent theme at play—the desire of each voluntourist to make a positive impact during their all-too-brief stay on Earth.

The collective impact of volunteers serving in any given location over the course of many years can be substantial, and prospective voluntourists can draw inspiration from these personal stories of purposeful travel.

IN THE NAME OF GOD

There are many roads leading to rewarding volunteer travel experiences. There are self-funded trips with tour operators; medical expeditions focused on a particular need such as dental, ophthalmic, or spinal issues; projects at work or school; and opportunities with your place of worship—an entry into voluntourism pursued by New Canaan, Connecticut's Marianna Kilbride, the mother of three adult daughters and director of missions and outreach at the 280-year-old Congregational Church of New Canaan.

Kilbride is staff liaison to the church's Missions and Social Action Committee, which manages 25 percent of the organization's annual budget set aside for outreach. Each year since 2003, a group of adults from the congregation have embarked on rehabilitation programs and building projects to a variety of domestic and international locations, including Belize, Baltimore, Exuma, Florida, New Orleans, and Nicaragua. The missions, typically held over seven to ten days in the spring, include various construction or renovation projects. Numerous US churches, synagogues, and mosques have outreach programs. The Congregational Church does it particularly well.

In response to the events of 9/11, the Congregational Church's Maasai Connection was created to be a force for good in an at-risk community in Kenya. The congregation has supported the Maasai through severe drought, food shortages, and political violence. Projects have included a water pipeline, water cisterns, drought-resistant goats, solar panels, a greenhouse, and laying hens, as well as the construction of dormitories—all vital improvements to the Maasai community. Yearly, thirty congregants support Maasai education scholarships for elementary and high school students. Participants on the trip pay their own way and avoid evangelizing.

"We're not there to preach, we're there to partner with local ministries and nonprofits," says Kilbride, who traveled to Nairobi, Kenya, shortly after a terrorist struck the upscale Westgate shopping mall in September 2013, resulting in at least sixty-seven deaths.[1]

"Yes, I was concerned. My trip sign-ups began the very next day after the attack. As a trip leader heading to a country with some degree of unrest, we had to decide whether it was reasonably safe or not. In fact, the trip was several months later, during which time there were other disturbances which I monitored closely.

"My point of view, hardened by living just forty-five miles from the worst terrorist attack in US history, is that anywhere you travel in today's world there is some degree of risk. But if you look at the odds, they are still very much in your favor. Bad things can happen anywhere at any time."

Kilbride continues, "Voluntourists need to be flexible and open to adventure. I tell those in our group to do their homework to understand local customs and etiquette. You might be in places with complicated histories with the United States. Understand and anticipate the country's mindset when you visit."

Kilbride and her group also traveled to León, Nicaragua's second largest city, with JustHope (justhope.org), a not-for-profit organization based in Tulsa, Oklahoma, that created a network of long-term partnerships between North American and Nicaraguan communities. During a nine-day visit, the Congregational Church delegation rehabilitated a clinic in the nearby farming community of Chacraseca that was in disrepair.

This time, they had an opportunity to be true voluntourists—working hard as well as taking time off to play tourist: visiting a pottery shop, photographing the Masaya volcano, and attending a Spanish-language service at the Cathedral of León.

Lest you think voluntourists always need a valid passport, the Congregational Church also travels to support domestic projects in the United States in places with substandard housing. For instance, in Mobile, Alabama, they work with Raise the Roof,[2] a home-repair ministry partnership of Dauphin Way United Methodist Church and St. Paul's Episcopal Church, and have conducted similar projects in Charlotte, North Carolina, and San Antonio, Texas, focusing on substandard homes.

"We cannot change the entire world, but we have changed this small part of it for the better," Kilbride believes.

Christian teachings take a much larger role during volunteer missions organized by the 1,300-member Cherry Creek Presbyterian Church (CCPC),[3] based in the Denver suburb of Englewood, Colorado. It's one of six hundred churches affiliated with the Evangelical Presbyterian Church and its world missions program that sends missionaries to remote communities.

Every other year a group of twelve to fifteen women from the Denver area travel to the Jewels of God Church in Pokuase, a suburb of Accra, Ghana, to teach leadership skills to approximately 150 local women who live in bush communities and speak Twi, which is spoken in southern and central Ghana by about six to nine million Ashanti people as a first and second language.

Al Johnson, CCPC's World Outreach director, has been at the church for the past fourteen years and supervises its Women's Mission Trip; there are also programs for youth volunteers to serve at a camp for physically challenged youth in Missouri and an Arizona Indian reservation.

"Our volunteers pay their own way—approximately $3,500 including airfare, lodging, meals, and a donation—to provide Ghanian women with leadership and life skills. During a ten-day visit to an annual teaching conference hosted by the Jewels of God Church, they advise about everyday issues, such as getting along with their husbands, menstrual hygiene management, and dealing with the symptoms of menopause.

"Our group offers hearing, blood pressure, and eye tests. Previously, volunteers raised money to help one local woman receive an operation to cure a case of goiter, which is unfortunately quite prevalent there," Johnson reports.

The Cherry Creek group has also assisted in funding the construction of a dormitory, established a seamstress school and a cooking school, and purchased kitchen equipment.

Through it all, Christian teaching remains the driving force behind the effort.

"The focus of the trip is on fostering their religious growth. About 99 percent of the Ghanians we reach are already practicing Christians, so the trip also includes gospel-centered lessons, and worship services translated from English to Twi. Bibles are distributed to the women and children—for many, these become their very first personal copies."

The CCPC volunteers come back profoundly changed, according to Johnson, who says the trip is so meaningful for his parishioners that many still regularly pray for the Ghanaians they met during their time in Africa.

Consider how your own place of worship can open doors to a lifetime of selfless volunteer work.

START YOUR OWN NONPROFIT

Sometimes you never know where a road can lead. That's especially true of Sylvia Allen, founder of Allen Consulting,[4] a successful public relations agency in Holmdel, New Jersey. Among her many projects over forty years is a fundraising effort to build a yellow brick path around a turn-of-the-century opera house in Aitkin, Minnesota, the first performance space where a young Judy Garland, known then as Baby Gumm, got her start on stage in 1925 long before her starring role in *The Wizard of Oz*.

Allen travels any path, any road that will lead to some new adventure. In fact, for business she has traveled the world providing media relations and corporate sponsorship advice in places as diverse as Beijing, Holland, Ireland, Japan, Kuala Lumpur, Okinawa, and Singapore, and as well as throughout the United States.

While teaching a class at New York University in January 2003, one of her students working for an African nonprofit invited her to the continent to visit. Allen, struck with wanderlust, didn't need much encouragement. By that May she was on a plane to Uganda, and soon thereafter, she became the adopted grandmother to hundreds of children at the Mbiriizi Advanced Primary and Day Care School near Masaka, located in the Central Region of Uganda, west of Lake Victoria.

Upon her return, she considered the options for helping her adopted grandchildren: donate to a local charity and perhaps watch as up to 15 percent of every dollar goes toward administrative costs, or start her own nonprofit, which is what she decided to do, asking her two adult children to serve as trustees. Allen incorporated first as a state charity and then as an IRS 501(c) organization to initially support 439 children in four buildings, of which

25 percent were orphans. Eventually she and Reverend Geofrey Kawuma, founder and head of the Mbiriizi Primary School, started a scholarship to pay tuition for any orphan student who wanted to enroll in secondary school and college or technical school.

Today, Sylvia's Children supports 1,024 primary schoolchildren in twenty-six buildings, on an eight thousand chicken farm, with forty pigs, seven acres of land planted in corn and tomatoes, five hundred thousand coffee tree seedlings, one hundred thousand mango trees, and a six-thousand-square-foot medical clinic that generates revenue for the school.[5]

"I run the organization only with volunteers, and 100 percent of the money goes to the school. So far, 150 orphans have moved on to secondary school, and 50 are in college or technical school, with 18 already having graduated," she says.

"We have students who are teachers, nurses, and information technologists. Our students are well educated, and they will make a worthwhile contribution to their country. I wanted to make it possible for them to have a better life than they would have experienced as an orphan. Plus, our students performed so well in 2017 that we are now one of the top one hundred schools in Uganda."

Her organization is a "Direct Participation" Charity—donors choose their level of involvement. Some decide to just send money, which is fine. The more the merrier. Others participate in voluntourism trips to Uganda led by Allen two times a year. Their cost is approximately $3,750. This covers airfare from New Jersey, accommodations in the Golf Lane Hotel in Masaka, food, car and driver, and a three-day excursion to the Mweya Safari Lodge in Queen Elizabeth National Park. Travelers coming from other parts of the country pay for airfare and overnight accommodations prior to leaving on the trip.

Volunteers are involved in teaching in the classrooms, playing with the children, helping in the kitchen, helping in the clinic, serving meals to the children, and, for the November trip, organizing a Christmas party for both primary and secondary school students.

Since 2003, the money raised by Sylvia's Children has helped construct a working well (in many developing countries, access to clean water is a critical issue), a library stocked with books, and the expansion of classrooms, new desks, and the purchase of land near the school, among other improvements.

"The joy of this trip is meeting these children who have so little and yet are so willing to give of their love and their hearts," she believes.

Sylvia Allen has made a significant difference in the children's lives, providing them with an education to have a better life than their parents.

THE KIDS ARE ALL RIGHT

The following extraordinary story of a preteen young girl from California demonstrates that passion to help others is more important than chronological age or one's financial wherewithal.

At the age of twelve, after returning from a year-long around-the-world vacation to twenty-seven countries with her parents, Claire Thomsen, from Malibu, California, already knew what she wanted to do with her life. The Thomsens visited a different city every week, living out of suitcases and backpacks. One stop of the family's odyssey was the Kingdom of Bhutan, a landlocked country in South Asia located in the Eastern Himalayas. Claire's short visit subsequently convinced her to dedicate her teen years to the children she met in Bhutan, a rugged, mountainous country where Gross National Happiness is considered more important than Gross Domestic Product. It's a tiny and remote nation with a stunning landscape and deep Buddhist spirituality.

Now a twenty-one-year-old junior at Chapman University in Orange, California, enrolled in the school's Department of Peace Studies, she tells how she was determined to raise $50,000 to build a library in a rural Bhutanese village near the Indian border.

"First of all, my friends couldn't understand why I'd spend twelve months traveling with my parents instead of lying on the beach. They thought it was lame. But the experience really changed me. I couldn't stop thinking about the children I met there and wanted to work to improve their education, especially literacy for girls," Thomsen says.

Upon her return, Thomsen learned about READ Global,[6] the San Francisco–based nonprofit that believes improved access to educational resources creates lasting social change in developing communities. For $50,000, Thomsen was told, she could fund the construction of the Chuzagang Library and Community Center in southern Bhutan.

Thus began a three-year on again/off again fundraising effort.

"I didn't know what $50,000 looked like, so had no idea how hard the fundraising would be," she tells me.

It was quite a disconnect for the teen who suddenly found herself reading books about tax deductions. She pitched to her parents' friends during dinner parties, attended Bhutanese festivals in nearby Los Angeles, and contacted anyone giving a TED Talk that even remotely mentioned the country.

After an initial letter-writing campaign sent to her parent's Christmas list, one personalized with stickers and stamps, she raised $5,000, but the effort bogged down for years until she was able to hold a fundraising party in the home of a family friend, the film actress Linda Hamilton of *Terminator* fame, whose son had been dating Thomsen's older sister for nine years. Over seventy-five guests attended, donating $10,000 in a single evening.

The event reinvigorated the campaign, and by 2013, at the age of fifteen, she had raised $45,000, enough for READ Global to begin construction of the library.

The next year, after scraping together the full $50,000, she and a group of fourteen, including her immediate family, traveled to the village for the first time in one of those sketchy buses with curtained windows and luggage racks on top—an arduous ten-hour bus ride over sheer cliffs, across rivers, and numerous hairpin turns, a bumpy, dusty journey in which a few passengers became violently carsick. Yet the ordeal faded from memory once the group arrived to a grand-opening celebration complete with an archery demonstration, dancing, and prayers, including one in which a Buddhist priest personally blessed Thomsen.

"I was so happy, I was crying my eyes out," she recalls.

"It was magical. The next two hours were the most beautiful of my life," she tells a TEDxMALIBU talk.[7]

Today the five-room READ Center has a three-thousand-book library, four computers, a TV room, women's counseling section, children's playroom, and training hall. And there above the entranceway is a plaque commemorating Thomsen's volunteer efforts.

The experience encouraged her to self-publish a travel photo essay in 2014 called *Girl Disrupted: How One Kid's Travels around the World Made It a Little Better* (2014). In it she explains how the key to happiness, something the Bhutanese know much about, is helping others and truly making a difference.

"Visiting Bhutan and raising funds for a library and community center completely changed my life and gave me a purpose and direction of what I wanted to do."

These days her focus is on graduating from college, but she is optimistic about what life will bring in the future, a life in which she expects the country of Bhutan will play a large role.

Another teen profoundly impacted by her volunteer time abroad is Sarah Cotton, from Edwards, Colorado, a young voluntourist and exceptional role model for teens contemplating spending their school vacations in the service of others. Now a nineteen-year-old college sophomore studying Political Science and Public Health at the University of Massachusetts, Amherst, she volunteered in Tanzania at age fifteen; Cambodia at sixteen; Morocco at age seventeen; Nepal, Cambodia, and Tanzania at the age of eighteen; and when we caught up with her in spring 2018 after she turned nineteen, she had recently returned from Nicaragua after helping special needs children.

Her parents were nervous at first sending her off to Africa at such an early age, but they were supportive of her passion to volunteer abroad. Cotton says they were accompanied by adult chaperones at all times and never strayed alone, which put her parents somewhat at ease.

"I've always felt 100 percent safe while abroad," she says, explaining that for all her volunteer work she traveled with Children's Global Alliance (CGA), a nonprofit created in 2010 to fill the void of large-scale volunteer experiences for students ages twelve to seventeen. CGA offers service-learning travel opportunities and a leadership development program for students from the United States to Cambodia, Nicaragua, Tanzania, Nepal, and Morocco.[8]

While abroad, students work, teach, and support children and families who are living in poverty. Students also experience the culture, make friendships that last a lifetime, and learn more about themselves and their capabilities than they ever have before, says CGA. The group requires its young volunteers to submit a fundraising plan and not to depend upon their parents to pay for it all. In Cotton's case, she earned money as a nanny for a local family, held dances and dinners, and worked at day camps to cover her travel expenses.

She spent her summers abroad mostly teaching English as a Second Language (ESL) but served in various other volunteer capacities as well: repairing buildings, picking up trash, cleaning, and gardening at an orphanage in Phnom Penh, Cambodia. In Rivas, Nicaragua, she assisted teachers in their classrooms and conducted home visits with the school's physical therapist; and in Tanzania she also assisted teachers, prepared lesson plans, and delivered supplies.

She taught an intensive, two-week ESL class at a middle school in Rabat, the capital city of Morocco, preparing lesson plans and English-language games and taught real-world phrases in conversational English—how to order food and conduct English-language tours of the city. That sort of thing. English grammar not so much.

"It's crazy to see how much English they picked up in two weeks and how passionate they were to learn it," she tells me. "They know that if they can speak English, they're almost guaranteed a job in the country's tourism industry."

It wasn't all work. Her Nicaragua service concluded with a trip to the beach on the Pacific Coast; in Nepal she and her fellow volunteers visited famous temples known as the birthplace of Buddha; in Morocco her group camped in the Sahara and rode camels; and following volunteer service in Tanzania, she participated in a one-day photo safari.

CGA requires its young volunteers to document their trips, something Cotton appreciates now that she can look back at her writing and learn more about her younger self.

"It's been a cool experience to see online how many people from across the world have read my blogs."

Reporting about her volunteer experiences, she believes, was an asset when the time came to apply for college. Her college essay explains how her Morocco trip and exposure to the Muslim culture offered her a broader view of the world, especially the similarities that exist between people of diverse backgrounds.

She writes in a summer 2016 blog about teaching ESL in Morocco: "The reward I get seeing their progress is worth each bead of sweat, the late nights and every ounce of effort. Education is the foundation to opportunity and to help develop this core [skill] in my students is an honor."[9]

In a comment that echoes what many young volunteers have told me, Cotton believes volunteering will always be part of her life as she graduates and goes out into the world. Of particular interest is possible future work in the Middle East. To that end, she plans to study Arabic at UMass. Clearly, this is one millennial going places.

For those contemplating a volunteer vacation, it's wise to consider the downsides of donating time and effort to one or more causes. Voluntourism is a field that has its share of detractors, which reminds me of the saying, "No good deed goes unpunished."

· VII ·

The Dark Side of Voluntourism

Times are vastly different, certainly from my days as a Boy Scout in the 1960s when we volunteered to restore trails or conduct roadside cleanups. Back then, our troop's activities would be covered in the local newspaper, or in the troop's own printed newsletter sent by snail mail to our parents.

Today we live at a time when, for some, the volunteer activity is all about producing a suitable selfie to share on social media.

Some volunteers try to create online personas that have no basis in reality. These activities, some more abhorrent than others, are readily mocked online and in mainstream media.

Maya Wesby writes in *Newsweek*, "The gaps in culture, background, and privilege are apparent on social media, where some participants post preening 'selfies' with indigenous children and use hashtags like #InstagrammingAfrica to share a filtered version of their glamorous lives. It all seems to devalue the original purpose of volunteering abroad, and makes one wonder if these participants' motives were charitable at all."[1]

Wesby adds, "Working in an underdeveloped region should result in meaningful change and an expansion of one's worldview, not a new profile picture."

Two anonymous twentysomethings brilliantly savage volunteers who make service trips to developing countries—and make it all about themselves. Their Barbie Savior site on Instagram had 155,000 followers in June 2018, the last time we looked. There's the popular children's doll, portraying a twenty-year-old service volunteer in Africa, with a selfie stick in an impoverished village, feeding a Coke to an African baby, and promoting a satirical line of Harness the Tears brand water.[2]

Dressed in a miniskirt, Barbie Savior is shown in front of a school blackboard. The Instagram post reads, "Who needs a formal education to teach in Africa. Not me! All I need is some chalk and a dose of optimism. It's so sad they don't have enough trained teachers here. I'm not trained either, but I'm from the West, so it all works out."

Barbie Savior lampoons the "white savior complex," a term used to describe white Westerners who travel abroad to swoop in and "save" impoverished people of color in developing countries, writes Savonne Anderson on Mashable.com.[3]

"Volunteers need to make sure their actions help communities in tangible, responsible ways—and aren't just driven by a desire to feel good about themselves," Anderson says.

"It can be easy to fall into this trap while helping those who are less fortunate in developing nations. For Westerners who have the privilege of clean water, access to education and modern utilities, exposure to such a different way of life can be panic-inducing—you can feel like you're an entire community's only hope."

One particularly amusing YouTube parody shows "Lilly Taylor" throwing food at African blacks, teaching them football, feeding baby goats, and participating in a mock game show, "Who Wants to Be a Volunteer?" To Save Africa she needs to answer the Grand Prize question: How many countries are there on the continent?

A. One B. Two C. Five or D. 54. (The answer is D.)

She gets it wrong, but nonetheless receives a trip to Save Africa and is carried away in a makeshift palanquin by four bare-chested men. The video, viewed 1.2 million times by June 2018, was sponsored by the Norwegian Students' and Academics' International Assistance Fund (SAIH) to emphasize that stereotypes harm dignity.[4]

Speaking of social media, SAIH has created a number of satirical videos including "Radi-Aid: Africa for Norway," a mock campaign for Africans to help Norwegians whose poor, suffering children get their tongues stuck to frozen metal. SAIH also created the Radi-Aid Awards celebrating the best—and the worst—of development fundraising videos.

Their goal is to challenge the perceptions around issues of poverty and development, to change the way fundraising campaigns communicate, and to break down dominating stereotypical representations. Most amusing is a short cartoon titled, "How to Get More Likes on Social Media?" Step one: Travel to Africa, and always remember to use hashtags. It's a brutally honest look at the temptation of some voluntourists to go overboard in a ceaseless campaign for more and more likes.[5]

An article in *The Onion* mocks voluntourism, brutally joking that a six-day visit to a rural African village can "completely change a woman's

Facebook profile picture." The parody quotes twenty-two-year-old "Angela Fisher" who says: "I don't think my profile photo will ever be the same, not after the experience of taking such incredible pictures with my arms around those small African children's shoulders."[6]

It reveals that Fisher "has been encouraging every one of her friends to visit Africa, promising that it would change their Facebook profile photos as well."[7]

"Much ink has been spilled about the white-savior industrial complex. It boils down to narcissistic Westerners asserting their perceived superiority by 'rescuing' a developing nation, and it is highly criticized by many," according to Michele L. Staton writing in Almost.TheDoctorsChannel.com.[8]

Certainly, not all volunteer vacation programs are equal. But many are designed for the travelers, not the local residents—programs that could cause more harm than good. Short-term solutions for complex problems.

What's more, building projects that are staffed by inexperienced volunteers may be taking jobs away from local workers, who can be hired cheaply and who rely upon those wages to survive. Or worse, create busywork for local laborers.

Consider Philippa (Pippa) Biddle, a New York–based writer, who volunteered in Tanzania and created an Internet shitstorm in 2014 with her blog post, "The Problem with Little White Girls (and Boys): Why I Stopped Being a Voluntourist," written after a series of voluntourism experiences over six years.[9] It went viral with over fifteen million hits, and instantly launched her as the poster child against privileged young white women volunteering overseas, according to a 2015 CBC documentary called *Volunteers Unleashed*, in which she appears.[10]

Biddle recounts how she was called upon to perform construction work in Tanzania.

"Our mission while at the orphanage was to build a library. Turns out that we, a group of highly educated private boarding school students, were so bad at the most basic construction work that each night the men had to take down the structurally unsound bricks we had laid and rebuild the structure so that, when we woke up in the morning, we would be unaware of our failure. It is likely that this was a daily ritual. Us mixing cement and laying bricks for 6+ hours, them undoing our work after the sunset, re-laying the bricks, and then acting as if nothing had happened so that the cycle could continue."

Biddle adds, "Basically, we failed at the sole purpose of our being there. It would have been more cost-effective, stimulative of the local economy, and efficient for the orphanage to take our money and hire locals to do the work, but there we were trying to build straight walls without a level."

Obviously, not all volunteer experiences are the same. That was not the experience of Jennifer Kimball Gasperini's family. Gasperini is a Minneapolis flight attendant for Sun Country Airlines who traveled to Jinotega in north-central Nicaragua to build a home for an impoverished family. The Gasperinis raised $1,200 one spring break vacation, enough to fund construction of a basic concrete home through AVODEC (Association of Volunteers for Community Development), a small, grassroots nonprofit that helps rural Nicaraguan communities where people are living in dirt-floor shacks, where there is a lack of sanitation, pure water, and medical care; and where educational opportunities are limited.[11]

Gasperini and her husband, Jim, and their two sons and a daughter, ages seven to fourteen, spent five days building the home they had funded. When I asked whether her family of five, without any construction experience, were perhaps pulling above their weight, Gasperini reports the menial labor they performed was entirely unskilled.

"It's not like we were doing electrical or plumbing work. This was hard, manual labor—we mixed concrete, transported it by shovels, cut blocks with serrated knives, and filled cinder blocks with small stones to make them stronger.

"It was pretty basic work. We couldn't screw anything up.

"At no time did we think we were displacing local workers. In fact, the locals seemed thrilled about receiving our support."

The Gasperini's were self-sufficient, purchasing their own food from local businesses, sharing that food with the family whose house they were helping to build, and donating a solar oven and clothing.

"My children came back with a greater understanding of the need for volunteer service and reported about the experience to their classmates, explaining the need for supporting one of the most impoverished communities in the second poorest country in the Western Hemisphere. Years later, our daughter worked as a WWOOF'er (Worldwide Opportunities on Organic Farms, also known as Willing Workers on Organic Farms) in Chile after her semester abroad."[12]

Constructing shelter in impoverished regions of the world is certainly a noble cause but is hardly enough. In her *Newsweek* story, Maya Wesby calls misguided efforts to build homes in a post-earthquake-shattered Haiti.

"While the foreign volunteers were well-intentioned, they misplaced their focus; it was necessary to build stable homes, but the real problem was crippling, multigenerational poverty.

"Lacking skills and employment to improve their condition, Haitian families continued to beg in the streets in the absence of tourists. The volunteers came and left, but nothing had really changed."[13]

Oxfam International, the nonprofit organization that addresses the root causes of poverty in over ninety countries, wasn't much help. In early 2018, Haiti suspended Oxfam GB operations as it launched an investigation of claims of sexual misconduct by charity staff after the 2010 earthquake.[14]

Thousands canceled their donations after it was revealed that aid workers hired prostitutes.

Children in orphanages or schools may form emotional bonds with people who come to volunteer, only to suffer abandonment issues when volunteers move in and out on conveyor belts, departing with empty promises to someday return. Nonprofit organizations that have formed long-term partnerships with local nongovernmental organizations are the ones most beneficial for the local communities.

What's worse, sex offenders disguise themselves as volunteers in orphanages and child care centers and arrange temporary housing in distant communities where they commit their crimes. According to the 2016 Global Study on the Sexual Exploitation of Children in Travel and Tourism, the sexual exploitation of children by travelers and tourists has expanded across the globe, outpacing every attempt to respond; more children are being victimized than ever before, and no country is immune.[15]

They find children via the Internet and "disguise themselves as volunteers in orphanages and child care centers and arrange temporary housing in distant communities where they commit their crimes," Dorothy Rozga, the executive director of ECPAT International, tells the *New York Times*.[16]

According to the *Times*, Nepal is one of Asia's poorest countries, and thousands of nongovernmental organizations (NGO) operate with limited government oversight.

The absence of strict regulations means aid groups can be used as cover for human traffickers and predatory behavior by humanitarian workers, said Pushkar Karki, the head of the country's Chief Investigation Bureau.[17]

Bibhuti Thakur has heard this all before. The founder of Himalayan Holidays based in Kathmandu, he started Mission Himalaya[18] in 2008 to assist Nepal's rural women, children, the elderly, and the sick. Shortly thereafter, he was part of the team that founded an orphanage called the Eco Home for Orphaned Children, supported by Dooley Intermed International, the nonprofit based in Forest Hills, New York. It's one of 1,500 orphanages located in the Kathmandu valley, and one of the few ethically run.

Located in a verdant valley about twenty-two miles from the capital city, the Eco Home's seven caretakers are responsible for the welfare of twenty-eight children, some orphaned by the 2015 earthquakes and some from abusive homes, who are enrolled through their completion of a secondary school education.

What most concerns Thakur are unscrupulous so-called orphanages in the country that mine rural villages for children and pay parents to whisk their sons and daughters away to what's promised as a better life.

"Often there are no orphans in these homes. The children serve as bait to lure donors, to pull on their heart strings," Thakur tells me in the garden of a Kathmandu restaurant during a December 2017 visit.

"Kidnapped is more like it," he continues. "These shady operators know donors will pull out more dollars for kids who are supposedly orphaned rather than merely underprivileged or from abusive homes.

"The children are provided minimum assistance—their clothes are dirty, the food is barely enough to get by, to make them seem more desperate."

Thakur advises, "Before you board that airplane and travel halfway around the world to volunteer someplace, know what you're getting into.

"Want to volunteer to help kids in Nepal? Make sure the facility and the children are registered with the local government. The Eco Home is inspected every three months and our caretakers live in a separate building," Thakur continues.

"The stories I hear about pedophiles posing as tourists and luring street children into their hotel rooms is simply disgusting."

Children have become a lucrative poverty commodity in Nepal, and the willingness of voluntourists and donors to provide funds ensures the ongoing demand for children to be unnecessarily displaced from their families, according to Next Generation Nepal's 2014 report, "The Paradox of Orphanage Volunteering."[19]

Next Generation Nepal is a nonprofit based in Eugene, Oregon, that reconnects trafficked Nepali children with their families. It was formed by Conor Grennan, who in 2004 left his job at the EastWest Institute in Brussels and set off on a solo, yearlong, round-the-world trip, starting with three months of volunteering at an orphanage in Nepal. He grew fond of the eighteen children in his care but was surprised to learn that the children were not orphans after all. In fact, Grennan discovered the existence of thousands of trafficked children who were beyond the reach of the system, children who were abandoned and forgotten, who had little or no food, shelter, or access to medical attention.[20]

"They had parents and siblings and friends somewhere in Nepal and were lured to orphanages by traffickers who offered the promise of a boarding school education in the capital. They tricked parents into handing over their children," Grennan says.

"These parents believed that they were not only saving their children's lives but giving them an opportunity. Sadly, this was not the case."

According to Grennan, there is evidence of traffickers falsifying documents declaring the children as orphans, meaning that children as young as two or three years old become "paper orphans." In some of the worst cases, orphanages are run by abusers who have succeeded in sexually abusing, beating, starving too, and even killing children. This adds to a culture of fear where children are too apprehensive to run away or report the abuse.

Once children are housed in the orphanages, the traffickers and orphanage managers fundraise and solicit foreign volunteers to work for free to support their profit-making enterprises. Children are forced to lie about their backgrounds, and the orphanage managers and traffickers profit from the generosity of well-intentioned volunteers. As a consequence, many "orphanages" have become lucrative businesses in Nepal with profit to be made from both the families and from tourists, volunteers, and donors, Grennan learned.

When he returned to the United States in 2006, Grennan formed Next Generation Nepal to protect trafficked children from exploitation and abuse and to reunite them with their parents.

Grennan would go on to recount his experiences in the *New York Times* bestseller, *Little Princes: One Man's Promise to Bring Home the Lost Children of Nepal* (2010).

The threat of children being trafficked was further compounded following the April 25 and May 12, 2015, earthquakes that killed roughly nine thousand people, and deeply affected the lives of millions more. Homes and schools were leveled, and crops and livestock were destroyed. Traffickers used the earthquakes in their fundraising pitches; many outside the country believe that the earthquakes left thousands of orphans, but in fact only 156 children lost both of their parents as a result of the quakes, and many of those children still have family that can care for them. Grennan tells of instances where parents trying to gain access to their children were routinely denied, and their children were sometimes punished for attempted contact by the parents.

Today NGN estimates there are hundreds of children living in "orphanages" in Nepal, yet at least two-thirds of these children are not orphans. The organization works with the Government of Nepal to rescue children who have been trafficked and need to be removed from the traffickers' facilities. While NGN does not run a children's home, it provides trauma counseling, medical treatment, nourishment, and education to all rescued children at a Transit Home in an undisclosed location until their families are found. Over the past decade, NGN has rescued and reconnected an impressive 577 children, Grennan reports.

The NGN-funded search teams travel for days on foot through the remote mountain villages of Nepal to find the families of trafficked children and to provide them with news and photos of these children, and to conduct thorough assessments of village conditions and family capacities all in an effort to permanently reunite as many children as possible with their parents. NGN follows up with each family, conducting regular monitoring visits to prevent retrafficking.

In 2018, NGN continued to implement rescues and organize reunions. It also has established a strong and effective advocacy effort by educating vulnerable families about child trafficking and the risk their children face. This is accomplished through town meetings, street drama, radio announcements, and through school conferences with teachers and the children themselves.

NGN also runs many advocacy programs back in the United States through its Ambassador Program—NGN's volunteer program in the States that recruits supporters interested in giving back but prefer not to travel to Nepal.

After all, there's nothing wrong with just being a responsible tourist. The 2014 NGN report recommends that if a person is unable to find an ethical voluntourism opportunity, or if it all just seems too complicated to research and organize, they should at least consider traveling ethically, spending money on services and goods that support local people and the local economy.

The NGN report continues: "Equally, it involves the foreigner talking with local people and sharing information about their own lives and interests. If appropriate, and if a local person requests it, the tourist could help with English language skills or other small tasks; for example, helping them write an English-language brochure for their small business.

"Most of all, an ethical tourist recognizes that they, and the local person with whom they are engaging, both have equal amounts of valuable knowledge to contribute to each other. Through this honest and sincere cultural transaction, both parties will benefit, and so will society more broadly."[21]

The core danger of voluntourism is that it creates a dependency between host communities and Western societies rather than the infrastructure needed for sustainable self-reliance, according to Wesby writing in *Newsweek*. "Yet because the industry shows no signs of stopping, voluntourism can only be modified, and not eliminated."

One positive note is that aid workers, inspired by the #MeToo movement, are starting to police themselves and have set up their own hashtag, #AidToo, to stay connected. Recent posts report the resignation of the CEO of Oxfam Great Britain; how journalists should cover sexual abuse in the aid sector; and distressing news about Peter Dalglish, a Canadian and former senior United Nations official charged with child rape in Nepal.

JUST HOW GREEN
IS THAT VOLUNTEER DESTINATION?

These days increasing numbers of responsible travelers are turning their backs on traditional resorts and heading for more sustainable destinations. Many of these promote a commitment to corporate social responsibility (CSR), providing guests the opportunity to make a positive contribution to the environment and to local communities.

Unfortunately, not all shades of "green" are the same. Many destinations offer activities that are not environmentally sustainable. Worse, many destinations do not follow widely accepted sustainable practices yet still call themselves "green," according to Gerald B. Goeden, Malayasian-based marine ecologist, Research Fellow and adviser to the National University of Malaysia, and marine consultant to Malaysia's Andaman Resort in Langkawi. Now semiretired, he leads conservation projects in Southeast Asia.

His handy checklist for considering volunteer opportunities suggest doing your homework and asking questions before packing your bags.

- Are volunteer activities regularly carried out by the hotel staff or only when guests want to participate?
- Where does the CSR funding come from, and is it all spent on the projects?
- If animals or plants are involved in the project, where do they come from, and are they native to the area?
- Is the CSR program supervised by a government department, university, or NGO?
- Can the hotel provide access to annual reports reporting CSR outcomes?

"This may all seem rather extreme, but from my experience many resort destinations rarely operate CSR programs with any insight into what they are doing and what is actually being achieved. Unfortunately, these can be little more than money-making exercises," Goeden believes.

"I'm told a Pacific Island resort offers coral transplanting to repair reef damage. This is accomplished by staff collecting healthy corals from another location and getting guests to 'transplant' them in front of the resort.

"At another resort, substantial funds are raised through guest contributions for environmental improvement, but is instead spent on building maintenance, wages, etc. Direct contributions of cash to CSR projects sometimes just disappear."

Goeden reveals a soon-to-open tourist attraction is offering guests a chance to propagate a few small corals at a price but will likely consume or kill at least a thousand or more large corals a year for display and pool snorkeling activities.

> For the past six years Goeden has worked with volunteers, as many as twenty groups per year, and knows it can be an internationally attractive activity.
>
> "It's important that volunteers obtain good information, find some inspiration, and above all, do some good with the money they have spent. Beware of the deceptions."

Lest this chapter scare off the prospective voluntourist, the takeaway here is to volunteer with your eyes open, as Michele L. Staton writes on the Almost. TheDoctorsChannel.com. "Make sure the organization you're going with is well-respected on the ground and is truly invested in the people or community that it is there to help, not just in the volunteers' experience. Many organizations have a mission statement, check to see if its focus is on the community or the voluntourists. . . . Then continue to invest in the cause when you return and use that newfound understanding of the world to help improve it."[22]

New York writer Pippa Biddle adds, "Before you sign up for a volunteer trip anywhere in the world this summer, consider whether you possess the skill set necessary for that trip to be successful. If yes, awesome. If not, it might be a good idea to reconsider your trip. Sadly, taking part in international aid where you aren't particularly helpful is not benign. It's detrimental. It slows down positive growth and perpetuates the 'white savior' complex that, for hundreds of years, has haunted both the countries we are trying to 'save' and our (more recently) own psyches."[23]

CharityNavigator.org, one major watchdog for charities in the United States, can help vet domestic projects and has a handy Guide to Volunteering. VolunteerMatch.org, the service I used to identify volunteer opportunities in US cities, calls itself the web's largest volunteer engagement network, with more than 117,000 active nonprofits, 150 network partners, and 13 million visitors annually. Also consult GuideStar.org and its searchable database of 1.8 million IRS-recognized charities.

Narrow the list, and then ask the tour operators or nonprofits to send you details on accommodations, fees, refund policy, and the precise nature of the work you'll be asked to perform. Request references, and contact volunteers listed in brochures and websites for their insight. Conduct a Google news search. No matter where in the world you're hoping to visit, even if it's as close as southern Nevada, be sure to properly vet the opportunity before you depart on that volunteer adventure.

· *VIII* ·

Funding Your Volunteer Project

$\mathcal{A}$s we learned from the story of Joe "Buffalo Joe" Watson, a small effort can make a huge difference in a Third World country such as Nepal. But often this requires rattling the cup and raising the necessary funds to accomplish your goals.

One way to see the world—and receive funding for it—is to design a trip that's bigger than yourself. Sarah Winters Papsun, a former marketing and investor relations consultant from Greenwich, Connecticut, has an interesting formula for seeing the world while helping others. At the age of thirty-seven, Papsun has already traveled to places most people only dream about . . . and has a rock band in Paris named after her (more on that later).

Papsun has been to every continent, including Antarctica, all fifty states, and has traveled to fifty-eight countries and counting. In her spare time, she is also a Rotarian, an accomplished cellist, and is actively involved with the Noroton, Connecticut, Presbyterian Church's Mission Team. She completed the Semester at Sea study aboard program and has a marketing degree from Quinnipiac University, which has served her well in her professional life and in helping to fundraise for charities. Her Facebook posts are a fascinating travelogue of her volunteer work abroad.

In 2010, she traveled with twelve women from around the world united by the Peaks Foundation (now part of No Barriers USA) to Kenya and Tanzania to hike the three highest peaks in those countries in three weeks.[1]

The group hiked Mt. Kenya to promote the environment, Mt. Meru to promote the importance of education, and Mt. Kilimanjaro to encourage better health through three nonprofits: the Laikipia Wildlife Forum, the School of St. Jude Tanzania, and Support for International Change.

Papsun raised over $17,000 individually for the causes, paid her own travel and expenses, and hand-carried her donations for the school, porters, and guides. She donated medical supplies, soccer balls, sunglasses, and extra hiking gear. When Papsun left Tanzania, she only had a small carry-on bag for the return flight, giving everything else away to those she had gotten to know.

In a modern take on the story of Cinderella, she even gave away her own hiking boots to a female porter who wore the same shoe size as she did.

"I felt so moved by the hardworking porters that made the trip work. They carried our food, our tents, and our pack. It was the least I could do, as some porters continuously hike Mt. Kilimanjaro in broken-down sneakers, dress shoes, or even sandals," she tells me.

In 2013, Papsun traveled to Machu Picchu in Peru—it was both a vacation and a chance to spend a portion of the trip with fellow Rotarians to install simple household water treatment devices, an improvement upon traditional slow sand filters specifically designed for intermittent use.[2]

A biosand filter (BSF) consists of a concrete or plastic container filled with specially selected and prepared sand and gravel. As water flows through the filter, physical straining removes pathogens, iron, turbidity, and manganese from drinking water. A shallow layer of water sits atop the sand, and a biofilm develops. The biofilm contributes to the removal of pathogens due to competition for food of nonharmful microorganisms contained in the biofilm and the harmful organisms in the water.

The big advantage is that the filter is simple to use and can be produced locally anywhere in the world because it is built using materials that are readily available.

Along with providing Peruvian families with a source for clean water, Papsun and other volunteers packed hundreds of toothbrushes, toothpaste, soap, adhesive bandages, vitamins, and small toys that they had collected from family and friends before they left.

In 2014, while on a Caribbean cruise vacation with friends, each cruiser packed an extra bag full of school supplies, which went to the Rotary Club in Roatán, Honduras.

"Small person-to-person donations can really add up, change the world, and break down stereotypes," she says.

After spending the past ten years as a voluntourist, Papsun knows a thing or two about providing fundraising advice for would-be world travelers.

START AN ONLINE FUNDRAISING PAGE

Even if you only have black-and-white skills in today's Technicolor world, learn how to use social media. Enlist the aid of a twelve-year-old if you have to. Do what it takes. When Papsun first conceives of a project, she logs on to First Giving to start the fundraising process.[3]

Papsun advises that it helps to have tax-exempt status, such as a 501(c)(3), or a tax ID (EIN). When collecting funds and money, it's important to tell people clearly what the organization is and how the funds are getting to the people you are helping. Transparency is critical. You want everything to be clear and simple. When soliciting donations, FirstGiving can help assure supporters that their contributions are tax deductible.

"Make up business cards you can pass out with your fundraising information, website, Twitter account, email, and telephone on it. It helps when meeting new people. Be able to strike up a conversation with anyone who asks you about your project, and pass them a card so they can make a donation later," says Papsun.

POST TO SOCIAL MEDIA FREQUENTLY

Each day blast out a Facebook, Tweet, or email asking friends to "rock your world" or "make your day" and donate just $5. If twenty friends do that, she believes these small amounts will really add up.

SELL POPULAR SNACKS

Another way Papsun has raised money was selling chocolate from Hershey Fundraising.[4] "I've also gone to Costco to buy snacks in bulk like granola bars, Clif bars, and candy bars to resell. Sometimes it seems like making a dollar here or there will take forever, but I assure you, it goes fast if you stay at it. I even set up a 'lemonade stand with a purpose' in the summer at my local MetroNorth train station, and people really started to take notice of my cause and made donations."

HOST HOME-COOKED DINNERS

Papsun hosts a wine, cheese, and pasta dinner night at her home.

"I would cook for my friends and at the end of the dinner I would place a pot on the table and ask if friends would donate 'what they felt was in their heart' or what they thought that dinner would have cost if they ate at a restaurant.

"I assure my guests that 100 percent of their donation will go to the charity, as I go to meet the people in need, work with the cause in the country I am visiting, and deliver the funds personally. At the dinner I talk about why the project means so much to me and answer any questions people have. You have to eat, breathe, and sleep your chosen volunteer project to make it happen."

PLAN A "TOP LESS" CAR WASH

Papsun advises, "Everyone needs a clean car, especially in the spring to wash off road salt. Plan a 'Top Less' car wash—a car wash where you don't wash the top of the cars (it's easier to wash that way). Identify the charity on signs you place all over town to raise awareness—and funds—for your trip."

Now about that band: Sarah W. Papsun is a Parisian rock group named after her in 2008. As you might imagine, she's a fan of their music.[5]

TURN YOUR WEDDING INTO A FUNDRAISER

It was a classic case of "meet-cute." In 2009, Suzanne Andre, a single banker living in the New York suburb of New Canaan, Connecticut, was attending an outdoor music concert in nearby Stamford. At five feet ten inches, she is naturally drawn to taller men. Across the crowd was a handsome young man named Jeff Anderson, who was taller still. Six feet six inches to be exact. They struck up a conversation and started dating, drawn to each other by a number of common interests, including a desire to help others in need.

Five years later, while planning a July 2014 wedding in the Italian Amalfi Coast resort village of Ravello, they both decided that instead of the usual "stuff" people give as wedding gifts—slow cookers, china, silverware—instead they would ask for money to fund a volunteer honeymoon. They would join a Habitat for Humanity Global Village[6] trip to Nepal in November 2014.

They called it a "Honeymoon for Humanity."

In their wedding invitation they wrote, "We will join volunteers from all over the world to bring attention to the problem of poverty housing. The partner families are either homeless or live in overcrowded, inadequate housing in constant threat of eviction. For the first time, these families will enjoy safe, decent shelter—something many of us take for granted."

Recently, she tells me, "We realized that with busy careers in banking, it was unlikely we'd get ten days off anytime soon to travel together to the other side of the world.

Suzanne and Jeff Anderson traveled to Nepal on a "Honeymoon for Humanity," raising $5,210 in lieu of gifts. Photo by Suzanne Anderson.

"A few months after our wedding was the right time to plan a big trip like this. We received an incredible reaction from family and friends. It seemed that our guests really supported the idea, and some even gave more than we believe they might have otherwise," Anderson says.

For additional funding, they turned to YouCaring, a free crowdfunding platform.[7] It was here they could post photos and outline their plans. As a result, they raised $5,210. Factoring in additional wedding gifts of $1,300, their total out-of-pocket costs including airfare were just $2,240.

The two journeyed to Kathmandu, Nepal, then to the district of Chitwan in south central Nepal where they helped build a home for five days on a banana plantation.

While Jeff and Suzanne had no prior construction experience, the work was fairly straightforward, echoing the experience of the Gasperini family in Nicaragua. Their American team leader taught them how to pour concrete and use woven bamboo to reinforce walls, working side by side with local construction workers. Habitat for Humanity arranged for local transportation, housing, food, and building materials, and provided opportunities to meet the locals and see the countryside. Habitat also supplied detailed packing lists, recommended vaccinations, and offered advice on staying safe and healthy upon arrival.

The two helped build a home with concrete floors and a tin roof for a twenty-five-year-old Nepalese mother with two children ages seven and eleven. Previously, the single mother had always lived with her parents in a crowded slum in Chitwan.

"Seeing her reaction when we led her through her very own home would make anyone's heart melt. It was more rewarding than anything we could have imagined," she recalls.

Anderson tells me in a call from her new home in London, "It was also a great thing to do together—it was hard, hot, manual labor, but a rewarding way to start our married life—working together to create a better world. Now, instead of a closet full of wine glasses and gravy boats, we have incredible memories about our trip and a sense of pride that we were able to give back."

Jeff and Suzanne hope to spend most Sundays on volunteer projects, although with a new baby girl in the family, they'll volunteer at nonprofits a lot closer to their London home.

BE POLITELY TENACIOUS

If you plan to travel on your own, well, you're likely to be on your own in terms of fundraising. But if you reserve a volunteer trip with one of the tour operators listed in this book, there's often a wealth of information and advice you can tap.

Such is the case with Projects Abroad's handy fundraising guide you can easily download to your home computer.[8]

Projects Abroad, the international volunteering organization founded in 1992, provides a number of important tips for fundraising, including:

1. *Know Your Facts*: Sponsors may ask what you are doing, your purpose in taking part in the program, and specifics about the organization. You must be able to explain exactly how their money will be spent and by whom. Many donors, including any businesses from whom you request sponsorship, will want to know where their money is going and how it is going to make a difference.
2. *Establish Aims and Objectives*: Projects Abroad suggests starting with the cost of the project. Work out exactly how much you owe, when

you need to pay, and how you want to pay. Don't forget medical expenses such as pretrip vaccinations and pocket money for weekend travel at the destination and the purchase of souvenirs. You may also need to buy extra clothing or necessities such as backpacks, first aid kits, and mosquito nets. Then set a target for how much money you'll need to raise each month as the departure date nears.

3. *Create a Fundraising Webpage*: Projects Abroad, for instance, can directly link a personalized webpage to your trip invoice so any donations will go directly toward paying off the program fee. Unlike crowdfunding sites, there are no processing fees. You can also share the page on Facebook and Twitter, email the link to friends and family, and give it out to attendees at your fundraising events.

4. *Plan Fundraising Events*: Speaking of which, once you have outlined your fundraising goals and established monthly targets, you can begin to plan events such as bake sales, car washes, community fashion shows, garage sales, pancake breakfasts, or sponsored runs, climbs, or hikes. How's this for a fundraising idea: a "crush" fundraiser for Valentine's Day. Typically it will be a type of flower (a rose, daisy, etc.) that someone can pay, let's say $5, to have it delivered by you to a crush, either anonymously or accompanied by a personal note.

"Be 'politely tenacious' when it comes to fundraising. Set a schedule to regularly follow up with everyone you think might be able to contribute to your goal, and make sure they fully understand what you are doing and how important it is to you," advises Christian Clark, Projects Abroad's US deputy director.

SEEK MATCHING DONATIONS FROM YOUR EMPLOYER

Many corporations match the donations their employees make to charities. This encourages charitable giving and extends corporate philanthropy. Matching donations, or matching gifts, are free money that nonprofits often miss out on because of limited information regarding donors' employers, complex corporate giving programs, and because the employees themselves may be unaware of the corporate matching process, according to Double the Donation LLC, which maintains a database of corporate matching gift and volunteer grant programs, plus application forms.

The database includes matching gift or volunteer grant information on 2,300 parent companies and approximately six thousand major subsidiaries that employ over eighteen million individuals.

For instance, United Airlines sponsors a United Volunteer Impact Grant program that provides grants to charities where its employees serve as dedicated and passionate volunteers. Full- or part-time United employees who complete forty hours of volunteer service in the previous twelve months with their favorite charity are eligible to apply for a United Airlines Foundation grant of $1,000 to that nonprofit.[9]

Nonprofits pay an annual fee to post their specific donation forms and incorporate Double the Donation's data into their websites. It's a popular site—charities benefit directly from the largesse of donors searching for matching grants from their employers; donors access the forms, guidelines, and instructions that they need.

According to an email from Adam Weinger, president of Double the Donation, companies change their programs frequently, but at the time of this writing, GE, for instance, will match donations from current employees to a wide range of nonprofits at a one-to-one ratio, up to $5,000; Exxon-Mobil matches donations from employees to higher education institutions up to three to one ($22,500 maximum); and if you work at Home Depot, as another example, in many cases they match donations up to a ceiling of $3,000.

"It's up to the company to determine their guidelines and we do our best to maintain that data from a variety of sources, investing a lot of time and money into the research," Weinger writes.

To find out if your company offers similar volunteer grants that you can apply to your next voluntourism project, view the Double the Donation website.[10]

CROWDSOURCE YOUR TRIP

When a national tragedy strikes, such as the death of sixteen members of a Canadian hockey team in a bus crash, when thousands of Houston residents become homeless after Hurricane Harvey, or a terrorist attack in New York kills eight cyclists, kindhearted donors often turn to crowdfunding websites to provide financial assistance. Personal fundraising sites go by names such as Fundly, FundRazr, Kickstarter, and Plumfund. One of the largest is Go-FundMe, since 2010 used by fifty-plus million people to raise over $5 billion, for causes ranging from the aforementioned disasters to funerals, animal and pet welfare, and, yes, volunteer trips.

The process is straightforward: set up the campaign, share it with family and friends, then receive the donated funds by check or bank transfer. You'll pay a processing fee of 2.9 percent plus thirty cents per donation.

A recent search of the site for voluntourism reveals 103 volunteer projects seeking funding, ranging from requests for airfare to travel to an orphanage in Thailand; a missionary trip to Liverpool, England, to assist refugees and asylum seekers; and a humanitarian trip to a remote community in Puerto Rico to assist victims of Hurricane Maria.[11] Most of the money raised falls in the low four figures, but still, every bit helps. It could mean the difference between paying your own airfare and using the money instead on accommodations, food, or supplies.

Adam Moore of the University of California San Diego writes in his appeal for funds to assist at an HIV/AIDS Clinic in Uganda, "This is different than your standard voluntourism. I'm not going to Africa to build a schoolhouse with no previous construction experience and take pictures with African children to feel better about myself.

"With this program, I will be helping treat patients that would otherwise not receive care due to the overwhelming patient-to-doctor ratio. This will help provide in-field experience to supplement the lab work I have been doing at the UCSD and Department of Veteran's Affairs Center for AIDS Research, and open my eyes to what public health is like in a developing country in preparation for eventually joining the Peace Corps."

He raised just over $2,000 from fifty-two donors in twenty-six months.[12]

Another handy fundraising tool is Volunteer Forever, sort of the Match .com of voluntourism, which helps sift through thousands of opportunities for volunteers, interns, or teach abroad programs. It not only assists in matching your special skills and interests with a nonprofit desperately needing assistance but also walks you through creating an online page for donor solicitation.

The first step in the process is to pick a program among an almost limitless variety of opportunities ranging from teaching English, volunteering for women's empowerment and girls' education, and working in health clinics to environmental projects on behalf of sea turtles, leopards, and elephants. In fact, the site maintains a database of 800 international volunteer organizations; 3,500 program reviews; and 11,600 volunteers who have collectively raised over $2 million for their trips. There are listings perfect for high schoolers, families and groups, couples, seniors, and those on gap years.

Let's say you'd like to coach sports. "It's definitely one of the most straightforward [volunteer opportunities] in knowing how you'll spend your time," posts Brittany Edwardes, a volunteer travel researcher.[13]

"Because sports and games are such a great way to hook children into academic activities, there is usually some element of teaching English in sports volunteering, especially if the kids are studying English as part of their school's curriculum."

The site goes on to suggest volunteer coaching opportunities in Ecuador, Fiji, India, Jamaica, South Africa, and Zambia, among other countries.

You then create a profile and fundraising page. It's painless. In sixty seconds you can upload personal information, a description of your planned trip, and images. All donations go directly to your personal account to help fund the project. Volunteer Forever charges 5 percent per transaction to conduct fundraising through the site. Depending on your account, PayPal or WePay will also charge 2.9 percent and thirty cents for each donation that you receive.[14]

After your project concludes, you're encouraged to post your trip so that other volunteers can learn from your experience. These trip reports fatten up your volunteer resume, which helps facilitate donations the next time you decide to hit the road and help make the world a better place for the less fortunate.

LAND A LOCAL BUSINESS SPONSOR

Both Papsun and Anderson experienced success with crowdfunding. Another way to raise funds for your trip is through local business sponsorship. Easier said than done.

No one said fundraising would be simple when you signed on to become a voluntourist. Sponsorship can cushion the financial impact on your budget, but it's time consuming and takes some effort to solicit local businesses to support your cause.

While it is certainly possible to convince law offices, real estate companies, dry cleaners, restaurants, and supermarkets to donate to your volunteer project, business owners aren't sitting around waiting for your call. They may already be donating to local chapters of the American Heart Association; National Kidney Foundation; or Susan G. Komen for the Cure, the breast cancer foundation—those causes they understand. A tougher sell is supporting a voluntourist's passion project.

Business owners may likely wonder how their businesses will benefit from supporting your plans to teach English in an African school, or volunteer at a biological research station in the Galápagos Islands.

Still, many companies may be receptive to your sponsorship pitch if approached correctly. Network with friends and loved ones to determine whether they have a lead on a potential sponsor. Then you'll need to describe clearly and concisely what's in it for the business owner. Your project isn't a run-of-the-mill charity. It's an opportunity for the business to become associated in a positive manner with a worthy cause.

Can they promote their involvement in online, radio, TV, and newspaper advertising? In a store window? With a special event in their store before you leave, then again once you return with a PowerPoint presentation and a head full of fascinating stories to tell? Can you meet with sales staff to motivate them to seek their own voluntourism opportunities? Does the business have the right to use your images?

Match your funding request with a related local business that already has an interest in your volunteer destination. Perhaps a Thai or Vietnamese restaurant? Are you volunteering in Africa to help provide dental care to impoverished villages? Pitch a local dentist office in your hometown for support. A clothing boutique might be interested in supporting your efforts to help Caribbean women create handicrafts for export. If your project involves granting microloans to a female-owned business in Zimbabwe, your hometown bank might be interested in assisting.

Develop a professional-looking sponsorship "deck" and carefully check for typos. These PowerPoint pages usually outline the project, explain who you are, and list sponsor benefits. Include a map of the destination, personal photographs, information about the organization you're assisting, and be sure to add a contact page so funders can easily find you. The sponsorship proposal should also be posted to a dedicated website and your Facebook and Instagram accounts. Savvy sponsors will check your social media presence; the more followers you have, the more credit a sponsor stands to receive.

Then reach out with a personalized email that reiterates your project and sponsor benefits. Do some homework and demonstrate in your solicitation that you have at least working knowledge of what the business actually does.

Remember, cash is always best, but you can bestow at least a small level of sponsor benefits if the company provides you with much-needed gear you would otherwise need to purchase, such as sturdy hiking boots, a comfortable backpack, or sleeping bag. Just remember, no matter how much value you receive in kind (known as VIK), a package of socks isn't going to help pay for that Singapore Airlines airfare to Borneo.

Companies are not the only organizations with sponsorship budgets. Local councils, religious centers, community groups, and youth or sports groups can also help, suggests Projects Abroad.[15]

As the Indian leader Mahatma Gandhi once said, "If you don't ask, you don't get it."

APPLY FOR HUMANITARIAN AIRFARE

If you're saving the world, or at least a small part of it, it might be possible to apply for reduced airfare. Fly For Good, based in Burnsville, Minnesota, are specialists in so-called humanitarian airfares.[16]

Major airlines create a "bucket" or reserved group of seats specifically for humanitarian travelers or those representing a nonprofit. These ticket prices are often significantly lower than the average published rate, which allow nonprofits and individuals to save money on their travel. Most people save 5 to 8 percent off what they might find online or directly through the airlines.

Unlike regular published rates, humanitarian rates do not increase with last-minute booking. You can also receive discounted rates for spontaneous volunteer trips, such as emergency responses for natural disasters. Plus, these discounts remain the same whether you're traveling for three days or one year; there may be no change fees; and often baggage fees are waived as well, making it easier to transport much-needed supplies.

There's just one catch: the fare is only available for humanitarians who work for, volunteer with, or are an immediate family member of an employee of a registered nonprofit organization involved in international humanitarian work. To qualify, you'll need an original letter of mission on the nonprofit's official letterhead, which should not be much of an obstacle.

LEARN TO GIVE THANKS

An important aspect of receiving funding for a voluntourism project is the simple concept of giving thanks to your benefactors. After all, no one owes you a nice trip to Nicaragua to spend a few days teaching English to secondary school students. This is your passion project, not that of your donors. Make them feel the best thing they could have done with their money was provide you with support.

Donors should never question your gratitude. Besides it being the right thing to do, informing them about the results of your effort this time will make it that much easier to gain their support the next time. While it takes some effort on your part, showing gratitude is not particularly difficult to achieve. Here are techniques to consider:

Pretrip

- Before you leave, prepare an email update you can send to all donors. If corporate sponsors have provided you with cash or gear, list those products in your pretrip communications. This also becomes an opportunity to describe the support you still need, such as donations to defray airfare, or specific outdoor travel products such as tents, sleeping bags, or a satellite telephone.

- Contact your local newspaper using a simple press release that summarizes the volunteer project. Prepare it yourself or have a journalism student or freelance writer craft an explanation of the "who, what, when, where, and how" of the trip. Be sure to credit all benefactors in the announcement and send them a copy as it goes to local radio, TV, print, and online media. Then once a story appears, share that press coverage as well.
- Ask your supporters for a banner, a logo to wear on your clothing, or some other item you can photograph in front of the school where you're teaching English, or the library you're helping construct. You can also use the image in your public talks after the project ends and in handwritten thank-you notes sent to donors (see Post-Trip Advice below).

During the Trip

- Purchase a small souvenir item from your destination to use later when expressing your appreciation of support. Volunteering on a farm in Iceland? Purchase Icelandic candleholders made from the country's iconic lava rock, or sample skin care kits from the famed Blue Lagoon Geothermal Spa.

   I chose to buy prayer flags during my volunteer mission to Nepal to thank the company that provided me with boots. For the sake of authenticity, I had to make sure they were "activated." Mere store-bought prayer flags aren't sufficient; they needed to be prayed over and "turned on." That entailed a solemn ceremony performed by a Buddhist monk involving rice, holy water, and a lengthy prayer—all for a payment equivalent to $2. Do the flags look any different once turned on? Hardly.

   In 2007, when Denver schoolteacher Mike Haugen climbed Everest, he was sponsored by the Coleman Company. Later, Coleman took the flags that went to the summit and framed them to present to employees and their outside public relations resources, myself included. I have one on my office wall. While it's impossible to determine whether they were activated with rice and holy water, it's one of my most treasured keepsakes.

- Keep in touch. After being first to reach the North Pole, it took months before American explorer Robert E. Peary (1856–1920) was able to send a telegram notifying the world of his success. Fast forward to 2018 and there's an expectation of instant communications worldwide from anywhere. When engaged in your volunteer activity, provide updates to your benefactors daily, or at least every few days. Too much information? Perhaps. But it's best to err on the side of too much communication than too little. Voluntourism is rife with stories of people who take the money and run, who are rarely heard from again. Don't be that person.

Communications from the field was sorely tested during my volunteer stint in December 2017 with Dooley Intermed International and its team of ophthalmologists based in remote Machhakhola, Nepal. Here I was, the volunteer communications director, unable to communicate. SIM cards weren't working, our unheated teahouse had no Wi-Fi—in fact, they only had electricity for three hours in the evening, assuming there was fuel for the generator.

Only by crossing a rickety steel footbridge suspended above the roaring Budhi Gandaki River, then climbing a set of concrete stairs almost straight up for ten minutes, could I reach one particular dead tree from whence a cell phone signal could be squeezed out of the ether. We called it the 4G tree, named after the cell phone network. The signal was strong enough to phone home but not send email. My daily updates, including praise for our sponsors, would have to wait until my return to Kathmandu.

This was not unexpected, by the way. We anticipated connectivity issues. After all, this impoverished hillside village was about as remote as you can be on the planet—an eight-hour 4WD ride from Kathmandu, followed by an eight-hour trek on foot along single-track trails perched precipitously above riverside cliffs.

One small consolation was our use of an inReach Explorer satellite communicator that allowed us to send 160-character text messages at a time. The text messages were posted to the mission's website and Facebook page. The inReach also had a slide switch that protected an SOS panic button that presumably would send out the calvary in the event of an emergency. Thankfully, we did not have to put this to the test.

Keep your posts short. Online attention spans necessitate messages that can be read in a minute or less. As the saying goes, tell them the time, not how to build a watch.

Post-Trip Advice

My least favorite part of a volunteer vacation is soliciting funding. But if you do it right, your donors can gain almost as much value as you do, as your friends and loved ones live vicariously through your trip reports, photos, blogs, and post-trip speaking engagements. Each message reinforces the importance of the effort and assures them their donation was money well spent.

- Remember that the voluntourism experience is not yet over when you return. Besides presenting the aforementioned trip souvenirs to your sponsors, and staying in touch frequently each week, create a final report to summarize the results of your trip. How many children were reached? How many books were donated to that library you helped rebuild? Where exactly were fuel-efficient cookstoves distributed? Provide quantitative measurement of your success.

  Send your supporters a coffee table–style photo book illustrating the project. Shutterfly or Mosaic, for instance, provide an easy way to become your own publisher. Insert your best images behind a cover containing the title of the project.

  Offer to conduct PowerPoint presentations to the sponsors' church, company, or civic organization. Speak at libraries, travel stores, or outdoor shops. Here in Boulder, Colorado, a travel store called Changes in Latitude has a full schedule of travel shows ranging from how to pack more efficiently, staying healthy on the road, and hiking in remote areas. While this particular store doesn't pay speakers, voluntourists use the opportunity to document how they provided credit to sponsors in a live, public setting.[17] Post retail store talks to YouTube.com and link to it for future sponsor outreach.

  These post-trip presentations help demonstrate to your future donors a willingness to go the extra mile to ensure they receive extra value from their support.

  My most memorable post-trip presentation was on a Celebrity Cruise oceanliner. I received a free week-long stay in return for three talks. "How is this a thing?" you might ask. The program was called "Beyond the Podium," and I was a featured speaker during days at sea. It was somewhat disconcerting to be in the 1,500-seat main theater and have only forty people in the audience, but I attributed that to a fierce Bingo tournament going on at the same time.

- Finally, don't underestimate the value of sending handwritten thank-you notes. At the conclusion of Jeff and Suzanne Anderson's Habitat for Humanity trip in 2014, the newleyweds thanked their friends and families personally, writing in part:

"Homes do more than just offer a roof over the head. In safe and stable housing children have a place to study and stay healthy. Thank you for helping us give a child a safe home."

Yes, that's right, you read correctly. Make it a handwritten note. A real piece of paper made from dead trees, using a grown-up's fountain pen, and actually mailed with the help of the good folks at the US Postal Service.

Who mails thank-you letters any more, you may ask? Precisely. When it comes to properly showing gratitude, you do.

SHARE YOUR TRIP

Your voluntourism project doesn't end when you return. There's more that can be done to motivate friends, families, and complete strangers to consider their own humanitarian missions, or at the least support your next project financially or with in-kind products and services. This requires you to document the project both while you're in the field and then upon your safe return back home.

When it comes down to it, a voluntourist has the responsibility of telling the rest of us, those who didn't get to go, what it was like and how we too can get involved.

Photography and videography are two important techniques for documenting your project. Often, it doesn't take any more gear than the smartphone you undoubtedly carry around every day.

Former Houston-area HR executive Pamela Johnston, until recently executive director of the Himalayan Stove Project,[18] pushes her iPhone 7 to the max and has returned from Nepal and Africa with stunning images of hardworking families and children living challenging Third World lives.

The funny thing is, she usually travels with what I call her "big boy" camera—an expensive Nikon D90 12.3MP DX-Format CMOS Digital SLR Camera with 18–105 mm f/3.5–5.6G ED AF-S VR DX Nikkor Zoom Lens. Sound confusing? Well it can be. She knows how to operate it but keeps it in her backpack as back up, preferring instead to use her unobtrusive smartphone, albeit one with as much memory as possible. In fact, she tells me there are twenty thousand images on her iPhone 7, all saved to iCloud storage.

Johnston refers to shoot from the hip with her compact smartphone, often recording video out of the window of foreign taxis or while walking down the street, knowing she can later capture still images from the footage.

"I much prefer to capture people as they really are, without them having to pose for me. I find joy in street photography. But if I want to shoot their faces, I'll always ask for permission first."

To ease the process, she'll often take along a Fujifilm Instax Instant camera and present her photo subjects with a color instant photo for them to keep. Recently, during a third trip to Nepal, she also carried ten pounds of framed iPhone 7 images to give to Nepalis she was revisiting.

"Walk into many homes and you'll see celebrity images on the walls taken from magazines, but few of their own family. Handing them a color image printed from my smartphone, especially a high-resolution photo of their elders, becomes an important keepsake."

Her Instagram account[19] is populated with thousands of creative, artsy images from her travels, many altered slightly by sharpening the image and using two Instagram applications, Rise and Skyline.

Johnston uses Rise to wash photos with a pleasing amber light. It softens the image with a yellowish-gold tint to fade away any blemishes. Rise will also lighten up photos that are too dark or underexposed.

Skyline allows Johnston to add interesting vignettes to the image.

"You can overwork an image, making it appear fake. These are simple alterations to enhance the photos' impact."

Johnston's images appear across multiple social media platforms, on the organization's website, in consumer and trade show booths, in brochures, and in emails sent to supporters.

"I couldn't imagine telling our story about the importance of fuel-efficient cookstoves without the visceral impact we achieve through photography."

During a backpacking trip through Bolivia and Peru, photographer Federico Cabrera was disturbed that tourists taking photos of the local people in low-income communities were often doing so without their knowledge or consent. It was as if they were on a "human safari," he writes on his Go-FundMe page.[20]

Then, in an ironic twist, and similar to what Pamela Johnston experienced in Nepal, he learned that most locals didn't own a single photo of themselves or their loved ones. That's when he came up with the idea for "Their Only Portrait," a one-man, 6,200-mile-plus bike tour along the Cordillera de los Andes on a mission to provide families with a physical record of their history.

His volunteer work has since expanded to include donations of Luci portable solar lights and Sawyer water filters to the families who need them most.

While Cabrera travels with technical photography equipment, you can easily share photos wherever you travel just as Pamela Johnston did while on the road for the Himalayan Stove Project.

Consider packing an instant camera such as the Fuji film Instax Instant Camera plus plenty of film. The camera costs about $60, and the photos come to about seventy cents each. Here's another option, although a bit more expensive: remember the Polaroid instant camera, a baby boomer favorite? It's been resurrected as the OneStep 2 i-Type camera. The camera is about $100 retail and its instant photos are a pricey $2.50 each.

Either way, handing out your own instant photos is a magical experience as the image develops right before your eyes. Sharing these photos with the people you meet along the way is an effective technique for connecting with locals and demonstrating a sincere desire to learn more than the average tourist would about their lifestyle and culture.

Instant cameras are fun, but for the best images, invest in a handy point-and-shoot camera and study the available light.

Professional photographer Marc Bryan-Brown,[21] based in New York's Hudson Valley, has traveled the world with his expensive professional camera gear, photographing expeditions, celebrities, real estate, and even the Emmy Awards. His go-to gear is the Nikon D5, Nikon D850, and a Nikon Df. Add in a case full of high-speed lenses and his equipment costs are over $25,000.

"The pro, by definition, is being paid to come through with the image for the client. The amateur, if they don't get the shot, they may be sad but it doesn't matter. I need to deliver in all conditions, whatever it takes," he says.

Yet even he will admit taking exceptional photos with his $380 point-and-shoot Canon PowerShot G9X digital camera. The vice president of membership for The Explorers Club, married father of two children, and incongruously, an heirloom garlic farmer in Upstate New York, Bryan-Brown advises that what counts more than a camera's technical features or ticket price is whether you can reach it easily and chase after optimal lighting for the best exposures.

This was certainly the case during my last Nepal trip when I left my bulky Nikon D40 digital camera home, preferring instead to take a pocket-sized Nikon Coolpix. I had it in a side pocket ready for action at a moment's notice. It worked so well, the photos were good enough for use in a book. This book, in fact.

Bryan-Brown reminds me that some of the most historic photos in the history of adventure were taken with small-for-their-day pocket cameras.

In 1915 to 1916, Sir Ernest Shackleton's photographer, Frank Hurley, recorded many of his best images with a large-view camera with glass plates, but some of the most iconic images were taken with what was, at the time, a groundbreaking Vest Pocket Kodak, one of the first truly compact cameras.[22] The Vest Pocket Kodak also figures highly in the story of English climber George Mallory, who disappeared on Mt. Everest in 1924. Mallory's body was found in 1999, sans camera, and some adventurers are still looking for the Kodak to prove whether he and his partner, Sandy Irvine, could have been first to summit the world's tallest peak.

Years later, Sir Edmund Hillary photographed his partner, Tenzing Norgay, on the top of Everest in 1953 with another pocket folding film camera—the circa 1935 Kodak Retina type 118.

Bryan-Brown speaks fondly about the convenience of the iPhone, and uses one himself, but he cautions that the ubiquitous smartphones have a narrow range. "They're limited in what they can do," he tells me. "An actual camera will perform better in low light and where the subject is moving."

Bryan-Brown offers a number of tips for voluntourists looking to improve the quality and impact of their photography:

- *Practice First*: Bryan-Brown tells the story of a friend who purchased an expensive Nikon just one week prior to departure on a safari.

    "He's about to leave and had no idea what he's doing. He missed a lot of Big Five images trying to figure out how to work his gear. Ask the camera salesman for tips, read the manuals, and remember that practice makes perfect," Bryan-Brown advises.
- *Keep a Camera Handy*: This is where smaller is better. Hang a camera on your belt, on your vest, or tucked into a pocket. Practice a "quick draw"—see how quickly you can take it out when something extraordinary happens that you want to capture. Remember that the best camera is the one you have with you.
- *Tell a Story*: Think ahead to the PowerPoint talk you might be called upon to present upon your return. Tell a story with your images. Start with an establishing shot, perhaps the entrance sign to the community. Record images of locals, take close-ups of hands, signs, animals, and other features of their environment. Zoom in to capture the color of someone's eyes, the lines on their hands, or wrinkles on their face. Consider shooting some action—hammering a tin roof, teaching ESL to schoolchildren, carrying boxes of supplies.

    "You get the picture," he says.
- *Position Subjects in the Light*: As a rule of thumb, if you shoot into the sun, the subject will come out dark. You want more light on the subject than in the background. If the background is bright, move the subject to where the light is better, rather than shoot right where they are.

    "Take control of the situation."

    Avoid using the camera flash as this tends to create images that look artificial; it kills the mood and tends to lack subtlety.
- *Keep Shooting*: Take multiple images of the same scene. If someone's eyes are closed, the next image may show them wide open. Bryan-Brown also suggests not looking at every photo after it's taken. "You

lose all spontaneity if you keep looking at each image. Take a string of them at one time."

- *Back Up Religiously*: Images should be backed up each night. Shoot with more than one digital card, just in case. Cameras have been known to fall, get soaked in water, even stolen. If that happens and you haven't backed up images on a laptop, thumb drive, or in the cloud, you won't have a good day.
- *Edit Your Work*: Friends and loved ones will be bored to tears if you come back and show them all 1,200 images on your digital cards. Bryan-Brown suggests editing your images relentlessly, perhaps down to the best forty or fifty.

"Go through your work, crop the images, and tweak them with simple editing software that comes with the camera or your computer's photo software."

Follow this advice, and your volunteer adventure will be a picture-perfect experience.

For voluntourists with videography experience, consider the advice of Polish explorer Milosz Pierwola,[23] thirty-four, founder of World in 360.[24] He travels the world with a 360-degree virtual reality (VR) camera that enables him to share experiences with bedridden patients who can feel as if they're actually there.

"This clever little gizmo allows me to shoot video in a complete circle. The camera records what it sees in front of it, behind it, on the sides, and even above and below all at once. It's light enough to connect to a drone, dunk underwater, and even strap to animals. The goal of the project is to share the final footage on virtual reality headsets with otherwise housebound patients in hospitals, foster homes, inpatient care centers, and elderly facilities, allowing the physically and mentally challenged to experience outdoor adventure and inspire individuals that anything is possible," Pierwola says.

The World in 360 program started with a simple consumer camera that was available to anyone. The first model Milosz owned was the Theta S released in December 2015 by Ricoh that retailed for $300. This was a simple camera that paired with Ricoh's dedicated website where the images and video could be uploaded.

Soon after, YouTube integrated 360 video, and many websites sprung up that offered fascinating new tools for these unique images.

It's technology like this that enables voluntourists to document their good work, credit sponsors, thank donors, and illustrate that it's simply not that hard to help others while on the road.

$\sim$

Together we've traveled the world in these pages learning about the inspiring stories of selfless voluntourists who are just like you and me, except with perhaps more frequent flier miles and passport stamps. Each has personally benefitted as they combined both time off from school or work with one form of altruism or another.

Traveling while making a difference is clearly the best of both worlds.

If travel expands the mind, one thing I've learned from my own volunteer missions and through research for this book is that *meaningful* travel expands the heart.

You're not going to save the world. In fact, you're likely to learn and gain more from your volunteer experience than you give. Voluntourism will be an experience that, hopefully, will enrich your life, give it extra meaning, and provide valuable insights on your fellow human beings—insights that will serve you well the rest of your life.

Voluntourists travel to lend a helping hand and learn about different cultures and how they struggle for everyday survival. Their work spreads awareness of the plight of the less fortunate.

Such is the beauty of volunteer travel.

Wherever voluntourism takes you, don't forget to write.

Jeff Blumenfeld
Boulder, Colorado
editor@expeditionnews.com

Appendixes

A. VOLUNTOURISM RESOURCES

What are the best resources for finding the volunteer program perfectly matched to your interests? One handy guide is Charity Navigator, America's largest independent charity watchdog, which evaluates and rates charities based on their financial health, accountability, and transparency, with the goal of helping donors and volunteers make informed decisions.[1]

Here are some other organizations that you can consult before your bags are packed. For each one listed, there may be many more right for you.

All Hands and Hearts—Smart Response (allhandsandhearts.org)
In fall 2017, Happy Hearts Fund merged with All Hands Volunteers to create All Hands and Hearts—Smart Response to efficiently and effectively address the immediate and long-term needs of communities impacted by natural disasters. The group arrives early for first response and stays late to rebuild schools and homes in a disaster-resilient manner. To date they have rebuilt 201 safe, disaster-resilient schools in nineteen countries empowering 105,400 children and uplifting 1,170,000 community members.

American Hiking Society Volunteer Vacations (americanhiking.org)
Join a week of building and maintaining trails in diverse locations across the country. Volunteer Vacations foster public land stewardship and provide volunteers the opportunity to give back to the trails they love, and have a great time meeting new people. Crews consist of six to fifteen volunteers accompanied by a crew leader. Trips involve backpacking or day hiking, and accommodations vary from primitive campsites to bunkhouses or cabins.

Tools and supervision are provided by the host agency or organization. Search the website for the desired state, project rating, accommodations, and hiking distances.

Americares (americares.org)

Health-focused relief and development organization that responds to people affected by poverty or disaster with life-changing medicine, medical supplies, and health programs. In vulnerable regions, the group prepositions emergency supplies and helps communities reduce risk and prepare for disaster while training health care providers. Its emergency team launches a disaster relief operation uniquely suited for the crisis and conditions on the ground. Then they stay in that country for months and years, rebuilding hospitals and clinics and addressing targeted health needs of the community and restoring health care access.

ARCAS (arcasguatemala.org)

A nonprofit Guatemalan NGO formed in 1989 by a group of local citizens who became concerned as they saw their precious natural heritage—especially their wildlife—rapidly disappearing before their eyes. Among its goals are the rescue, rehabilitation, and release of wildlife, especially sea turtles.

Biosphere Expeditions (biosphere-expeditions.org)

Runs citizen science wildlife conservation research expeditions worldwide. Projects are not tours, photographic safaris, or excursions but research expeditions and citizen science wildlife conservation projects. The organization promotes sustainable conservation and preservation of the planet's wildlife by forging alliances between scientists and the public.

Cambodian Children's Fund (cambodianchildrensfund.org)

CCF transforms the country's most impoverished kids into tomorrow's leaders by delivering education, family support, and community development programs into the heart of Cambodia's most impoverished communities. The CCF Volunteer Program focuses on recruiting skilled volunteers with professional experience to assist in building capacity for ongoing development within the organization. Aside from some specific projects advertised, volunteers must be able to commit to at least three months.

Children's Global Alliance (childrensglobalalliance.org)

The organization was created in 2010 to fill the void of large-scale volunteer experiences for children ages twelve to seventeen. This most impressionable age group is capable of extraordinary things yet is rarely trusted with extraordinary opportunities.

Conservation Volunteers International Program (conservationvip.org)
This organization is dedicated to helping sustain some of the world's greatest landscapes, cultural sites, and biodiversity. Projects include maintaining and building trails, restoring archaeological sites, and protecting and restoring critical habitats.

Cross-Cultural Solutions (crossculturalsolutions.org)
Empowers passionate volunteers to work alongside an experienced team of local nationals to implement a proven approach to improving children's education and health. This collaboration ensures CCS generates a sustainable impact on individual children, as well as impacts that can scale to entire communities. The organization believes that through meaningful volunteer service it can build relationships and connections that are essential components to increased tolerance and global awareness. Its geographic focus is upon health, education, and economic volunteer opportunities in Central and South America, Europe, Asia, and Africa.

Cultural Vistas (culturalvistas.org)
A nonprofit exchange organization promoting global understanding and collaboration among individuals and institutions. It develops international professional experiences that create more informed, skilled, and engaged citizens. The group believes sustained immersion in a country and language and professional experience, even more than travel or study abroad, promotes confidence and skills that create successful careers and nurture leaders, whether they are community activists or change agents at a global level.

Discover Corps (discovercorps.com)
Aims to foster peace by forging ties of cultural understanding between people of different cultures. Founded upon the core tenets of volunteer service, sustainable travel, and cultural sensitivity, its social mission is to protect and preserve the geographic, ecological, and cultural environments they visit.

dZi foundation (dzi.org)
Since 1998, the dZi foundation has partnered with communities in the Everest region to build schools and community centers, start an agriculture program, and assist in earthquake recovery.

Earthwatch Institute (earthwatch.org)
Approximately one hundred thousand people have joined Earthwatch in the field, contributing roughly ten million hours of data collection—far more than scientists could have collected alone. A scientific background is not

required to be a volunteer, and no prior skills are necessary (except for a scuba certification for diving projects).

Fly for Good (flyforgood.com)
Specialists in humanitarian airfares—reserved groups of seats specifically for humanitarian travelers or those representing a nonprofit. These ticket prices are often significantly lower than the average published rate, which allow nonprofits and individuals to save money on their travel. Most people save 5 to 8 percent off what they might find online or directly through the airlines.

Give a Day Global (giveadayglobal.org)
Connects travelers with short-term volunteer opportunities at nonprofit organizations around the world with an emphasis on those located near an urban hub or tourist destination that involve the community they are serving and have staff that speak English fluently for interacting with volunteers.

GivingWay (givingway.com)
A social impact, for-profit tech company bringing "volunteering back to its roots, before all the noise, clutter and expensive middlemen took over. Just people & causes putting good intentions to good use." They connect volunteers and nonprofits at no cost—at last count 1,900 organizations in more than 115 countries.

GlobalGiving (globalgiving.org)
The largest global crowdfunding community connecting nonprofits, donors, and companies in nearly every country. It helps nonprofits access the tools, training, and support they need to be more effective.

Global Leadership Adventures (experiencegla.com)
Offers what they consider is a fresh, new approach to service learning abroad for intellectually curious and socially oriented teenagers. The program involves exploring historic and natural sites in different countries; learning the local culture, language, and history; and serving the community through meaningful volunteer efforts. Ultimately, GLA hopes these life-changing experiences will cultivate a global perspective and open-mindedness in students that will ultimately inspire them to become great leaders and global thinkers and seek positive change in their own communities.

Global Volunteers (globalvolunteers.org)
One of the oldest and largest human and economic development organizations engaging short-term volunteers on long-term development projects

internationally. Its service projects offer a renewable resource of expertise, energy, and compassion. GV has engaged more than thirty-three thousand international volunteers in more than two hundred communities in thirty-four countries on six continents since 1984, and they call themselves the "granddaddy of the volunteer vacation movement."

GoEco (goeco.org)
Eco-tourism company with a varied selection of affordable volunteer projects abroad. Opportunities include teenage volunteering, which is promoted as resume-builders for college and job applications. Teenage volunteering abroad through GoEco is also a way to cultivate a foreign language, meet people, and do your part to give back to less fortunate communities abroad.

Go Overseas (gooverseas.com)
The small company of twenty- and thirtysomething travelers facilitates travel opportunities around the world. Go Overseas shares volunteer opportunities, study and teach abroad programs, gap-year travel, language studies, and more.

GVI USA (gviusa.com)
Since 1998, GVI has been running multiple-award-winning high-impact conservation and community development programs worldwide. Volunteers gain practical experience, find new passions, and develop career or employability skills.

Habitat for Humanity (habitat.org)
Habitat for Humanity is a global nonprofit housing organization working in nearly 1,400 communities across the United States and in approximately seventy countries. Habitat's vision is of a world where everyone has a decent place to live and works toward that vision by building strength, stability, and self-reliance in partnership with people and families in need of a decent and affordable home.

HelpX (helpx.net)
An online listing of host organic farms, nonorganic farms, farmstays, homestays, ranches, lodges, B&Bs, hostels, and even sailboats that invite volunteer helpers to stay with them short term in exchange for food and accommodation.

Himalayan Voluntourism (himalayanvoluntourism.org)
The nonprofit provides a wide range of volunteering opportunities in rural Nepal depending upon the interest and skills of volunteers and also the needs

of local communities. It connects groups of volunteers from international schools, universities, corporate groups, and gap-year students with Nepalese communities.

Honduras Outreach (hoi.org)
Works in communities long term, empowering them to reach their full potential, and arranges short-term volunteer mission trips to accomplish long-range goals. HOI has a rich history in communities of Central America using an integrated approach that includes education, medical care, agriculture, facility construction, and spiritual development. By investing in communities over decades, it strives to see permanent and total transformation.

International Institute for Peace through Tourism (IIPT) (iipt.org)
Nonprofit organization dedicated to fostering and facilitating tourism initiatives that contribute to international understanding and cooperation, an improved environment, and the preservation of heritage, with the goal of helping to bring about a peaceful and sustainable world.

International Volunteer HQ (volunteerhq.org)
A volunteer travel company, working in over forty destinations around the world and placing thousands of volunteers abroad every year. IVHQ believes any traveler, anywhere in the world, is empowered to make a meaningful difference in the community they are visiting. It focuses on providing affordable volunteer travel experiences that are responsible, safe, and high quality. Programs heighten global awareness and cultural understanding through the skills and expertise volunteers bring to their host communities, and through the experiences and lessons that volunteers take back to their own countries and cultures.

Lead Adventures (lead-adventures.com)
Ecuadorian tour operator offering volunteer trips in Ecuador and the Galapágos Islands. The staff is born and bred Ecuadorian and circulates its revenues within the local community, significantly increasing employment and development. They generate jobs by hiring local guides and host families and porters, and they offer assistance to other local businesses in the tourism industry.

Leave No Trace (lnt.org)
Leave No Trace educates visitors on conservation, environmental stewardship, and responsible recreation. Volunteers may give presentations, run a booth at outdoor shows, or take on other tasks.

North Dakota Geological Survey Fossil Digs (dmr.nd.gov/ndfossil/digs/)
The North Dakota Geological Survey was created by an act of the North Dakota legislature in 1895. After more than 120 years, the Survey still serves as the primary source of geological information in the state. North Dakota is known for a plethora of fossil plants and animals and organizes volunteer digs from late June through August. Digs are offered in three categories: beginner, intermediate, and experienced. Volunteer tasks might include washing off dirt, chiseling rocks, organizing books, or typing.

Responsible Travel (responsiblevacation.com)
Founded in 2001, this organization promotes the concept of responsible tourism—treating local people with respect and fairness, which in turn pays back by delivering a more rewarding experience for the traveler. As an option, when you book a vacation, they will pay for a day trip for a disadvantaged child from a developing country to a game park, mountain, or museum.

Sea Turtle Conservancy (conserveturtles.org)
The world's oldest sea turtle research and conservation group dedicated to saving sea turtles from eminent extinction through rigorous science-based conservation. The organization carries out worldwide programs to conserve and recover sea turtle populations through research, education, advocacy, and protection of the natural habitats.

SEEDS (seeds.is)
SEEDS enables volunteers to get to know Iceland from a different perspective, to meet the locals, develop insight into Icelandic culture, learn new skills, gain international understanding, and give something back to the environment. Main activities relate to the promotion of environmental protection and awareness and intercultural understanding and peace through work on social, cultural, and environmental projects in the country.

ShelterBox USA (shelterboxusa.org)
This organization seeks volunteers to commit for a period of five years by deploying twice each year for three weeks at a time. The ShelterBox Response Team (SRT) delivers essential aid that people need to begin rebuilding their lives in the aftermath of a disaster. Sturdy, green ShelterBoxes contain family-sized tents specially designed to withstand the elements and provide people with temporary shelter until they are able to start the process of rebuilding a home. ShelterKits contain all the essential tools people need to start repairing and rebuilding homes.

Sierra Club (sierraclub.org)
The nation's largest and most influential grassroots environmental organization—with three million members and supporters. The group sponsors dozens of service trips per year, with more projects offered through sixty-four local chapters nationwide.

Thula Thula Volunteers Academy (thulathula.com)
Part of the South African Conservation Fund. Volunteers learn about game reserve and wildlife management (from survival skills to wildlife monitoring) and community skill development and education in the local communities. Includes a "back to nature" adventure in a bush camp at the Thula Thula Game Reserve. Only eight volunteers can apply per session. Proceeds of what volunteers pay are redistributed toward conservation projects.

Travel2Change (travel2change.org)
Honolulu-based nonprofit that connects tourists with service-oriented activities. The organization posts opportunities for travelers to take part in free, socially conscious service projects and excursions that wouldn't otherwise be available.

Travel with a Challenge (travelwithachallenge.com)
Travel with a Challenge is an eighteen-year-old globally popular travel information website largely addressing the interests and agendas of the educated, proactive, mature traveler, aged forty-five to eighty years old. It covers alternative travel including ecological, educational, cultural/historical, and volunteer vacations worldwide. There is also a selection of recommended volunteer vacation organizations and operators.

Trekking for Kids (trekkingforkids.org)
Organizes purpose-driven treks for socially conscious hikers in some of the world's most remote and iconic locations. A Trekking for Kids expedition provides trekkers with an opportunity to combine their thirst for adventure and the outdoors with their desire to help those less fortunate. TFK focuses on the orphans who live in the shadows of the world's most coveted adventure destinations.

Volunteer Forever (volunteerforever.com)
Takes the guesswork out of choosing a volunteer abroad program. Uses a database of eight hundred international volunteer organizations; 3,500 program reviews; and 11,600 volunteer-abroad fundraisers who have collectively raised $2 million for their trips.

Volunteer.gov (volunteer.gov)
America's Natural and Cultural Resources Volunteer Portal built and maintained by the Federal Interagency Team on Volunteerism (FITV) comprised of volunteer program coordinators from three cabinet-level departments. It's an e-government site with volunteer positions and events for citizens interested in volunteer service benefitting the nation's resources. The portal is a free, fast, and efficient way to match personal requirements and choice of volunteer work throughout America's vast land base and expansive resources. Requires a commitment to share one's knowledge, skills, time, and effort with others (the volunteering "ethos" or spirit), and a willingness to serve in a nonsalaried, nonstipend volunteer position with little or no remuneration beyond incidental expenses (arranged on a case-by-case basis and subject to the availability of funds).

VolunteerMatch (volunteermatch.org)
Free database of 120,000 volunteer organizations seeking to recruit upward of four million volunteers. In effect, it's a search engine for volunteer opportunities nationwide. Nonprofits sign up, and volunteers can search for them based on the location, the causes, and other criteria.

Volunteers for Outdoors Colorado (voc.org)
Enables volunteers to become active stewards of Colorado's natural resources. VOC works with conservation and land agencies and relies on thousands of people annually to provide a volunteer workforce for outdoor projects that take place across Colorado—from city parks and open spaces, to grasslands and foothills, to alpine meadows and peaks. The group offers projects for the general public as well as customized youth and business group projects in trail construction and maintenance, invasive species management, habitat restoration, gardening and planting, forestry management, flood and fire restoration, recreational improvement, and historic preservation. Volunteer assignments vary in type and difficulty level.

Volunteers for Peace (vfp.org)
This nonprofit offers over three thousand voluntary service opportunities around the world as an effective means of intercultural education, service learning, and community development. It also empowers host communities to work cooperatively for environmental sustainability, social justice, and peace. As advocates for civic engagement, the group encourages volunteers to apply their new skills as citizen diplomats, community activists, and global leaders.

Workaway (workaway.info)
Promotes fair exchange between budget travelers, language learners, or culture seekers who can stay with thousands of families, individuals, or organizations that are looking for help in over 165 countries.

WWOOF—Worldwide Opportunities on Organic Farms (wwoof.net)
A cultural and educational exchange that links people who are passionate about healthy food, healthy living, and a healthy planet. Volunteers live alongside their hosts in sixty-plus countries helping with daily tasks and experiencing life as a farmer.

B. BEST TRAVEL APPS

Finding the right app for your smartphone can be a daunting experience. In 2017, Android users were able to choose between 2.8 million apps. Apple's App Store remained the second-largest app store with 2.2 million available apps.[2]

Four percent of those are related to travel, or approximately eighty-eight thousand apps, some more obscure than others. Apps are available to read airport terminal restaurant menus (Grab), locate vegan and vegetarian restaurants in nearly 10,500 cities worldwide (HappyCow), find local hotels for a few hours of shut-eye (Dayuse), or rent cars directly from their owners (Turo).

For my volunteer trips, both domestic and international, I have a limited number of go-to apps that have worked for me. See if they work for you as well.

I consistently use Airbnb while searching for an alternative to expensive hotels and want to meet more locals; FlightAware to check the status of my flight; Google Translate to ask "where is the bathroom" in Spanish; Netflix for those unbearable airport delays; TripAdvisor to consult for the best local hotels and restaurants; Tile, to keep track of my keys and luggage; Uber, for ground transportation; and Yelp to locate services such as coffee shops, locksmiths, and gas stations.

Skype and WhatsApp allow me to call home at virtually no cost so long as I have a Wi-Fi connection.

Then there's Flightradar24, an ingenious Swedish Internet-based service that shows real-time aircraft flight information on a map. It includes flight tracks, origins and destinations, flight numbers, aircraft types, positions, altitudes, headings, and speeds. Flightradar24 has no real application and is sort of a time waster, but it is fascinating nonetheless.

For safety, consider CloseCircle, the lifestyle personal and travel security membership service that offers timely alerts relevant to your location; and Sitata, a community-based app that helps avoid tourist scams, quickly find hospitals, and stay up to date with real-time travel alerts.

The more you travel, the more you'll determine your own favorites as well.

C. FAVORITE TRAVEL BOOKS

I love the feel of paper books. Their heft. The tactile sensation of each page. The ability to dog-ear a corner and pick up exactly where I left off. When I travel, I do so without the paper jacket. I want to preserve the book on my bookshelf when I return. Another keepsake of my journey.

My dirty little secret, maybe you do this as well, is to handwrite somewhere on the inside cover where I was and what I was doing when I first cracked it open and dug in. When I'm gone and someone finds it in Goodwill, or buys it for $1 at a garage sale, they'll know those pages have been somewhere special.

Books on the road are especially meaningful thanks to another habit of mine: I tend to read those that relate to the destination. Lining my bookshelves at home are:

Annapurna by Maurice Herzog (1997), which I read in Nepal, where the tenth-highest mountain in the world (26,545 feet) looms over the north-central region of the country.

Arctic Dreams by Barry Lopez (1986). I consumed this voraciously during a visit to the Canadian town of Iqaluit, Baffin Island, Nunavut, while volunteering as communications director for explorers training for an Antarctic expedition.

Crossing Antarctica by Will Steger and Jon Bowermaster (1992). I know both adventurers, so I was eager to reread this again years later while off the coast of the Antarctic Peninsula. Plus, I was honored to be acknowledged within its pages for my role in helping the 1989–1990 Trans-Antarctica Expedition raise funding.

During the same trip, I also read *Endurance: Shackleton's Incredible Voyage* by Alfred Lansing (1959), *Shackleton* by Roland Huntford (1985), and *South: The Story of Shackleton's Last Expedition* (1919), written by Ernest Shackleton himself, the great polar explorer. It was particularly impactful to be engrossed in this memoir in 2010 while on a research vessel moored just off Point Wild on Elephant Island, the very same island that provided refuge for twenty-eight of Shackleton's men left imperiled after their ship, *Endurance*, sank in Weddell Sea ice.

Despite my decidedly old-school preference for reading ink on dead trees, there are times, I'll admit, when I succumb to the digital age and travel with an e-book. My Kindle accompanied me to Antarctica, to Nepal, and Norway, on extended trips where I preferred not to burden myself with added weight. The Kindle was perfectly fine, although I find that its reproduction of photographs and maps leave much to be desired.

If you're like me and view a long flight as a gift of time and not the horrid experience it can be, especially if trapped in a center seat in coach for thirteen hours from Qatar to JFK, you might enjoy reading one or more these other well-known travel books. They have accompanied me, in one form or another, for years. These are my favorites. They may become yours as well.

A Short Walk in the Hindu Kush by Eric Newby (2008). Humorous mountain-climbing expedition in the wild and remote Hindu Kush, in northeastern Afghanistan.

Arabian Sands by Wilfred Thesiger (1959). Travels across the Empty Quarter of the Arabian Peninsula—ten thousand miles by camel from 1945 to 1950.

How Not to Travel the World by Lauren Juliff (2015). Good thing you've gotten this far reading *Travel with Purpose*. Juliff's travelogue will make you want to destroy your luggage and burn your passport as she tells of bad luck and near-death experiences on the road. Ah, but then she meets a handsome New Zealander with a love of challenges.

In a Sunburned Country by Bill Bryson (2000). Australia is not all Foster's Lager and Crocodile Dundee. After you read this one, crack open *A Walk in the Woods.* Actually, all his travel books make you want to hold your mail, seek a sabbatical from work, and hit the road.

In Patagonia by Bruce Chatwin (1977). Full of anecdotes, history, and lots of raw details about a little-known area of the world.

Kon-Tiki, by Thor Heyerdahl (1950). It awakened feelings of wanderlust in many impressionable young readers, myself included.

Microadventures by Alastair Humphreys (2014). What's a "microadventure"? Quite simply it's an experience close to home, cheap, simple, short, and 100 percent guaranteed to refresh your life. A microadventure takes the spirit of a big adventure and squeezes it into a day or even a few hours.

On the Road, by Jack Kerouac (1957). This timeless classic tells of colorful characters who live life against a backdrop of jazz, poetry, and drug use.

Sea of Glory by Nathaniel Philbrick (2003). Lewis and Clark got all the publicity thirty years before, but the US exploring expedition of 1838 to 1842 was the granddaddy of American seagoing expeditions.

Seven Years in Tibet by Heinrich Harrer (1952). Harrer's autobiography details his dramatic escape from a British internment camp in India and his trek across the Himalayas, becoming one of the first Europeans to enter and settle in Lhasa. The book is better than the movie, for sure.

The Great Railway Bazaar by Paul Theroux (1975). You like trains? You'll like this one. Read it before long-distance travel by trains is no longer a thing.

The Innocents Abroad by Mark Twain (1869). An account of voyages from New York City to Europe and the Holy Land in June 1867. The book that made Twain an international star.

The Sun Also Rises by Ernest Hemingway (1926). Follows American expats and their love story as they meet up with a motley crew of British expats.

The Worst Journey in the World by Apsley Cherry-Garrard (1922). Best definition of the word *epic* you'll ever read.

Travels with Charley in Search of America by John Steinbeck (1962). The author's ten-thousand-mile adventure around the United States in 1960 with his French poodle, Charley, riding in a truck named Rocinante.

Video Night in Kathmandu by Pico Iyer (1988). Humorous and poignant essays about travel to Bali, Tibet, Nepal, China, the Philippines, Burma, Hong Kong, India, Thailand, and Japan.

D. VOLUNTOURISM VIDEOS

Before you depart, before you buy a backpack full of adventure clothing, before those inoculations, before you apply for that visa and renew your passport, it makes sense to fully understand what you're about to do—both the good, the bad, and the ugly. In researching this book, we found more videos pointing out the cons than the pros of voluntourism. No need to be discouraged. There are plenty of positive programs to consider. Just go in with your eyes open. These online videos will help you do so.

The Ethical Volunteer—An Introduction. The Ethical Volunteer identifies how to select the best volunteering opportunities that don't exploit the volunteer or the people they're helping.[3]

Being the Difference. Documentary about the importance and significance of teen volunteer work. Posted by Spotlight Story Productions and Young Dreamer Network.[4]

Travel Report—Voluntourism. Includes key questions to ask, such as "Am I going to make a difference? Am I going to be safe?" Includes television coverage about Fly for Good, international airfare experts who negotiate reduced humanitarian rates for nonprofits and their volunteers.[5]

The Voluntourism Experience. Video produced by Holbrook Travel based in Gainesville, Florida. Stephanie Kowacz discusses voluntourism and the rewarding experience of traveling while also lending a hand in a community abroad. Kowacz has participated in sea turtle conservation projects, reforestation projects, school renovations, and more.[6]

What You Should Know before Your Next Volunteer Trip. TEDxWalla-WallaUniversity talk by Heather Ruiz, who talks about her experiences as a volunteer working abroad and identifies the differences between volunteering and touring. Great advice here.[7]

The Voluntourist: Is Voluntourism Doing More Harm Than Good? Thirty-minute documentary questioning the impact of international volunteering on local communities.[8]

Volunteers Unleashed. 2015 CBC documentary follows volunteers to South America, Southeast Asia, and Africa, showing how "voluntourism" has become the fastest growing and the most controversial travel sector.[9] (Available in Canada online, or anywhere through rental on Amazon for $3.99.)

Who Wants to Be a Volunteer? Norwegian satire produced in English. Brutally honest. You'd expect to view something like this on *Saturday Night Live.* Seen over 1.2 million times.[10]

Notes

INTRODUCTION

1. Rajan Pokhrel, "Kathmandu Airport Ranked One of the Worst in the World," *Himalayan Times*, October 23, 2016, https://thehimalayantimes.com/nepal/kathmandu-airport-ranked-one-worst-world/.
2. Alison Gardner, "Learning to Love Voluntourists—Harnessing Their Energy and Curiosity for Volunteer Service Vacations," December 2008, http://www.transitionsabroad.com/listings/work/volunteer/articles/learning-to-love-voluntourists.shtml.
3. www.travelwithachallenge.com, accessed May 28, 2018.
4. Oxford Dictionaries, accessed May 28, 2018, https://en.oxforddictionaries.com/definition/voluntourism.
5. Goodreads.com, accessed May 28, 2018, https://www.goodreads.com/quotes/964873-wherever-you-turn-you-can-find-someone-who-needs-you.

CHAPTER I

1. Goodreads.com, accessed May 28, 2018, https://www.goodreads.com/quotes/1716-travel-is-fatal-to-prejudice-bigotry-and-narrow-mindedness-and-many.
2. Alexandra Wolfe, "Rick Steves's Plan for a Better World: More Travel," *Wall Street Journal*, February 2, 2018, https://www.wsj.com/articles/rick-stevess-plan-for-a-better-world-more-travel-1517598663.
3. Loren Grush, "Jeff Bezos: 'I Don't Want a Plan B for Earth,'" TheVerge.com, June 1, 2016, https://www.theverge.com/2016/6/1/11830206/jeff-bezos-blue-origin-save-earth-code-conference-interview.

4. Adventure Travel Trade Association, "20 Adventure Travel Trends to Watch in 2018," accessed May 28, 2018, https://www.adventuretravel.biz/research/20-adventure-trends-to-watch-for-2018/.

5. Rachel Pannett, "Anger Over Tourists Swarming Vacation Hot Spots Sparks Global Backlash," *Wall Street Journal*, May 22, 2018, https://www.wsj.com/articles/anger-over-tourists-swarming-vacation-hot-spots-sparks-global-backlash-1527000130.

6. Transformational.travel, accessed May 28, 2018, www.transformational.travel.

7. Everett Potter, "Transformational Travel with Michael Bennett," EverettPotter.com, June 21, 2016, https://www.everettpotter.com/2016/06/transformational-travel-with-michael-bennett/.

8. Diamond Resorts International, "New Research and Infographic: Vacation Much More Important Than 'Nice to Have,'" PRNewswire, August 26, 2014, https://www.prnewswire.com/news-releases/new-research-and-infographic-vacation-much-more-important-than-nice-to-have-272758061.html.

9. Maya Wesby, "The Exploitative Selfishness of Volunteering Abroad," *Newsweek*, August 18, 2015, http://www.newsweek.com/exploitative-selfishness-volunteering-abroad-363768.

10. Peter Greenberg, "When a Destination Is Too Popular: The Problem with Overtourism," PeterGreenberg.com, February 16, 2018, https://petergreenberg.com/2018/02/16/destination-popular-problem-overtourism/.

11. Peter Greenberg, "Travel Tip: Travel to the U.S. Continues to Drop," PeterGreenberg.com, February 9, 2018, https://petergreenberg.com/2018/02/09/travel-to-us-continues-to-drop/.

CHAPTER II

1. Starfish Project, "The Parable," accessed May 28, 2018, https://starfishproject.com/the-parable/.

2. HOI, Inc., accessed May 28, 2018, www.hoi.org.

3. HOI, Inc., accessed May 28, 2018, http://hoi.org/where-we-serve-rancho-el-paraiso/.

4. Maya Wesby, "The Help and Harm of the $2 Billion 'Voluntourism' Industry," *Wilson Quarterly*, July 23, 2015, https://webcache.googleusercontent.com/search?q=cache:mjfaltwZ-uQJ:https://wilsonquarterly.com/stories/the-help-and-harm-of-the-173-billion-voluntourism-industry/+&cd=1&hl=en&ct=clnk&gl=us&client=safari.

5. Carrie Kahn, "As 'Voluntourism' Explodes in Popularity, Who's It Helping Most?" *National Public Radio*, July 31, 2014, https://www.npr.org/sections/goatsandsoda/2014/07/31/336600290/as-volunteerism-explodes-in-popularity-whos-it-helping-most.

6. Eric Hartman, Cody Morris Paris, and Brandon Blache-Cohen, "Fair Trade Learning: Ethical Standards for Community-Engaged International Volunteer

Tourism," Middlesex University Research Repository, Middlesex University London, 108–16, http://eprints.mdx.ac.uk/17476/1/Pre-Proof%20Draft%20FINAL%20 FTL%20Ethical%20Prin%20THR.pdf.

7. Alison Gardner, "Learning to Love Voluntourists—Harnessing Their Energy and Curiosity for Volunteer Service Vacations," December 2008, http://www.tran sitionsabroad.com/listings/work/volunteer/articles/learning-to-love-voluntourists. shtml.

8. Voluntourism Institute, "Fresh (Mis)Perceptions on Voluntourism," March 24, 2014, https://voluntourisminstitute.wordpress.com/tag/voluntourists/.

9. Rachel Taft, "How to Make a Difference in the World While Traveling," *Travel & Leisure*, April 22, 2017, http://www.travelandleisure.com/trip-ideas/green-travel/travelers-as-citizen-diplomats.

10. Taft, "How to Make a Difference in the World While Traveling."

11. UnitedHealth Group, "Doing Good Is Good for You—2013 Health and Volunteering Study," accessed May 28, 2018, http://www.unitedhealthgroup.com/~/ media/UHG/PDF/2013/UNH-Health-Volunteering-Study.ashx.

12. Demetria Gallegos, "Research Finds Volunteering Can Be Good for Your Health," *Wall Street Journal*, April 22, 2018, https://www.wsj.com/articles/research-finds-volunteering-can-be-good-for-your-health-1524449280?mod=searchresults& page=1&pos=1.

13. UnitedHealthcare, "UnitedHealthcare Study Finds Americans Who Volunteer Feel Healthier and Happier," September 13, 2017, news release, https://news-room.uhc.com/news-releases/volunteering-for-all.html.

14. Sumedha Gupta, "Impact of Volunteering on Cognitive Decline of the Elderly," *Journal of the Economics of Ageing* 12 (February 2018), https://www .researchgate.net/publication/322894669_Impact_of_Volunteering_on_Cognitive_ Decline_of_the_Elderly.

15. Gallegos, "Research Finds Volunteering Can Be Good for Your Health."

16. Chase, "Millennials More Likely to Travel Abroad to Volunteer Than Other Generations, Marriott Rewards Credit Card from Chase Survey Reveals," *BusinessWire* press release, May 27, 2015, https://www.businesswire.com/news/ home/20150527005936/en/Millennials-Travel-Volunteer-Generations-Marriott-Rewards-Credit.

17. Kahn, "As 'Voluntourism' Explodes in Popularity, Who's It Helping Most?"

18. Matt Wastradowski, "Traveling for Good: Voluntourism Continues to Be a Top Travel Trend," RootsRated.com, June 12, 2017, https://rootsrated.media/blog/ traveling-for-good-voluntourism-continues-to-be-a-top-travel-trend/.

19. Dr. Marc Mancini, "The Five Things You Must Know about Millennials," The Travel Institute, accessed April 2, 2018, https://www.thetravelinstitute. com/2015/10/30/the-five-things-you-must-know-about-millennials/.

20. Nekton Deep Ocean Exploration, accessed May 28, 2018, www.nektonmis sion.org.

21. FreshWater Watch, "An Earthwatch Research Project Investigating the Health of Global Freshwater Ecosystems on a Scale Never Seen Before," accessed May 28, 2018, https://freshwaterwatch.thewaterhub.org.

22. National Biodiversity Network, accessed May 28, 2018, https://nbn.org.uk/.

23. Encyclopedia of Life, "Making Observations through iNaturalist," accessed May 28, 2018, http://eol.org/info/making_observations.

24. Nigel Winser, *"Half-Earth: Our Planet's Fight for Life* by Edward O Wilson," *Geographical*, September 3, 2016, http://geographical.co.uk/reviews/books/item/1886-half-earth-our-planet-s-fight-for-life-by-edward-o-wilson.

25. Hartman, Paris, and Blache-Cohen, "Fair Trade Learning."

26. GlobalSL, "Fair Trade Learning—Video, Tools, Research," accessed video May 28, 2018, https://globalsl.org/ftl/.

27. GlobalSL, "Fair Trade Learning."

28. Kaplan, "Going Global: Are Graduates Prepared for a Global Workforce?" accessed May 28, 2018, https://kaplan.com/wp-content/uploads/2016/09/Going-Global-Are-graduates-prepared-for-a-global-workforce-EIU-Kaplan-WhitePaper-2016.pdf.

29. Family Travel Association, accessed May 28, 2018, https://familytravel.org/welcome-to-the-family-travel-association/.

30. GVI, accessed May 28, 2018, https://www.gviusa.com.

31. Wikipedia, accessed May 28, 2018, https://en.wikipedia.org/wiki/List_of_countries_by_GDP_(PPP)_per_capita.

32. Touch the Sky Foundation, accessed May 28, 2018, https://touchtheskyfoundation.org.

33. Katherine Cassidy, "Walk This Way: Helping Orphans Thrive in Sierra Leone," *Ellsworth American*, September 8, 2017, https://www.ellsworthamerican.com/opinions/commentary/walk-way-helping-orphans-thrive-sierra-leone/.

34. GoFundMe, "Opening Our Orphanage for Girls," accessed May 28, 2018, https://www.gofundme.com/opening-our-orphanage-for-girls.

35. Alison Gardner, "Volunteer Vacations for Seniors," accessed May 28, 2018, http://www.transitionsabroad.com/publications/magazine/0409/volunteer_vacations_for_seniors.shtml.

36. Airbnb, "Social Impact Experiences," accessed May 28, 2018, https://www.airbnb.com/experiences/social-impact.

37. Airbnb, "Social Impact Experiences," accessed May 28, 2018, https://www.airbnb.com/experiences/82265.

38. Airbnb, "Social Impact Experiences," accessed May 28, 2018, https://www.airbnb.se/experiences/44548.

39. Airbnb, "Social Impact Experiences," accessed May 28, 2018, https://www.airbnb.com/experiences/106637.

40. Children's Global Alliance, accessed May 28, 2018, www.childrensglobalalliance.org.

41. GoEco, accessed May 28, 2018, www.goeco.org.

42. Farewell Travels, accessed May 28, 2018, www.farewelltravels.com.

43. Family Travel Association, accessed May 28, 2018, https://familytravel.org/welcome-to-the-family-travel-association/.

44. Pacific Blue Foundation, "The Beqa Lagoon Initiative," accessed May 28, 2018, http://pacificbluefoundation.org/projects/the-beqa-lagoon-initiative/.

45. Sefano Katz, Beqa Lagoon Initiative (BLI) with Pacific Blue Foundation (PBF), email received April 5, 2018, https://www.dropbox.com/s/x5iox5y4avjhsqz/TWP%20-%20BeqaLagoonInitiativeEmailApr52018.docx?dl=0.

46. The Andaman, accessed May 28, 2018, http://www.theandaman.com.

47. Eco-Business.com, "Discovery of an Underwater Treasure at the Andaman," accessed May 28, 2018, http://www.eco-business.com/press-releases/discovery-of-an-underwater-treasure-at-the-andaman/.

48. Zen Harmony Diving, accessed May 28, 2018, http://www.zenharmonydiving.com.

CHAPTER III

1. Shivani Vora, "How to Plan a Volunteering Vacation," *New York Times*, January 16, 2017, https://www.nytimes.com/2017/01/16/travel/how-to-plan-a-volunteering-vacation.html.

2. Dooley Intermed International, accessed May 28, 2018, dooleyintermed.org.

3. John Vidal, "Almost Half the World Cooking as If It Were the Stone Age, WHO Warns," *The Guardian*, March 21, 2016, http://www.theguardian.com/global-development/2016/mar/21/half-world-cooking-stone-age-world-health-organisation-report-dr-maria-neira.

4. Himalayan Stove Project, accessed May 28, 2018, www.himlayanstoveproject.org.

5. VolunteerMatch, accessed May 28, 2018, www.volunteermatch.org.

6. Thomas Moore, "Las Vegas Sees Record Tourism, Visitor Spending in 2016," *Las Vegas Sun*, March 14, 2017, https://lasvegassun.com/news/2017/mar/14/las-vegas-sees-record-tourism-visitor-spending-in/.

7. KNPR, Las Vegas radio station, "Poverty Is Rising in the Las Vegas Suburbs," March 2, 2016, https://knpr.org/knpr/2016-03/poverty-rising-las-vegas-suburbs.

8. Baby's Bounty, accessed May 28, 2018, www.babysbounty.org.

9. Lighthouse Charities, accessed May 28, 2018, www.lighthousecharities.net.

10. Lighthouse Charities, accessed May 28, 2018, http://www.lighthousecharities.net/new-blog/.

11. Three Square, accessed May 28, 2108, www.threesquare.org.

12. United States Census Bureau, "Quick Facts, Lake Havasu City, Arizona," accessed May 28, 2018, https://www.census.gov/quickfacts/fact/table/lakehavasucitycityarizona/PST045216.

13. Lake Havasu City Convention & Visitors Bureau, Lake Havasu City, Arizona, accessed May 28, 2018, www.golakehavasu.com.

14. Friends of the Bill Williams River and Havasu National Wildlife Refuges, accessed May 28, 2018, www.billwilliamsriver-havasufriends.org.

15. Adventure Scientists, accessed May 28, 2018, adventurescientists.org.

16. Richard Pérez-Peña, "What to Give Up for Lent? Smoking? Cursing? How about Plastic?" *New York Times*, February 15, 2018, https://www.nytimes.com/2018/02/15/world/europe/lent-plastic-church-of-england.html.

17. *Guinness World Records*, "Fastest Time to Visit All Sovereign Countries (Female)," accessed May 28, 2018, http://guinnessworldrecords.com/world-records/400940-fastest-time-to-visit-all-sovereign-countries-female.

18. *National Geographic*, "Explorers Festival," Friday, June 16, 2017, presentation by Gregg Treinish, Adventure Scientists, https://www.youtube.com/watch?v=wpYsv1YH3aw#t=02h25m11s.

19. *Insurance Journal*, "Car and Deer Collisions Cause 200 Deaths, Cost $4 Billion a Year," October 24, 2012, https://www.insurancejournal.com/news/national/2012/10/24/267786.htm.

20. Scienceinthewild.com, accessed May 28, 2018, scienceinthewild.com.

21. RickHodes.org, accessed May 28, 2018, www.RickHodes.org.

22. Airlines Ambassadors International, accessed May 28, 2018, http://airlineamb.org/eforms/nepal_air-intermed_mission/.

23. US Customs and Border Protection, "How to Apply for Global Entry," accessed May 28, 2018, https://www.cbp.gov/travel/trusted-traveler-programs/global-entry/how-apply.

24. World Health Organization, "Blindness and Vision Impairment Prevention," October 12, 2017, http://www.who.int/blindness/world_sight_day/2017/en/.

25. Andrew Jacobs, "A Simple Way to Improve a Billion Lives: Eyeglasses," *New York Times*, May 5, 2018, https://www.nytimes.com/2018/05/05/health/glasses-developing-world-global-health.html.

26. Skyship Films, "Gorkha: Gift of Sight," video accessed May 28, 2018, https://vimeo.com/256732590.

27. ShelterBox USA, accessed May 28, 2018, www.shelterboxusa.org.

28. Water Mission, accessed May 28, 2018, www.watermission.org.

29. Eagle Creek, accessed May 28, 2018, http://www.eaglecreek.com/live-work-travel.

30. ASAE (The Center for Association Leadership), accessed May 28, 2018, https://www.thepowerofa.org/power-of-a-research/.

31. ASAE, "Annual Meeting & Exposition," accessed May 28, 2018, https://annual.asaecenter.org/community.cfm.

32. The Borgen Project, "Causes of Poverty in Antigua and Barbuda," September 25, 2017, https://borgenproject.org/causes-of-poverty-in-antigua-and-barbuda/.

33. John Roberts, "Cruise Voluntourism: Ways to Give Back at Sea," *Cruise Critic*, September 21, 2017, https://www.cruisecritic.com/articles.cfm?ID=885.

34. HopeFloats, accessed May 28, 2018, http://www.hopefloats.org.

35. Princess Cruises, "Princess Cruises and Fathom Travel Add Impact Sailings to Caribbean," *PR Newswire* press release, March 2, 2018, https://www.prnewswire.com/news-releases/princess-cruises-and-fathom-travel-add-impact-sailings-to-caribbean-300607455.html.

36. Holland American Line, accessed May 28, 2018, https://www.hollandamerica.com/cruise-destinations/ExcursionDetails.action?excursionCode=100027144&portCode=CIO&destCode=&requestSource=shoreExcursions.

37. Holland American Line.

38. Holland American Line.

39. Holland American Line.

40. Holland American Line.

41. Lucas Peterson, "A 7-Night, $250 Cruise? Yes, and You Might Also Do Some Good," *New York Times*, September 29, 2016, https://www.nytimes.com/2016/10/02/travel/cheap-cruise-fathom-voluntourism-frugal.html.

42. Pack for a Purpose, accessed May 28, 2018, https://www.packforapurpose.org.

43. George W. Stone, "Traveler of the Year: Rebecca Rothney," National Geographic.com, accessed May 28, 2018, https://www.nationalgeographic.com/travel/travelers-of-the-year-2014/rebecca-rothney/.

44. Appalachian Mountain Club, "2018 Adult Volunteer Vacations," accessed May 28, 2018, https://www.outdoors.org/volunteer/volunteer-trails/adult-crews-full-list.

45. Leave No Trace, accessed May 28, 2018, www.LNT.org.

46. Volunteers for Outdoor Colorado, accessed May 28, 2018, http://www.voc.org.

47. World Wide Opportunities on Organic Farms, accessed May 28, 2018, http://wwoof.net.

48. Kibbutz Volunteer, accessed May 28, 2018, https://kibbutzvolunteer.com.

49. HelpX, accessed May 28, 2018, www.helpx.net.

50. Workaway.Info, accessed May 28, 2018, www.workaway.info.

51. TE on TV, "New Nomad: Christine Maxfield (Ep 8)," January 28, 2013, bitly.com/TravelAndEscape.

52. ARCAS, "ARCAS Volunteering in Hawaii (Guatemala)," accessed May 28, 2018, http://arcasguatemala.org/volunteering/volunteering-in-hawaii/.

53. Britt Stephens, "The Real Reason Princess Diana Had a Public Funeral," PopSugar, March 29, 2018, https://www.popsugar.com/celebrity/Princess-Diana-Funeral-Details-43518804.

54. Americares, "Airlift Benefit 2017," accessed May 28, 2018, https://www.americares.org/en/events/aab/2017/.

55. Trent Lott and Jason Grumet, "How to Fix Our $350 Billion Disaster Relief Problem," CNBC, November 10, 2017, https://www.cnbc.com/2017/11/10/hurricane-disaster-relief-costs-unsustainable-how-to-fix-it-commentary.html.

56. Americares, "Hurricanes 2017: The Road Back to Health," accessed May 28, 2018, https://www.americares.org/en/what-we-do/emergency-programs/ep-hurricanes2017/.

57. F. Scott Fitzgerald, *The Complete Short Stories and Essays, Volume 2*, 752, Simon and Schuster, 2004, https://books.google.com/books?id=YNN4kjbFY-CoC&pg=PA752&dq=This+is+worse+than+a+calamity;+it's+getting+to+be+a+nuisance.%22&hl=en&sa=X&ved=0ahUKEwipi6j5-NraAhUW3YMKHRYMCCkQ6AEILzAB#v=onepage&q=This%20is%20worse%20than%20a%20calamity%3B%20it's%20getting%20to%20be%20a%20nuisance.%22&f=false.

58. Elaine Glusac, "How Travelers Can Help Hurricane-Damaged Islands," *New York Times*, April 3, 2018, https://www.nytimes.com/2018/04/03/travel/volunteer-vacations-caribbean.html.

59. Friends of Virgin Islands National Park, accessed May 28, 2018, https://friendsvinp.org/.

60. Para la Naturaleza, accessed May 28, 2018, www.paralanaturaleza.org/en/.

61. Starwood Capital Group, "Anguilla's Largest Private Employers & Real Estate Owners Partner to Form Hurricane Irma Emergency Relief Fund," *PR Newswire* press release, October 4, 2017, https://www.prnewswire.com/news-releases/anguillas-largest-private-employers--real-estate-owners-partner-to-form-hurricane-irma-emergency-relief-fund-300531110.html.

62. Lila Battis, "Why You Should Go to Puerto Rico Now—and How to Help Once You're There," *Travel & Leisure*, May 2, 2018, http://www.travelandleisure.com/travel-news/why-you-should-go-to-puerto-rico-now.

63. Battis, "Why You Should Go to Puerto Rico Now."

64. US Fish & Wildlife Service, "National Key Deer Refuge," accessed May 28, 2018, https://www.fws.gov/refuge/National_Key_Deer_Refuge/what_we_do/get_involved.html.

65. All Hands and Hearts Smart Response, accessed May 28, 2018, www.allhandsandhearts.org.

66. Petra Němcová, "All Hands and Hearts," accessed May 28, 2018, https://www.hands.org/team/petra-nemcova-copy/.

CHAPTER IV

1. Plenty International, accessed May 28, 2018, www.plenty.org.

2. David Sheldrick Wildlife Trust, accessed May 28, 2018, www.sheldrickwildlifetrust.org.

3. Empowerment International, accessed May 28, 2018, www.empowermentinternational.org.

4. Walking Tree Travel, accessed May 28, 2018, www.walkingtree.org.

5. Cambodian Children's Fund, accessed May 28, 2018, www.cambodianchildrensfund.org.

6. Habitat for Humanity, accessed May 28, 2018, https://www.habitat.org/restores/volunteer.

7. VolunteerMatch, accessed May 28, 2018, https://www.volunteermatch.org/search?c=United+States&l=Denver%2C+CO&r=10&na=&k=denver&partner=&specialGroupsData.groupSize=noselection&advanced=1.

8. ReStore Volunteer Safety Video, Youtube.com, July 3, 2014, https://www.youtube.com/watch?v=TmWF8KlTwqE.

9. Restore Donation Valuation Guide, accessed May 28, 2018, https://restore.tchabitat.org/hubfs/DONATION%20VALUATION%20GUIDE%20(2).pdf?t=1524860060133.

CHAPTER V

1. US Department of State—Bureau of Consular Affairs, accessed May 28, 2018, https://travel.state.gov/content/travel/en/traveladvisories/traveladvisories.html.

2. Peter Greenberg, "US State Department Changes Travel Warning System," PeterGreenberg.com, January 16, 2018, https://petergreenberg.com/2018/01/16/us-state-department-travel-warning/.

3. U.S. Department of State—Bureau of Consular Affairs, Smart Traveler Enrollment Program (STEP), accessed May 28, 2018, https://travel.state.gov/con tent/travel/en/international-travel/before-you-go/about-our-new-products/staying-connected.html.

4. Stephanie Rosenbloom, "New Country Rankings Aim to Help Travelers Choose Safe Destinations," *New York Times*, January 19, 2018, https://www.nytimes.com/2018/01/19/travel/new-state-department-travel-advisories.html.

5. David O. Freedman, Lin H. Chen, and Phyllis E. Kozarsky, "Medical Considerations before International Travel," *New England Journal of Medicine*, July 21, 2016, https://www.nejm.org/doi/full/10.1056/NEJMra1508815.

6. Centers for Disease Control and Prevention, Vaccines & Immunizations, accessed May 28, 2018, www.CDC.gov/vaccines.

7. World Health Organization, "World Health Statistics," accessed May 28, 2018, http://www.who.int.

8. Centers for Disease Control, "Vaccine Information Statements (VISs)," accessed May 28, 2018, https://www.cdc.gov/vaccines/hcp/vis/index.html.

9. Passport Health, accessed May 28, 2018, www.passporthealthusa.com.

10. International Association for Medical Assistance to Travellers (IAMAT), accessed May 28, 2018, https://www.iamat.org.

11. Travel Guard, accessed May 28, 2018, www.travelguard.com.

12. Himalayan Holidays (P) Ltd., accessed May 28, 2018, www.himalayanholidaysnepal.com.

13. Nick Enoch, "French Boy, 10, Dies from Rabies after Being Bitten by a Puppy While on Holiday in Sri Lanka," DailyMail.com, October 19, 2017.

14. Bobos, accessed May 28, 2018, https://eatbobos.com/.

15. U.S. Environmental Protection Agency, "How to Find Bed Bugs," EPA.com, accessed January 17, 2018, https://www.epa.gov/bedbugs/how-find-bed-bugs.

CHAPTER VI

1. Wikipedia, "Westgate Shopping Mall Attack," accessed May 29, 2018, https://en.wikipedia.org/wiki/Westgate_shopping_mall_attack.

2. Raise the Roof Project, accessed May 29, 2018, www.raisetheroofproject.org.

3. Cherry Creek Presbyterian Church, accessed May 29, 2018, https://cherrycreekpres.org.

4. Allen Consulting, Inc., accessed May 29, 2018, www.allenconsulting.com.

5. Sylvia's Children, accessed May 29, 2018, www.sylviaschildren.org.

6. READ Global, accessed May 29, 2018, www.readglobal.org.

7. Claire Thomsen, "Chuzagang Library and Community Center," accessed May 29, 2018, http://www.clairethomsen.com/the-library/.

8. Children's Global Alliance, accessed May 29, 2018, www.childrensglobalalliance.org.

9. Sarah Cotton, "CGA 2017: Nepal Cambodia & Tanzania," accessed May 29, 2018, https://cottonsarah.blogspot.com/2016/06/up-high-down-low-too-slow.html.

CHAPTER VII

1. Maya Wesby, "The Exploitative Selfishness of Volunteering Abroad," *Newsweek*, August 8, 2015, http://www.newsweek.com/exploitative-selfishness-volunteering-abroad-363768.

2. Barbie Savior, Instagram site, accessed May 29, 2108, https://www.instagram.com/barbiesavior/.

3. Savonne Anderson, "'White Savior Barbie' Brilliantly Mocks Insincere Volunteer Selfies in Africa," Mashable.com, April 19, 2016, https://mashable.com/2016/04/19/white-savior-barbie/#NgLeH3OCnuqw.

4. Norwegian Students' and Academics' International Assistance Fund (SATH), "Who Wants to Be a Volunteer?," YouTube.com, November 7, 2014, https://www.youtube.com/watch?v=ymcflrj_rRc.

5. Radi-Aid, "How to Communicate the World," accessed May 29, 2018, https://www.radiaid.com/social-media-guide/.

6. *The Onion*, "6-Day Visit to Rural African Village Completely Changes Woman's Facebook Profile Picture," January 28, 2014, https://www.theonion.com/6-day-visit-to-rural-african-village-completely-changes-1819576037.

7. Lauren Kascak with Sayantani DasGupta, "#InstagrammingAfrica: The Narcissism of Global Voluntourism," *The Society Pages*, December 29, 2014, https://thesocietypages.org/socimages/2014/12/29/instragrammingafrica-the-narcissism-of-global-voluntourism/.

8. Michelle Staton, "7 Reasons Why Your Two-Week Trip to Haiti Doesn't Matter: Calling Bull on 'Service Trips' and Voluntourism," *Almost Doctor's Channel*, December 15, 2015, http://almost.thedoctorschannel.com/143232/#bOEbXEEXYejaIKZW.99.

9. Pippa Biddle, "The Problem with Little White Girls (and Boys): Why I Stopped Being a Voluntourist," Pippabiddle.com, accessed May 29, 2018, http://pippabiddle.com/2014/02/18/the-problem-with-little-white-girls-and-boys/.

10. CBC, Doc Zone, "Volunteers Unleashed," October 10, 2015, http://www.cbc.ca/doczone/episodes/volunteers-unleashed.

11. Association of Volunteers for Community Development (AVODEC), accessed May 29, 2018, http://www.avodec.brightnewideas.org.

12. Worldwide Opportunities on Organic Farms, accessed May 28, 2018, www.wwoofinternational.org.

13. Wesby, "The Exploitative Selfishness of Volunteering Abroad."

14. BBC, "Oxfam Sex Scandal: Haiti Suspends Charity's Operations," February 22, 2018, http://www.bbc.com/news/uk-43163620.

15. Angela Hawke and Alison Raphael, "Global Study on Sexual Exploitation of Children in Travel and Tourism 2016," Ministry of Foreign Affairs of the Netherlands, Defence for Children, and ECPAT, May 2016, http://globalstudysectt.org/wp-content/uploads/2016/05/Global-Report-Offenders-on-the-Move-Final.pdf.

16. Daniela Petrova, "A Vacation with a Purpose: Fighting Trafficking in Thailand," *New York Times*, May 11, 2017, https://www.nytimes.com/2017/05/11/travel/thailand-vacation-fighting-trafficking-exploitation-altruvistas.html.

17. Kai Schultz and Rajneesh Bhandari, "Noted Humanitarian Charged with Child Rape in Nepal, Stunning a Village," *New York Times*, May 11, 2018, https://www.nytimes.com/2018/05/11/world/asia/nepal-peter-dalglish-aid-pedophilia.html.

18. Mission Himalaya, accessed May 29, 2018, www.missionhimalaya.org.np.

19. Next Generation Nepal, "The Paradox of Orphanage Volunteering," accessed May 29, 2018, https://nextgenerationnepal.org/wp-content/uploads/2017/08/The-Paradox-of-Orphanage-Volunteering.pdf.

20. Next Generation Nepal, accessed May 29, 2018, www.nextgenerationnepal.org.

21. Next Generation Nepal, accessed May 29, 2018, https://www.nextgenerationnepal.org/ethical-volunteering/.

22. Staton, "7 Reasons Why Your Two-Week Trip to Haiti Doesn't Matter."

23. Biddle, "The Problem with Little White Girls (and Boys)."

CHAPTER VIII

1. No Barriers USA, accessed May 30, 2018, www.nobarriersusa.org.

2. SSWM, "Sustainable Sanitation and Water Management Toolbox," accessed May 30, 2018, www.sswm.info.

3. FirstGiving, accessed May 30, 2018, www.firstgiving.com.

4. The Hershey Company, "Hershey's Fund Raising," accessed May 30, 2018, www.hersheys.com/fundraising.

5. Sarah W. Papsun, music video, YouTube, accessed May 30, 2018, https://www.youtube.com/user/sarahwpapsun.

6. Jeff Anderson and Suzanne Andre, "Honeymoon for Humanity," YouCaring.com.

7. Anderson and Andre, "Honeymoon for Humanity."

8. Projects Abroad, Fundraising with Projects Abroad, "Get Our Fundraising Guide," accessed May 30, 2018, https://www.projects-abroad.org/how-it-works/fundraising/.

9. Double the Donation, "United Airlines' Corporate Responsibility Team," accessed May 30, 2018, https://doublethedonation.com/matching-gifts/united-continental-holdings.

10. Double the Donation, "Top Matching Gift Companies," accessed May 30, 2018, https://doublethedonation.com/matching-grant-resources/list-matching-gifts-companies/.

11. GoFundMe, "Results for Voluntourism," accessed May 30, 2018, https://www.gofundme.com/mvc.php?route=category&term=voluntourism.

12. Adam Moore, "HIV/AIDS Clinic Work in Uganda," GoFundMe.com, CCESSED May 30, 2018, https://www.gofundme.com/AdamUganda.

13. Brittany Edwardes, "Sports and Coaching Volunteer Abroad Programs," VolunteerForever.com, June 12, 2015, https://www.volunteerforever.com/article_post/sports-and-coaching-volunteer-abroad-programs.

14. Volunteer Forever, "Frequently Asked Questions," accessed May 30, 2018, https://www.volunteerforever.com/cms/faq.

15. Projects Abroad, Fundraising with Projects Abroad, "Get Our Fundraising Guide."

16. Fly For Good, accessed May 30, 2018, www.flyforgood.com.

17. Changes in Latitude Travel Store, accessed May 30, 2018, http://www.cil.com/travelshows/.

18. Himalayan Stove Project, accessed May 30, 2018, www.HimalayanStoveProject.org.

19. Pamela Johnston, Instagram, accessed May 30, 2018, @psj1970.

20. Fede Cabrera, "Their Only Portrait Argentina," GoFundMe.com, accessed May 30, 2018, https://www.gofundme.com/theironlyportrait2.

21. Marc Bryan-Brown, accessed May 30, 2018, www.Bryan-brown.com.

22. David Arnold, "Frank Hurley, Antarctica, the Kodak Vest Pocket," David Arnold Photography, January 25, 2016, http://davidarnoldphotographyplus.com/2016/01/25/frank-hurley-antarctica-the-kodak-vest-pocket/.

23. Milosz Pierwola, accessed May 30, 2018, http://AdventureMilo.com.

24. Milosz Pierwola, World in 360, accessed May 30, 2018, http://Worldin360.com.

APPENDIXES

1. Charity Navigator, accessed May 30, 2018, https://www.charitynavigator.org/.

2. Statista—The Statistics Portal, "Number of Apps Available in Leading App Stores as of 1st Quarter 2018," accessed May 30, 2018, https://www.statista.com/statistics/276623/number-of-apps-available-in-leading-app-stores/.

3. Robert Kelly, "The Ethical Volunteer—An introduction," YouTube.com, August 15, 2013, https://www.youtube.com/watch?v=a4TFIRCgV9E.

4. BeingTheDifferenceTV, "Being the Difference—2012 Documentary Film," YouTube.com video, March 9, 2013, Spotlight Story Productions and Young Dreamer Network, https://www.youtube.com/watch?v=h9FN-XHdUjQ.

5. Fly for Good, "Travel Report—Voluntourism," YouTube.com video, December 9, 2008, https://www.youtube.com/watch?v=mZsFd1KzaAs.

6. Holbrook Travel, "The Voluntourism Experience," YouTube.com video, July 25, 2013, https://www.youtube.com/watch?v=aTQ6JNygW6Q.

7. Heather Ruiz, "What You Should Know before Your Next Volunteer Trip," TEDxWallaWallaUniversity, YouTube.com video, June 13, 2016, https://www.you tube.com/watch?v=3NvNSNepz8Y&t=279s.

8. The Voluntourist, "Documentary 'The Voluntourist': Is Voluntourism Doing More Harm Than Good?" YouTube.com video, September 10, 2015, https://www.youtube.com/watch?v=E16iOaAP4SQ&t=1304s.

9. CBC, Doc Zone, "Volunteers Unleashed," YouTube.com video, October 10, 2015, http://www.cbc.ca/doczone/episodes/volunteers-unleashed.

10. Norwegian Students' and Academics' International Assistance Fund (SAIH), "Who Wants to Be a Volunteer?," YouTube.com, November 7, 2014, https://www.youtube.com/watch?v=ymcflrj_rRc.

ABOUT THE AUTHOR

1. Expedition News, accessed May 30, 2018, www.expeditionnews.com.

2. The Explorers Club, accessed May 30, 2018, www.explorers.org.

3. Dooley Intermed International, "Gorkha: Gift of Sight," Vimeo.com video, accessed May 30, 2018, https://vimeo.com/256732590.

Bibliography

Adventure Scientists, accessed May 28, 2018, adventurescientists.org.

Adventure Travel Trade Association, "20 Adventure Trends to Watch in 2018," accessed May 28, 2018, https://www.adventuretravel.biz/research/20-adventure-trends-to-watch-for-2018/.

Airbnb, "Social Impact Experiences," accessed May 28, 2018, https://www.airbnb.com/experiences/social-impact.

Airbnb, "Social Impact Experiences," accessed May 28, 2018, https://www.airbnb.com/experiences/82265.

Airbnb, "Social Impact Experiences," accessed May 28, 2018, https://www.airbnb.se/experiences/44548.

Airbnb, "Social Impact Experiences," accessed May 28, 2018, https://www.airbnb.com/experiences/106637.

Airline Ambassadors International, accessed May 28, 2018, http://airlineamb.org/eforms/nepal_air-intermed_mission/.

Alila Hotels, accessed May 28, 2018, https://www.alilahotels.com/manggis.

Allen Consulting, Inc., accessed May 29, 2018, www.allenconsulting.com.

All Hands and Hearts Smart Response, accessed May 28, 2018, www.allhandsand hearts.org.

Americares, "Airlift Benefit 2017," accessed May 28, 2018, https://www.americares.org/en/events/aab/2017/.

Americares, "Hurricanes 2017: The Road Back to Health," accessed May 28, 2018, https://www.americares.org/en/what-we-do/emergency-programs/ep-hur ricanes2017/.

Andaman, accessed May 28, 2018, http://www.theandaman.com.

Anderson, Jeff, and Suzanne Andre, "Honeymoon for Humanity," YouCaring.com.

Anderson, Savonne, "'White Savior Barbie' Brilliantly Mocks Insincere Volunteer Selfies in Africa," Mashable.com, accessed April 19, 2016, https://mashable.com/2016/04/19/white-savior-barbie/#NgLeH3OCnuqw.

175

Appalachian Mountain Club, "2018 Adult Volunteer Vacations," accessed May 28, 2018, https://www.outdoors.org/volunteer/volunteer-trails/adult-crews-full-list.

ARCAS, "ARCAS Volunteering in Hawaii (Guatemala)," accessed May 28, 2018, http://arcasguatemala.org/volunteering/volunteering-in-hawaii/.

Arnold, David, "Frank Hurley, Antarctica, the Kodak Vest Pocket," David Arnold Photography, accessed January 25, 2016, http://davidarnoldphotographyplus. com/2016/01/25/frank-hurley-antarctica-the-kodak-vest-pocket/.

ASAE, "Annual Meeting & Exposition," accessed May 28, 2018, https://annual. asaecenter.org/community.cfm.

ASAE (The Center for Association Leadership), accessed May 28, 2018, https:// www.thepowerofa.org/power-of-a-research/.

Association of Volunteers for Community Development (AVODEC), accessed May 29, 2018, http://www.avodec.brightnewideas.org.

Baby's Bounty, accessed May 28, 2018, www.babysbounty.org.

Barbie Savior, Instagram site, accessed May 29, 2108, https://www.instagram.com/ barbiesavior/.

Battis, Lila, "Why You Should Go to Puerto Rico Now—and How to Help Once You're There," *Travel & Leisure*, May 2, 2018, http://www.travelandleisure.com/ travel-news/why-you-should-go-to-puerto-rico-now.

BBC, "Oxfam Sex Scandal: Haiti Suspends Charity's Operations," February 22, 2018, http://www.bbc.com/news/uk-43163620.

BeingTheDifferenceTV, "Being the Difference—2012 Documentary Film," You-Tube.com video, March 9, 2013, Spotlight Story Productions and Young Dreamer Network, https://www.youtube.com/watch?v=h9FN-XHdUjQ.

Biddle, Pippa, "The Problem with Little White Girls (and Boys): Why I Stopped Being a Voluntourist," Pippabiddle.com, accessed May 29, 2018, http://pippabiddle. com/2014/02/18/the-problem-with-little-white-girls-and-boys/.

Bobos, accessed May 28, 2018, https://eatbobos.com/.

Borgen Project, "Causes of Poverty in Antigua and Barbuda," September 25, 2017, https://borgenproject.org/causes-of-poverty-in-antigua-and-barbuda/.

Bryan-Brown, Marc, accessed May 30, 2018, www.Bryan-brown.com.

Cambodian Children's Fund, accessed May 28, 2018, www.cambodianchildrensfund. org.

Cassidy, Katherine, "Walk This Way: Helping Orphans Thrive in Sierra Leone," *Ellsworth American*, September 8, 2017, https://www.ellsworthamerican.com/ opinions/commentary/walk-way-helping-orphans-thrive-sierra-leone/.

CBC, Doc Zone, "Volunteers Unleashed," YouTube.com video, October 10, 2015, http://www.cbc.ca/doczone/episodes/volunteers-unleashed.

Centers for Disease Control and Prevention, "Vaccines & Immunizations," accessed May 28, 2018, www.CDC.gov/vaccines.

Changes in Latitude Travel Store, accessed May 30, 2018, http://www.cil.com/ travelshows/.

Charity Navigator, accessed May 30, 2018, https://www.charitynavigator.org/.

Chase, "Millennials More Likely to Travel Abroad to Volunteer Than Other Generations, Marriott Rewards Credit Card from Chase Survey Reveals,"

BusinessWire press release, May 27, 2015, https://www.businesswire.com/news/home/20150527005936/en/Millennials-Travel-Volunteer-Generations-Marriott-Rewards-Credit.

Cherry Creek Presbyterian Church, accessed May 29, 2018, https://cherrycreekpres.org.

Children's Global Alliance, accessed May 28, 2018, www.childrensglobalalliance.org.

Cotton, Sarah, "CGA 2017: Nepal Cambodia & Tanzania," accessed May 29, 2018, https://cottonsarah.blogspot.com/2016/06/up-high-down-low-too-slow.html.

Diamond Resorts International, "New Research and Infographic: Vacation Much More Important Than 'Nice to Have,'" *PRNewswire*, August 26, 2014, https://www.prnewswire.com/news-releases/new-research-and-infographic-vacation-much-more-important-than-nice-to-have-272758061.html.

Dooley Intermed International, accessed May 28, 2018, Dooleyintermed.org.

Dooley Intermed International, "Gorkha: Gift of Sight," Vimeo.com video, accessed May 30, 2018, https://vimeo.com/256732590.

Double the Donation, "Top Matching Gift Companies," accessed May 30, 2018, https://doublethedonation.com/matching-grant-resources/list-matching-gifts-companies/.

Double the Donation, "United Airlines' Corporate Responsibility Team," accessed May 30, 2018, https://doublethedonation.com/matching-gifts/united-continental-holdings.

Eagle Creek, accessed May 28, 2018, http://www.eaglecreek.com/live-work-travel.

Eco-Business.com, "Discovery of an Underwater Treasure at The Andaman," accessed May 28, 2018, http://www.eco-business.com/press-releases/discovery-of-an-underwater-treasure-at-the-andaman/.

Edwardes, Brittany, "Sports and Coaching Volunteer Abroad Programs," VolunteerForever.com, June 12, 2015, https://www.volunteerforever.com/article_post/sports-and-coaching-volunteer-abroad-programs.

Empowerment International, accessed May 28, 2018, www.empowermentinternational.org.

Encyclopedia of Life, "Making Observations through iNaturalist," accessed May 28, 2018, http://eol.org/info/making_observations.

Enoch, Nick, "French Boy, 10, Dies from Rabies after Being Bitten by a Puppy While on Holiday in Sri Lanka," DailyMail.com, October 19, 2017, http://www.dailymail.co.uk/news/article-4997552/French-boy-dies-rabies-puppy-bit-him.html#ixzz52IlxLa7V.

Expedition News, accessed May 30, 2018, www.expeditionnews.com.

Explorers Club, accessed May 30, 2018, www.explorers.org.

Family Travel Association, accessed May 28, 2018, https://familytravel.org/welcome-to-the-family-travel-association/.

Farewell Travels, accessed May 28, 2018, www.farewelltravels.com.

FirstGiving, accessed May 30, 2018, www.firstgiving.com.

Fitzgerald, F. Scott Fitzgerald, *The Complete Short Stories and Essays, Volume 2* (New York: Simon and Schuster, 2004), 752, https://books.google.com/books?id=YNN-4kjbFYCoC&pg=PA752&dq=This+is+worse+than+a+calamity;+it's+getting+to+

be+a+nuisance.%22&hl=en&sa=X&ved=0ahUKEwipi6j5-NraAhUW3YMKHR
YMCCkQ6AEILzAB#v=onepage&q=This%20is%20worse%20than%20a%20
calamity%3B%20it's%20getting%20to%20be%20a%20nuisance.%22&f=false.

Fly For Good, accessed May 30, 2018, www.flyforgood.com.

Fly For Good, "Travel Report—Voluntourism," YouTube.com video, December 9, 2008, https://www.youtube.com/watch?v=mZsFd1KzaAs.

Freedman, David O., Lin H. Chen, and Phyllis E. Kozarsky, "Medical Considerations before International Travel," *New England Journal of Medicine*, July 21, 2016, https://www.nejm.org/doi/full/10.1056/NEJMra1508815.

FreshWater Watch, "An Earthwatch Research Project Investigating the Health of Global Freshwater Ecosystems on a Scale Never Seen Before," accessed May 28, 2018, https://freshwaterwatch.thewaterhub.org.

Friends of the Bill Williams River and Havasu National Wildlife Refuges, accessed May 28, 2018, www.billwilliamsriver-havasufriends.org.

Friends of Virgin Islands National Park, accessed May 28, 2018, https://friendsvinp.org/.

Gallegos, Demetria, "Research Finds Volunteering Can Be Good for Your Health," *Wall Street Journal*, April 22, 2018, https://www.wsj.com/articles/research-finds-volunteering-can-be-good-for-your-health-1524449280?mod=searchresults&page=1&pos=1.

Gardner, Alison, "Learning to Love Voluntourists—Harnessing Their Energy and Curiosity for Volunteer Service Vacations," December 2008, http://www.transitionsabroad.com/listings/work/volunteer/articles/learning-to-love-voluntourists.shtml.

Gardner, Alison, "Volunteer Vacations for Seniors," accessed May 28, 2018, http://www.transitionsabroad.com/publications/magazine/0409/volunteer_vacations_for_seniors.shtml.

GlobalSL, "Fair Trade Learning—Video, Tools, Research," accessed video May 28, 2018, https://globalsl.org/ftl/.

Glusac, Elaine, "How Travelers Can Help Hurricane-Damaged Islands," *New York Times*, April 3, 2018, https://www.nytimes.com/2018/04/03/travel/volunteer-vacations-caribbean.html.

GoEco, accessed May 28, 2018, www.goeco.org.

GoFundMe, "Opening Our Orphanage for Girls," accessed May 28, 2018, https://www.gofundme.com/opening-our-orphanage-for-girls.

GoFundMe, Results for Voluntourism, accessed May 30, 2018, https://www.gofundme.com/mvc.php?route=category&term=voluntourism.

Goodreads.com, Albert Schweitzer quote, accessed May 28, 2018, https://www.goodreads.com/quotes/964873-wherever-you-turn-you-can-find-someone-who-needs-you.

Goodreads.com, Mark Twain quote, accessed May 28, 2018, https://www.goodreads.com/quotes/1716-travel-is-fatal-to-prejudice-bigotry-and-narrow-mindedness-and-many.

Greenberg, Peter, "Travel Tip: Travel to the U.S. Continues to Drop," PeterGreenberg.com, February 9, 2018, https://petergreenberg.com/2018/02/09/travel-to-us-continues-to-drop/.

Greenberg, Peter. "U.S. State Department Changes Travel Warning System," Pe terGreenberg.com, January 16, 2018, https://petergreenberg.com/2018/01/16/us-state-department-travel-warning/.

Greenberg, Peter, "When a Destination Is Too Popular: The Problem with Overtourism," PeterGreenberg.com, February 16, 2018, https://petergreenberg.com/2018/02/16/destination-popular-problem-overtourism/.

Grush, Loren, "Jeff Bezos: 'I Don't Want a Plan B for Earth,'" TheVerge.com, June 1, 2016, https://www.theverge.com/2016/6/1/11830206/jeff-bezos-blue-origin-save-earth-code-conference-interview.

Guinness World Records, "Fastest Time to Visit All Sovereign Countries (Female)," accessed May 28, 2018, http://guinnessworldrecords.com/world-records/400940-fastest-time-to-visit-all-sovereign-countries-female.

Gupta, Sumedha, "Impact of Volunteering on Cognitive Decline of the Elderly," *Journal of the Economics of Ageing*," February 12, 2018, https://www.researchgate.net/publication/322894669_Impact_of_Volunteering_on_Cognitive_Decline_of_the_Elderly.

GVI, accessed May 28, 2018, https://www.gviusa.com.

Habitat for Humanity, accessed May 28, 2018, https://www.habitat.org/restores/volunteer.

Hartman, Eric, Cody Morris Paris, and Brandon Blache-Cohen, "Fair Trade Learning: Ethical Standards for Community-Engaged International Volunteer Tourism," Middlesex University Research Repository, Middlesex University London, 2014, 108–16. http://eprints.mdx.ac.uk/17476/1/Pre-Proof%20Draft%20FINAL%20FTL%20Ethical%20Prin%20THR.pdf.

Hawke, Angela, and Alison Raphael, "Global Study on Sexual Exploitation of Children in Travel and Tourism 2016," Ministry of Foreign Affairs of the Netherlands, Defence for Children, and ECPAT, May 2016, http://globalstudysectt.org/wp-content/uploads/2016/05/Global-Report-Offenders-on-the-Move-Final.pdf.

HelpX, accessed May 28, 2018, www.helpx.net.

Hershey Company, "Hershey's Fund Raising," accessed May 30, 2018, www.hersheys.com/fundraising.

Himalayan Holidays (P) Ltd., accessed May 28, 2018, www.himalayanholidaysnepal.com.

Himalayan Stove Project, accessed May 28, 2018, www.himlayanstoveproject.org.

HOI, Inc., accessed May 28, 2018, www.hoi.org.

HOI, Inc., accessed May 28, 2018, http://hoi.org/where-we-serve-rancho-el-para iso/.

Holbrook Travel, "The Voluntourism Experience," YouTube.com video, July 25, 2013, https://www.youtube.com/watch?v=aTQ6JNygW6Q.

Holland American Line, accessed May 28, 2018, https://www.hollandamerica.com/cruise-destinations/ExcursionDetails.action?excursionCode=100027144&portCode=CIO&destCode=&requestSource=shoreExcursions.

Holland American Line, accessed May 28, 2018, http://www.hollandamerica.com/cruise-destinations/ExcursionDetails.action?excursionCode=2013&portCode=AM1&destCode=&requestSource=shoreExcursions.

Holland American Line, accessed May 28, 2018, http://www.hollandamerica.com/ cruise-destinations/ExcursionDetails.action?excursioncode=100025206&portCod e=HUX&destCode=&requestSource=shoreExcursions.

Holland American Line, accessed May 28, 2018, https://www.hollandamerica.com/ cruise-destinations/ExcursionDetails.action?excursioncode=1010048231&portCo de=AMB&destCode=&requestSource=shoreExcursions.

Hope Floats, accessed May 28, 2018, http://www.hopefloats.org.

Insurance Journal, "Car and Deer Collisions Cause 200 Deaths, Cost $4 Billion a Year," October 24, 2012, https://www.insurancejournal.com/news/na tional/2012/10/24/267786.htm.

International Association for Medical Assistance to Travellers (IAMAT), accessed May 28, 2018, https://www.iamat.org.

Jacobs, Andrew, "A Simple Way to Improve a Billion Lives: Eyeglasses," *New York Times*, May 5, 2018, https://www.nytimes.com/2018/05/05/health/glasses-devel oping-world-global-health.html.

Johnston, Pamela, Instagram account, accessed May 30, 2018, @psj1970.

Kahn, Carrie, "As 'Voluntourism' Explodes in Popularity, Who's It Helping Most?" *National Public Radio*, July 31, 2014, https://www.npr.org/sections/goatsand soda/2014/07/31/336600290/as-voluntourism-explodes-in-popularity-whos-it-helping-most.

Kaplan, "Going Global—Are Graduates Prepared for a Global Workforce?" accessed May 28, 2018, https://kaplan.com/wp-content/uploads/2016/09/Going-Global-Are-graduates-prepared-for-a-global-workforce-EIU-Kaplan-WhitePaper-2016. pdf.

Kascak, Lauren, with Sayantani DasGupta, MD MPH, "#InstagrammingAfrica: The Narcissism of Global Voluntourism," *The Society Pages*, December 29, 2014, https://thesocietypages.org/socimages/2014/12/29/instragrammingafrica-the-nar cissism-of-global-voluntourism/.

Katz, Stefano, Beqa Lagoon Initiative (BLI) with Pacific Blue Foundation (PBF), email received April 5, 2018, https://www.dropbox.com/s/x5iox5y4avjhsqz/ TWP%20-%20BeqaLagoonInitiativeEmailApr52018.docx?dl=0.

Kelly, Robert, "The Ethical Volunteer—An Introduction," YouTube.com video, August 15, 2013, https://www.youtube.com/watch?v=a4TFIRCgV9E.

Kibbutz Volunteer, accessed May 28, 2018, https://kibbutzvolunteer.com.

KNPR, Las Vegas radio station, "Poverty Is Rising in the Las Vegas Suburbs," March 2, 2016, https://knpr.org/knpr/2016-03/poverty-rising-las-vegas-suburbs.

Lake Havasu City Convention & Visitors Bureau, website, Lake Havasu City, Arizona, accessed May 28, 2018, www.golakehavasu.com.

Leave No Trace, accessed May 28, 2018, www.LNT.org.

Lighthouse Charities, accessed May 28, 2018, www.lighthousecharities.net.

Lighthouse Charities, accessed May 28, 2018, http://www.lighthousecharities.net/ new-blog/.

Lott, Trent, and Jason Grumet, "How to Fix Our $350 Billion Disaster Relief Problem," CNBC, November 10, 2017, https://www.cnbc.com/2017/11/10/hurricane-disaster-relief-costs-unsustainable-how-to-fix-it-commentary.html.

Mancini, Marc, "The Five Things You Must Know about Millennials," The Travel Institute, accessed April 2, 2018, https://www.thetravelinstitute.com/2015/10/30/the-five-things-you-must-know-about-millennials/.

Mission Himalaya, accessed May 29, 2018, www.missionhimalaya.org.np.

Moore, Adam, "HIV/AIDS Clinic Work in Uganda," GoFundMe.com, accessed May 30, 2018, https://www.gofundme.com/AdamUganda.

Moore, Thomas, "Las Vegas Sees Record Tourism, Visitor Spending in 2016," *Las Vegas Sun*, March 14, 2017, https://lasvegassun.com/news/2017/mar/14/las-vegas-sees-record-tourism-visitor-spending-in/.

National Biodiversity Network, accessed May 28, 2018, https://nbn.org.uk/.

National Geographic, "Explorers Festival," June 16, 2017, presentation by Gregg Treinish Adventure Scientists, https://www.youtube.com/watch?v=wpYsvlYH3a w#t=02h25m11s.

Nekton Deep Ocean Exploration, accessed May 28, 2018, www.nektonmission.org.

Němcová, Petra, "All Hands and Hearts," accessed May 28, 2018, https://www.hands.org/team/petra-nemcova-copy/.

Next Generation Nepal, accessed May 29, 2018, www.nextgenerationnepal.org.

Next Generation Nepal, accessed May 29, 2018, https://www.nextgenerationnepal.org/ethical-volunteering/.

Next Generation Nepal, "The Paradox of Orphanage Volunteering," accessed May 29, 2018, https://nextgenerationnepal.org/wp-content/uploads/2017/08/The-Paradox-of-Orphanage-Volunteering.pdf.

No Barriers USA, accessed May 30, 2018, www.nobarriersusa.org.

Norwegian Students' and Academics' International Assistance Fund (SAIH), "Who Wants to Be a Volunteer?" YouTube.com, November 7, 2014, https://www.youtube.com/watch?v=ymcflrj_rRc.

Onion, The, "6-Day Visit to Rural African Village Completely Changes Woman's Facebook Profile Picture," January 28, 2014, https://www.theonion.com/6-day-visit-to-rural-african-village-completely-changes-1819576037.

Oxford Dictionaries, accessed May 28, 2018, https://en.oxforddictionaries.com/definition/voluntourism.

Pacific Blue Foundation, "The Beqa Lagoon Initiative," accessed May 28, 2018, http://pacificbluefoundation.org/projects/the-beqa-lagoon-initiative/.

Pack for a Purpose, accessed May 28, 2018, https://www.packforapurpose.org.

Pannett, Rachel, "Anger over Tourists Swarming Vacation Hot Spots Sparks Global Backlash," *Wall Street Journal*, May 22, 2018, https://www.wsj.com/articles/anger-over-tourists-swarming-vacation-hot-spots-sparks-global-backlash-1527000130.

Papsun, Sarah W., music video, YouTube, accessed May 30, 2018, https://www.youtube.com/user/sarahwpapsun.

Para la Naturaleza, accessed May 28, 2018, www.paralanaturaleza.org/en/.

Passport Health, accessed May 28, 2018, www.passporthealthusa.com.

Pérez-Peña, Richard, "What to Give Up for Lent? Smoking? Cursing? How about Plastic?" *New York Times*, February 15, 2018, https://www.nytimes.com/2018/02/15/world/europe/lent-plastic-church-of-england.html.

Peterson, Lucas, "A 7-Night, $250 Cruise? Yes, and You Might Also Do Some Good," *New York Times*, September 29, 2016, https://www.nytimes.com/2016/10/02/travel/cheap-cruise-fathom-voluntourism-frugal.html.

Petrova, Daniela, "A Vacation with a Purpose: Fighting Trafficking in Thailand," *New York Times*, May 11, 2017, https://www.nytimes.com/2017/05/11/travel/thailand-vacation-fighting-trafficking-exploitation-altruvistas.html.

Pierwola, Milosz, accessed May 30, 2018, http://AdventureMilo.com.

Pierwola, Milosz, World in 360, accessed May 30, 2018, http://Worldin360.com.

Plenty International, accessed May 28, 2018, www.plenty.org.

Pokhrel, Rajan, "Kathmandu Airport Ranked One of the Worst in the World," *Himalayan Times*, October 23, 2016, https://thehimalayantimes.com/nepal/kathmandu-airport-ranked-one-worst-world/.

Potter, Everett, "Transformational Travel with Michael Bennett," EverettPotter.com, June 21, 2016, https://www.everettpotter.com/2016/06/transformational-travel-with-michael-bennett/.

Princess Cruises, "Princess Cruises and Fathom Travel Add Impact Sailings to Caribbean," *PR Newswire* press release, March 2, 2018, https://www.prnewswire.com/news-releases/princess-cruises-and-fathom-travel-add-impact-sailings-to-caribbean-300607455.html.

Projects Abroad, Fundraising with Projects Abroad, "Get Our Fundraising Guide," accessed May 30, 2018, https://www.projects-abroad.org/how-it-works/fundraising/.

Radi-Aid, "How to Communicate the World," accessed May 29, 2018, https://www.radiaid.com/social-media-guide/.

Raise the Roof Project, accessed May 29, 2018, www.raisetheroofproject.org.

READ Global, accessed May 29, 2018, www.readglobal.org.

Restore Donation Valuation Guide, accessed May 28, 2018, https://restore.tchabitat.org/hubfs/DONATION%20VALUATION%20GUIDE%20(2).pdf?t=1524860060133.

ReStore Volunteer Safety Video, Youtube.com, July 3, 2014, https://www.youtube.com/watch?v=TmWF8KlTwqE.

RickHodes.org, accessed May 28, 2018, www.RickHodes.org.

Roberts, John, "Cruise Voluntourism: Ways to Give Back at Sea," *Cruise Critic*, September 21, 2017, https://www.cruisecritic.com/articles.cfm?ID=885https://www.cruisecritic.com/articles.cfm?ID=885https://www.cruisecritic.com/articles.cfm?ID=885.

Rosenbloom, Stephanie, "New Country Rankings Aim to Help Travelers Choose Safe Destinations," *New York Times*, January 19, 2018, https://www.nytimes.com/2018/01/19/travel/new-state-department-travel-advisories.html.

Ruiz, Heather, "What You Should Know Before Your Next Volunteer Trip," TEDxWallaWallaUniversity, YouTube.com video, June 13, 2016, https://www.youtube.com/watch?v=3NvNSNepz8Y&t=279s.

Schultz, Kai, and Rajneesh Bhandari, "Noted Humanitarian Charged with Child Rape in Nepal, Stunning a Village," *New York Times*, May 11, 2018, https://www.nytimes.com/2018/05/11/world/asia/nepal-peter-dalglish-aid-pedophilia.html.

Scienceinthewild.com, accessed May 28, 2018, scienceinthewild.com.

Sheldrick Wildlife Trust, accessed May 28, 2018, www.sheldrickwildlifetrust.org.

ShelterBox USA, accessed May 28, 2018, www.shelterboxusa.org.

Skyship Films, "Gorkha: Gift of Sight," video accessed May 28, 2018, https://vimeo.com/256732590.

SSWM, "Sustainable Sanitation and Water Management Toolbox," accessed May 30, 2018, www.sswm.info.

Starfish Project, "The Parable," accessed May 28, 2018, https://starfishproject.com/the-parable/.

Starwood Capital Group, "Anguilla's Largest Private Employers & Real Estate Owners Partner to Form Hurricane Irma Emergency Relief Fund," *PR Newswire* press release, October 4, 2017, https://www.prnewswire.com/news-releases/anguillas-largest-private-employers--real-estate-owners-partner-to-form-hurricane-irma-emergency-relief-fund-300531110.html.

Statista—The Statistics Portal, "Number of Apps Available in Leading App Stores as of 1st Quarter 2018," accessed May 30, 2018, https://www.statista.com/statistics/276623/number-of-apps-available-in-leading-app-stores/.

Staton, Michelle, "7 Reasons Why Your Two-Week Trip to Haiti Doesn't Matter: Calling Bull on 'Service Trips' and Voluntourism," *Almost Doctor's Channel*, December 15, 2015, http://almost.thedoctorschannel.com/143232/#bOEbXEEXYejaIKZW.99.

Stephens, Britt, "The Real Reason Princess Diana Had a Public Funeral," PopSugar, March 29, 2018, https://www.popsugar.com/celebrity/Princess-Diana-Funeral-Details-43518804.

Stone, George W., "Traveler of the Year: Rebecca Rothney," National Geographic.com, accessed May 28, 2018, https://www.nationalgeographic.com/travel/travelers-of-the-year-2014/rebecca-rothney/.

Sylvia's Children, accessed May 29, 2018, www.sylviaschildren.org.

Taft, Rachel, "How to Make a Difference in the World While Traveling," *Travel & Leisure*, April 22, 2017, http://www.travelandleisure.com/trip-ideas/green-travel/travelers-as-citizen-diplomats.

TE on TV, "New Nomad: Christine Maxfield (Ep 8)," January 28, 2013, bitly.com/TravelAndEscape.

Thomsen, Claire, "Chuzagang Library and Community Center," accessed May 29, 2018, http://www.clairethomsen.com/the-library/.

Three Square, accessed May 28, 2108, www.threesquare.org.

Touch the Sky Foundation, accessed May 28, 2018, https://touchtheskyfoundation.org.

Transformational.travel, accessed May 28, 2018, www.transformational.travel.

Travel Guard, accessed May 28, 2018, www.travelguard.com.

TravelWithaChallenge.com, accessed May 28, 2018, www.travelwithachallenge.com.

UnitedHealthcare, "UnitedHealthcare Study Finds Americans Who Volunteer Feel Healthier and Happier," September 13, 2017, news release, https://newsroom.uhc.com/news-releases/volunteering-for-all.html.

UnitedHealth Group, "Doing Good Is Good for You—2013 Health and Volunteer-ing Study," accessed May 28, 2018, http://www.unitedhealthgroup.com/~/media/UHG/PDF/2013/UNH-Health-Volunteering-Study.ashx.

U.S. Census Bureau, "Quick Facts, Lake Havasu City, Arizona," accessed May 28, 2018, https://www.census.gov/quickfacts/fact/table/lakehavasucitycityarizona/PST045216.

U.S. Customs and Border Protection, "How to Apply for Global Entry," accessed May 28, 2018, https://www.cbp.gov/travel/trusted-traveler-programs/global-en try/how-apply.

U.S. Department of State—Bureau of Consular Affairs, accessed May 28, 2018, https://travel.state.gov/content/travel/en/traveladvisories/traveladvisories.html.

U.S. Department of State—Bureau of Consular Affairs, "Smart Traveler Enroll-ment Program (STEP)," accessed May 28, 2018, https://travel.state.gov/content/travel/en/international-travel/before-you-go/about-our-new-products/staying-connected.html.

U.S. Environmental Protection Agency, "How to Find Bed Bugs," EPA.com, ac-cessed January 17, 2018, https://www.epa.gov/bedbugs/how-find-bed-bugs.

U.S. Fish & Wildlife Service, National Key Deer Refuge, accessed May 28, 2018, https://www.fws.gov/refuge/National_Key_Deer_Refuge/what_we_do/get_in volved.html.

Vidal, John, "Almost Half the World Cooking as If It Were the Stone Age, WHO Warns," *The Guardian*, March 21, 2016, http://www.theguardian.com/global-development/2016/mar/21/half-world-cooking-stone-age-world-health-organisa tion-report-dr-maria-neira.

Volunteer Forever, Frequently Asked Questions, accessed May 30, 2018, https://www.volunteerforever.com/cms/faq.

VolunteerMatch, accessed May 28, 2018, www.volunteermatch.org.

VolunteerMatch, accessed May 28, 2018, https://www.volunteermatch.org/search?c =United+States&l=Denver%2C+CO&r=10&na=&k=denver&partner=&specialG roupsData.groupSize=noselection&advanced=1.

Volunteers for Outdoor Colorado, accessed May 28, 2018, http://www.voc.org.

Voluntourism Institute, "Fresh (Mis)Perceptions on Voluntourism," March 24, 2014, https://voluntourisminstitute.wordpress.com/tag/voluntourists/.

Voluntourist, "Documentary 'The Voluntourist': Is Voluntourism Doing More Harm Than Good?" YouTube.com video, September 10, 2015, https://www.youtube.com/watch?v=E16iOaAP4SQ&t=1304s.

Vora, Shivani, "How to Plan a Volunteering Vacation," *New York Times*, January 16, 2017, https://www.nytimes.com/2017/01/16/travel/how-to-plan-a-volunteering-vacation.html.

Walking Tree Travel, accessed May 28, 2018, www.walkingtree.org.

Wastradowski, Matt, "Traveling for Good: Voluntourism Continues to Be a Top Travel Trend," RootsRated.com, June 12, 2017, https://rootsrated.media/blog/traveling-for-good-voluntourism-continues-to-be-a-top-travel-trend/.

Water Mission, accessed May 28, 2018, www.watermission.org.

Wesby, Maya, "The Exploitative Selfishness of Volunteering Abroad," *Newsweek*, August 18, 2015, http://www.newsweek.com/exploitative-selfishness-volunteering-abroad-363768.

Wesby, Maya, "The Help and Harm of the $2 Billion 'Voluntourism' Industry," *Wilson Quarterly*, July 23, 2015, https://webcache.googleusercontent.com/search?q=cache:mjfaltwZ-uQJ:https://wilsonquarterly.com/stories/the-help-and-harm-of-the-173-billion-voluntourism-industry/+&cd=1&hl=en&ct=clnk&gl=us&client=safari.

Wikipedia, accessed May 28, 2018, https://en.wikipedia.org/wiki/List_of_countries_by_GDP_(PPP)_per_capita.

Wikipedia, "Westgate Shopping Mall Attack," accessed May 29, 2018, https://en.wikipedia.org/wiki/Westgate_shopping_mall_attack.

Winser, Nigel, "*Half-Earth: Our Planet's Fight for Life* by Edward O. Wilson," *Geographical*, September 3, 2016, http://geographical.co.uk/reviews/books/item/1886-half-earth-our-planet-s-fight-for-life-by-edward-o-wilson.

Wolfe, Alexandra, "Rick Steves's Plan for a Better World: More Travel," *Wall Street Journal*, February 2, 2018, https://www.wsj.com/articles/rick-stevess-plan-for-a-better-world-more-travel-1517598663.

Workaway.Info, accessed May 28, 2018, www.workaway.info.

World Health Organization, "Blindness and Vision Impairment Prevention," October 12, 2017, http://www.who.int/blindness/world_sight_day/2017/en/.

World Health Organization, "World Health Statistics," accessed May 28, 2018, http://www.who.int.

World Wide Opportunities on Organic Farms, accessed May 28, 2018, http://wwoof.net.

Zen Harmony Diving, accessed May 28, 2018, http://www.zenharmonydiving.com.

Index

About the Author

Jeff Blumenfeld is founder and president of Blumenfeld and Associates PR, LLC, a public relations and adventure marketing agency based in Boulder, Colorado, that has represented some of the largest outdoor recreation companies in the United States. Clients have included Coleman, Duofold, DuPont, Eddie Bauer, Lands' End, LEKI, Lewmar, Mares, Michelin, Orvis, Timberland, Timex, and W. L. Gore & Associates.

Blumenfeld is also editor and publisher of *Expedition News*, a newsletter, blog, and website[1] he founded in 1994 to cover news about the adventure marketing field. Excerpts from *Expedition News* also appear in The Explorers Club quarterly *Explorers Journal.* A Fellow of The Explorers Club[2] based in New York, he is the organization's former director of communications and is currently chairman of its Rocky Mountain chapter and member of its Flags & Honors Committee.

In 2009, he released his first book, *You Want to Go Where?: How to Get Someone to Pay for the Trip of Your Dreams.* A guide to expedition and adventure sponsorship, it received favorable reviews from a variety of outdoor media. The book was re-released in paperback in 2014 under the new title, *Get Sponsored: A Funding Guide for Explorers, Adventurers, and Would-Be World Travelers.*

He has presented over forty book talks throughout the United States, once off the coast of Antarctica. For a few years he was a guest speaker aboard two separate Celebrity cruise ships, the *Silhouette* and *Reflection.*

Blumenfeld also belongs to the American Alpine Club, based in Golden, Colorado, and is a Fellow of the Royal Geographical Society in London, where he has presented two talks on adventure marketing.

In May 2013 he served as communications director for Dooley Intermed International's "Gift of Sight" Expedition to Nepal—an effort to deliver badly needed quality eye care to seven hundred impoverished villagers. He returned to Nepal in December 2017 to continue his work there. The latter trip was the subject of a documentary that can be seen on Vimeo.com.[3]

Blumenfeld is a former adjunct faculty member of the New York University School of Continuing and Professional Studies/Marketing and Management Institute, and is a part-time lecturer at the University of Colorado, Boulder. He serves on the board of Voices of September 11, the leading advocacy group for the friends and families of victims of 9/11 (voicesofsept11. org), the International Skiing History Association (skiinghistory.org), and is vice president of the North American Snowsports Journalists Association (nasja.org).

An avid sea kayaker, hiker, fly-fishing angler, downhill skier, and sailor, he resides in Boulder with his wife, Joan, near their two adult daughters and one grandson.

Learn more at: BlumenfeldPR.com and expeditionnews.com.